A Journey through Music and Poetry

"Where Retro is, there's harmony, music, and poetry—
And few can match Retro's artistry..."

A Journey through Music and Poetry

RETRO
MUSE
SOCIETY

Rebels and Romantics

by   Sonia Maria Anda Cristolțean

This work was first penned in Romanian and has been translated
into English by the author, with the assistance of AI-supported
translation tools.

Cover photo credit: Anni Roenkae – Pexels
Printed in the United States of America

This book is inspired by real stories, real places, and real people
— except when it's not.
If you think you recognize yourself in here, well... maybe it's just a
wild coincidence.
And to those who preferred not to be mentioned: don't worry,
your secret is safe with me.

Translator's Note

This book was first written in Romanian, inspired by the shared journey of a community close to my heart: *Cenaclul Retro*, founded in 2017.

The word *cenaclu* has no exact English equivalent. It evokes a gathering of creatives — poets, musicians, storytellers, dreamers — coming together to share their voices, ideas, and passions. *Cenaclul Retro* was such a space: a living, evolving circle where rebels and romantics alike found room to be seen and heard.

For the English edition, I've chosen to render its name as *The Retro Muse Society*. While not literal, it captures the spirit of what *Cenaclul Retro* has become — a society of voices, laughter, performances, and reflection. *Muse* evokes both inspiration and creativity, the twin hearts of every gathering.

Throughout this book, the terms *Cenaclul Retro*, *The Retro Muse Society*, and *Retro circle* are used interchangeably; all refer to the same community of voices, laughter, and creative gathering.

This translation was guided by AI language tools, yet every sentence was lovingly edited by me to preserve the rhythm, emotion, and personality of the original. If you are reading these pages, you are now part of our circle — welcome.

On Anonymized Dialogues

To protect privacy, dialogues in the original manuscript that used bold and underlined capital letters (A, B, C, etc.) have been adapted here as capital letters only (A, B, C). Clarity is preserved, as is the intention behind each voice.

This manuscript was born in Romanian, and while every effort has been made to translate it faithfully, some jokes, rhythms, and cultural quirks may take on a slightly different flavor in English. Consider it the same recipe with a pinch of new spice — the spirit remains, the fun endures.

Author's Note

In Romania, I am known simply as **Anda**, the name under which the original version of this book was created. In the United States, I am known as **Sonia**, the name by which my colleagues and friends know me today.

Because this English edition includes original images and WhatsApp inserts that preserve the authentic Romanian context, both names appear throughout the book. Whether you encounter **Anda** or **Sonia**, both refer to me—the author—at different moments of my life and in different cultural spaces. To honor this continuity, I sign this edition as **Sonia Maria Anda**.

DEDICATION

To the members of Cenaclul Retro,

who turned longing into lyrics,

memories into verses,

and distance into something beautiful.

And to everyone who believes

art and friendship can bridge any ocean.

Dear Reader,

Welcome to the world of the Retro Muse Society! Thank you for taking the time to be here and for accompanying me on this journey. Together, we'll wander through Retro's craziness and quiet moments — through memories, lyrics, songs, and poems...

At first, I wrote this book just for Retro — this wonderful group of talented people who made my life (and the lives of those around them) more beautiful. But then I thought:
These moments are too beautiful not to share with anyone eager to read and fill their soul with the harmony of Retro's art...

So let's dive into this five-year journey, through my eyes and imagination. Simply.

Many who read this book will find pieces of themselves within its pages. And to those who get easily offended — I kindly recommend that you stop here and keep the memories of Retro safe and warm in your heart.

I hope this book will inspire future generations to carve their own harmonious path through art. If you have a talent — something that can bring joy to those around you — I urge you to use it. The world needs it more than ever.

This journey was not easy, and I was deeply inspired and supported along the way by my family, to whom I am endlessly grateful.

To *Paul*, who published a book at 20, and helped me transcribe texts, images, and notes from the Retro "notebook" (which I originally wrote by hand).
To *Andrei*, who encouraged me to continue — especially when I felt lost on the wings of time.

To *Sonia,* who worked with great dedication on the book cover, trying to capture the whirlwind of thoughts and emotions I poured into these pages.

To *Ştefan,* who supported all my ideas — and played his guitar to anchor me, even as I laughed and warned him, "Careful... you don't know what tune is coming next.

And last but not least, I thank the **Retro Muse Society**. Without each of you — those deeply or lightly involved — this book wouldn't exist.

With gratitude,
Sonia Maria Anda

Reader Impressions

"I read the book. It's the most heartfelt book I've read."

"You know what I appreciate about you? You've created a space where creativity and curiosity can thrive — fueled by the wealth you carried with you from home. That, to me, is the essence of the Retro Muse Society. In a deeply personal and familial phenomenon, you've generously welcomed those who had the courage to pack **dor** *in their immigration suitcases — in all its forms.*

I say **dor** because it cannot be translated. 'Romanian longing' is a pleonasm.

And when I say *in all forms,* I mean: longing for the country, for family, for youth, for school, for that first apartment...
For the traditions and joy life gave us, for our social roots, for mountain hikes, for opportunities missed and taken — the very things that shaped us and brought us here.

How lucky we are that we still feel this **dor**."

— *Laetitia Alex-St. Patrick, journalist*

Table of Contents

A NEW BEGINNING

They say the eyes are the windows to the soul...
"I'll keep my windows open. You keep yours open too. Who knows—
between us, we might just start a little breeze in this world."

January 2020   **A conversation** — somewhere, sometime...
Anda & Ștefan

"There are two ways to live life," I said with a smile, recalling the
famous words tucked somewhere in my memory. "One, to not
believe in miracles — and the other, to believe that everything is
a miracle."
"Or to create your own miracles," Ștefan added.

From the moment we met, we chose not only to believe in
miracles, but to make them happen. Retro is one of those miracles
— a cultural phenomenon born out of our wish to bring joy to as
many people as possible, to help them feel and live their
Romanian identity, even far from home.
Sometimes I wish I could freeze time - to stay suspended on the
wing of an hour, and simply revel in moments like these.

Spring 2011

"What do you think — how about starting a circle of arts and
stories?"
And that's how it all began: an idea that would grow into a unique
way of living and feeling Romanian, right in the heart of Chicago's
diaspora. (For more information, visit: www.cenaclulretro.org)

Ligia and Anişoara

Once upon a time... a cherished memory, lost in a season of longing, which I now try to bring back to light — just as I remember it.

I first met Ligia and her mother, Anişoara, along with Iulian, Olezia, and Sorin, many years ago at the home of dear friends — Mihaela and Nicu. Much later, and entirely by chance, I discovered that those friends were actually distant cousins — family, nonetheless.

Mihaela and Nicu, devoted lovers of music and poetry, often invited us to their gatherings. They always asked us to bring the guitar, and each party turned into a kind of cultural evening — a space where anyone who wanted to sing, recite, or simply enjoy the moment felt free to do so.

If we brought a microphone (and we usually did), it was bound to be hijacked by someone — talented or not — and I would inevitably find myself "managing" the flow, whether I liked it or not. I'd juggle the microphone from one person to the next, trying to keep things fair. It became a story in itself — full of humor, improvisation, and good-natured chaos.

At one such gathering — I can't recall the exact occasion, only that it wasn't a large crowd — Mihaela introduced us to Ligia and Iulian, Olezia and Sorin. That's also when I met Ligia's mother: Ana from Sighişoara — a woman with poetry in her soul, and a soul made of poetry.

None of us could have known that on that lovely summer evening in 2010, in the warm, art-filled home of such kind-hearted people, we were planting the seeds of something lasting.

2

As the evening unfolded, we exchanged stories about Cluj and our shared love for music and verse — everything flowing easily, with warmth and sincerity.

In May 2011, when we hosted the very first meeting of the Retro Muse Society (then called Cenaclul Vox Maris) in the event space of the Romanian library — thanks to Steven's support — Ligia and Anişoara were the first to volunteer. They came forward to read poetry, their own and others', and their presence helped shape the evening's success.

For the longest time, I meant to write these memories down — to offer readers a glimpse into the beginnings of Retro. Life, of course, had its own plans. But one day I picked up my pen and let the memories pour out, just as I remembered them.

A Journey Through Time
From "Cireşarii" to Vox Maris Cenacle and Vox Maris Band

The *Cireşarii* hold a special place in our hearts.

Who were they? And why write about them?
In short, *Cireşarii* was a rock band made up of children between the ages of seven and twelve — radiant, talented kids who, between 2009 and 2010, became a sensation at Romanian community events around Chicago.

Now, the full story.

Like many other families with children that age, every Friday we'd take ours to church — first for religious studies, then for traditional Romanian dance.

It wasn't easy. The church was in Chicago; we lived in the suburbs. Every trip meant at least an hour and a half each way —

especially on traffic-heavy Fridays. But we did it, wanting our children to stay connected to their language, culture, and traditions.

Then one day, Ștefan had an idea.
"I'm thinking of starting a rock band for the kids. What do you think? Andrei plays violin, Paul's on piano... if we gather a few more, we could start something special."
I smiled, admiring his eternal drive to bring joy wherever he goes. "It's not a bad idea," I said. "It'll keep the kids busy doing what they love. And honestly — a rock band made entirely of children? That's something unique."

The idea was announced at church, and soon enough, a few eager young musicians joined. So, in the winter of 2009, Ștefan began rehearsals.

The lineup:
Andrei — violin
Paul — keyboard
Giani — drums
Alicia — vocals
Diana — vocals
Loredana — vocals
Răzvan — violin
Dragoș — keyboard
Radu — bass guitar

Word spread quickly. One sunny day, Dan appeared — enthusiastic and ready to help in any way he could. That's how we met Dan, Mirela, and their children. And so began a wonderful adventure in the world of rock.

Cireşarii became an extraordinary artistic phenomenon.

I hope those children — now grown — remember those days with joy: the rehearsals, the performances, the laughter. They were phenomenal. And their parents? So supportive. Some… perhaps too supportive.

One evening, we got a call from N., the father of one of the band members. I watched Ștefan's face change.
"What happened?" I asked.
"We need to make a decision about *Cireșarii*," he said gravely.

What followed was hard to believe. Despite all our efforts, a handful of adults — the parents — had cast shadows over the project with gossip and petty drama… "acts that scandalized us," as the Romanian poet George Topârceanu, known for his ironic social commentary, might have put it.

Ștefan was upset but resolute.
"We can't continue like this. *Cireșarii* is over."

With heavy hearts, we brought it to a close.

We knew it wasn't the children's fault. And believe me — no one suffered more than we did.

But Dan and Ștefan kept playing — at home, at each other's houses — and their unofficial debut as *Ștefan & Dan* happened in June 2010, in Rockford.

We'd been invited to *a Sânziene celebration*, a Romanian midsummer festival, in Rockford — a sister city of Cluj-Napoca, one of Transylvania's cultural centers. The music began softly, hesitantly at first, like a gentle ripple, and then the audience joined in, their voices rising with the melody. I smiled, filmed them, and let myself be carried away by their joy. Later, they would perform at other community events — from church festivals to the Romanian Heritage Festival organized by Steven Bonica — each time bringing a little piece of home to this distant city.

May 2011

We organized the first meeting of the **Retro Muse Society** (then *Cenaclul Vox Maris*) at the Romanian Heritage Center's library, with the support of Steven Bonica. I didn't know Steven very well at the time, but Ştefan had known him for a while. Steven was deeply passionate about promoting Romanian culture, tradition, and art. He was receptive to Ştefan's ideas and offered us the venue for this event.

Only a few lovers of beauty gathered that evening — Ligia, Anişoara, Călin (that's actually when we first met Călin), Doru, Dan, and Ştefan — along with Adi and Dan R., who had just heard about the event.

Imagine it: May 2011, in the cozy library of the Romanian Heritage Center, at the very first meeting of what would become the Retro Muse Society. Everything flowed beautifully — music and poetry blending in harmony, books seeming to vibrate and dance with us. A beautiful collaboration was taking shape — the foundation of what would later become the Vox Maris Band.

At the end, Steven took the microphone and, with sincerity and warmth, shared his story — how he came to America, how he continued to live and feel as a Romanian, and why he did what he did for the community.

It moved me deeply. That moment, when Steven opened his heart and spoke of his journey, touched me profoundly. I felt even closer to our mission.

"I fled Romania filled with anger and an indescribable rage.
I was so deeply affected by what had happened to me that the first thing I did was change my name from Ştefan to Steven.
But now, after these moments you've given me — moments that made me feel close to my homeland again — this is the first time I've regretted changing my name."

And that was the beginning of the Vox Maris Band.

The guys kept meeting, organizing performances, bringing something fresh and original to the community. And what a joy to know that, as I write these words, the Vox Maris Band is celebrating its ten-year anniversary — still connected to its roots.

Excerpt from our Retro Muse group chat after watching the Vox Maris anniversary video.

Ligia
Nice recording. Congratulations. Sorin, for your idea contribution, Stefan, for your idea and the Vox Maris Baand. The memories remai. I liked how you presented by year: 10, 9, 8... history, lots of work and dedication. 8:30 PM

Glad you pointed that out, Ligia. I thought it was a live recording, which I watched (and commented on with passion). Actually, this is a video celebrating the 10 years. Nicely done indeed. And I saw Stefan in there too. Congratulations, dear one! 8:30 PM

Now it's Sorin, as I said earlier. Bravo Vox Maris! We need to come up with something AWESOME for the 5-year mark! 8:30 PM

Ligia
What a joy to meet you all and to open pages of poetry and music together. And what a joy to know you 🤎 8:49 PM

Anakin
Thank you, dears. Let's not forget that Ligia, Anisoara, and Calin took part in the first edition on May 21, 2011. 8:37 PM

(P.S. — Ștefan goes by "Anakin" in my contacts — yes, really.)

He was part of Vox Maris Band until early 2016. At some point, he told me:

"It's just not fun anymore. What if we kept going — but as a literary and musical circle instead? We could involve more people, bring joy to more hearts."

Said and done.

Beginnings

We Are Reborn by Celebrating Romanian Emotions, Wherever We May Be...

Looking back, the heart of our story can be traced through moments that brought us together long before we carried the name RETRO. What began as a spark between friends grew into something much greater — a shared passion for music, poetry, and the arts that refused to fade, no matter where life carried us.

It started with two good friends — troubadours forever in love with beauty — who, through their songs, brought joy to the audience that summer of 2010 at the Romanian Festival in Rockford. They simply called themselves Ştefan and Dan. Soon after, they they began performing at other cultural events in Chicago.

In May 2011, the first show of Cenaclul Vox Maris took place, hosted by Steven Bonica at the Romanian Heritage Center. That evening brought together wonderful people whose art enriched the souls of those present. Alongside Ştefan Cristolţean, Anda Cristolţean, and Dan Păduraru, musical pieces were performed by Adrian Nechiti, Dan Rizo, Monica Mureşan, and Doru Bândilă (on the flute). The poets Ana Munteanu Drăghici and Ligia Ana Grindeanu (mother and daughter) recited their own works, conveying emotions and feelings we never imagined possible so far from home. Călin Mărincaş delighted the audience with a

8

selection of epigrams and poems written by his uncle, Florea Florescu.

A delightful surprise was the children's group *Cireșarii*, guided by Ștefan Cristolțean and Dan Păduraru — including Diana and Ștefan Păduraru-Iovănescu, and Andrei and Paul Cristolțean.

Following that event, the Vox Maris Band began to take shape. It remains active to this day, performing and recording successfully. Ștefan remained part of the band until early 2016, after which the idea of reviving the literary circle resurfaced. Together with Anda, they gathered friends and fellow artists from the Romanian community around a roundtable of friendship, welcoming all who wished to take part.

And so, in early December 2016, still carrying the emotion of Romania's National Day, the creative circle was reborn with a performance held at the Romanian Heritage Center, sponsored by the company Diversital.

The founding members were joined by Corina Vlad, Bogdan Iuhas, Costin Movilă, Liviu Roman, and mezzo-soprano Nicoleta Roman.

The great lady of Romanian poetry, Ana Munteanu Drăghici, remained close to the members of the circle, promoting their creations and events in magazines and publications in Romania. Her kind and warm words from home — turned into verse — reminded us that *"distances are close when thoughts call them forth..."*

As the circle's popularity and potential grew, in January 2017, at the invitation of the Holy Nativity Church in Chicago and through the gracious efforts of Father and Presbytera Lupescu, we held a performance dedicated to our national poet, Mihai Eminescu.

That show was conceptualized by Ligia Grindeanu and hosted by Anda Cristolțean. The circle welcomed more beloved souls who contributed to the event's success: Laura Sisu (actress), Cătălin Nicolae (actor), Roxana Iacob, Laurențiu Cristian Nicolae, Iulian Grindeanu, Monica Mihaela Voicu, and Ionel Voicu.

In April 2017, with the arrival of spring, the literary circle blossomed in fresh new colors — and a new name: Cenaclul RETRO. (Retro Muse Society)

More artists and beauty lovers joined: Alina Celia Cumpan (poet), Traian Bălan, Oana Moise (visual artist), and Decebal Sorin Griza. The event was hosted by Mariana Torz at the Romanian Heritage Center.

Our wish is to bring beauty into your life and light into your soul.

We invite you to sing along with us songs from home, to remember the verses from the libraries of our childhood, to create new poems, images, and melodies — to feel Romanian and to dream together.

If you leave our shows feeling richer, with "a star" in your heart, we've fulfilled our mission.

Our story continues, like any story does, with: To be continued...

— Ligia Grindeanu & Anda Cristolțean
Motto by Corina Vlad
Chicago, May 2017

(Originally published on www.cenaclulretro.org and Facebook, December 2016. Adapted in December 2022 for inclusion in this book.)

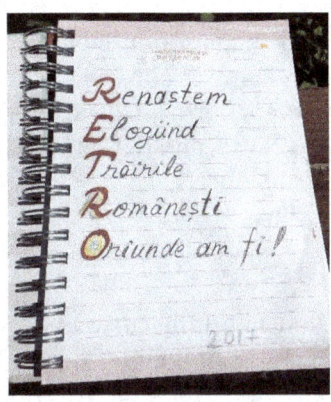

RETRO – Our Artistic Creed

We Are Reborn by Celebrating Romanian Emotions, Wherever We May Be!
(Renaştem Elogiind Trăirile Româneşti, Oriunde am fi! — an acrostic spelling RETRO)

Our story found a second beginning at an event organized by Mariana, my sister-in-law, who, at that time, was renting an office in the Romanian Heritage Center. There, she had access to the library hall and wanted to gather a few friends to celebrate a promotion.

And so, I invite you to join me on a little journey back in time.

It was a cold November evening when the phone rang. Ştefan answered.
"I have a favor to ask you," came her voice on the other end.
"Could you bring your guitar to Sunday's event and play something to lighten the atmosphere?"

That was all Ştefan needed. Asking him to bring his guitar and sing is like telling him to breathe. He hung up the phone and, with complete calm, turned to me:
"We have an event on Sunday. We'll be playing at Mariana's."

11

I looked at him, puzzled and a little skeptical.
"And who exactly will be playing? And what?"
"Don't worry," he said. "Many of our friends will be there. We'll also talk to Ligia, Anişoara, Corina, Laura, Cătălin..."
I knew Ligia, Anişoara, Laura, and Cătălin... but Corina was a name I had never heard before.

Corina

"Who's Corina?" I asked, naturally curious.
"You've probably seen her, but maybe you don't remember," Ştefan replied. "She's sung a few times at Vox Maris events... Don't worry, it'll be fine."
Saturday arrives, and we take Charley, our dog, out for a walk. The winter day is cold, but the sun smiles at us through the bare branches, showing its frosty teeth. Ştefan's phone buzzes. He pulls it from his pocket, reads the message, and turns to me.

Note: *To preserve anonymity, dialogue excerpts in this book use single-letter initials (A, B, C, etc.).*

"It's from **A***. She had to go to the hospital unexpectedly. She can't make it tomorrow."

I freeze for a moment. "I hope she's okay!"
"Me too. She didn't give details, but if she's there, she's in good hands." Mental note: *I'll pray for her.*

I look him straight in the eyes. "So... what do we do tomorrow? Our program is pretty thin now."
"Don't worry," he says.

That's one of Ştefan's qualities that sets him apart from almost everyone else—there's something in his calm that soothes even in the tensest moments. But for me, the idea of presenting an artistic program in front of a crowd the next day was stressful, daunting even.

12

"How can I not worry?" I mutter. Who would present? What would we present? My mind races—when it comes to organizing, I go all in. Without **A**, it would be just Ștefan, Corina, Ligia, Anișoara, and a few friends who had offered to add a little something to the program. And, of course, Ștefan would accompany everyone on his guitar. Our entire "arsenal" consisted of a guitar, an amplifier, and a microphone.

"You'll present," Ștefan says.
"Me?" I stare at him. He isn't joking. "Why me? You know I'm not comfortable speaking into a microphone... and I have no idea what to say."
"Anda, you need to have more faith in yourself. I know you can do much more than you let people see. Besides, who else do you want to introduce me? You have stage presence, and the words will come naturally... Don't worry."

Then he changes the subject. "I asked Corina what she's going to sing. Look, she just replied."
We stop at a street corner—Charley puzzled, me smiling but a bit doubtful. Ștefan shows me the message: *Decembre, La o cană cu vin, Și totuși iubirea, Doru, La fereastra ta.* [*These are well-loved Romanian songs — classics that nearly everyone in Romania knows by heart.*]

I can't believe it. I already like this girl. She's decisive, she knows what she wants.

The next day we load everything into the car and head to the library hall. The place is ready for the event—food set out on tables at the back, chairs neatly arranged for the performance. We love this library; it holds the memory of our very first creative circle meeting back in 2011. The air, heavy with the scent of books, always brings me home to Romania. Perhaps that's why, whenever we had the chance to use this room for Cenaclul Retro events, we never hesitated

Ştefan sets up his gear—amplifier, microphone, guitar, cables—while we mingle with guests, most of whom we know. The only unfamiliar faces are Mariana's business partners. Then Corina arrives. Ştefan introduces us. She's petite, delicate, but radiates a special energy. I smile, remembering her message from the day before.

I show her the program. She admits she's nervous—she's never sung in such a setting before. I encourage her, telling her to look at me if the nerves start to take over. I'll send her strength and confidence. I glance toward the almost-full room and deliberately avoid looking at her—she doesn't need to absorb my unease.

The "business" part ends, and Mariana gives us the cue. Ştefan picks up his guitar and starts strumming a few simple chords. I step timidly toward the microphone—only I know what's in my heart at that moment.

"Good evening, friends! We invite you to an evening of music and poetry. And since it's December, we'll start with *Treceţi batalioane române Carpaţii* (*March, Romanian Battalions in the Carpathians*), a patriotic song traditionally sung on Romania's National Day, December 1st."

A friend steps to the front — the spot where we'd set up the mic — and lets out the opening note. The audience joins in, encouraged by his strong, commanding voice.

What follows is a string of beautiful moments—poems recited by Ligia and Anişoara, intertwined with romances, folk songs, and rock ballads. My voice shakes, but I manage to control it, and in the end... it's not so bad. In fact, I enjoy it.

Then it's Corina's turn. I can feel her trembling, yet also her bravery—bold, unbroken in her flight. Our eyes meet, and I

encourage her silently: *It's good, Corina, it's good. Keep going!*
Applause. Applause. Applause.

After Ștefan's last song, the clapping continues... then silence. The
audience sits still, unwilling to leave. True, the show had lasted
only about 45 minutes, but their eyes (and not only their eyes)
say: *We want more.*

Ștefan announces, "This is where our show ends, as I mentioned
earlier..." The audience waits. Silence. Suspense. Finally, Ștefan
relents: "I'll sing one more song... but that's all we have in the
program."

Joy, excitement, more applause—*More! More!*

Afterward: congratulations, photos, questions—"Who are you?
What name should we look for on Facebook?" Strange...
memories flood in. We are, in fact, Cenaclul Vox Maris.

 From Facebook Memories

 Anda și Stefan
Sep. 11, 2016 · 🔒

A journey into the world of music and poetry.
Cenaclul Vox Maris then, Cenaclul Retro now.

We are reborn by celebrating Romanian emotions,
wherever we may be!

 4 Years Ago — See Your Memories
Cenaclul Vox Maris
Unforgettable moments n'pecty, Chicago ara

A journey to
the world of music
and poetry.

Cenaclul Vox Maris then,
Cenaclul Retro now.
We are reborn by celebrating
Romanian emotions,
wherever we may be

 4 Years Ago – See Your Memories
Cenaclul Vox Maris · P Chicago area

 Anda si Stefan
And they've even blossomed in many other
hearts... Did you imagine it back then?

 Corina Vlad
Thank you for the challenge! Timid about the first
time and borrowing a guitar, I've no regret that I
broke the ice, as in memories you can still feel the
vibrations of the first chords and lose yourself in
that "once upon a time' and to come!

Love · Reply · 24w   4

 Anda Si Stefan
A timid presence then, explosive and captivating
now. A living flame 🔥

Like · Reply · 24w   2

January 2017 - **And because all of this needed a name, they called it Eminescu.**

Note: *The phrase is born from a verse of Nichita Stănescu, who once wrote in homage to our national poet that whenever one seeks a name vast enough to contain poetry itself— the tremor of love, the echo of memory, the breath of a people — that name can only be Eminescu. In this way, the performance was no longer just a gathering of voices and instruments, but a rebirth under the sign of the poet whose very name has become the language of eternity.*

We were invited by the priest of the Holy Nativity Church to organize a performance dedicated to our national poet, Mihai Eminescu. We began preparing, reaching out to friends and acquaintances to see who might want to participate. A few years earlier, shortly after arriving in America, we ourselves had taken part in a similar event, organized back then by the *Mihai Eminescu Literary Circle*.

Volunteers stepped forward, and rehearsals began. In truth—if I recall correctly—we managed only one, at Ligia and Iulian's home, where Ligia had prepared a script she had once used in a similar setting.

The day of the event greeted us with a full hall, a full stage, and an audience thrilled by what was unfolding—the music and poetry that filled the air with energy. We, too, were uplifted by it all, by the way we connected through song and verse. You could truly say there is a need for more events like this. We even joked, *"Let Eminescu judge us,"* referencing a verse from a poem dedicated to Romania's beloved national poet.

Somewhere in the back of the room, I spotted two members of the Vox Maris Band. I was happy to see them and thought how kind it was of them to come and support us. Ştefan had left the band in early 2016, yet we had all remained friends, and at that moment, we truly needed each other's support.

Later, Ștefan told me they had actually come to suggest we change our name from *Cenaclul Vox Maris* to something else—so as to avoid confusion in the community. Still, I like to believe that what happened on that stage moved them and brightened their hearts. And the proof? I saw them at other performances, long after that day...

Their suggestion about the name turned out to be a good one. Many names were proposed. We had a great time joking around in our group chat. I wish I had kept all the messages from back then.

> What about Cenaclul
> Eternitatea? Sounds poetic!

Ștefan

> You don't know there's a
> cemetery in Cluj called
> Eternitatea? 😵

Sonia

> I think every city has a cemetery
> named Eternity...

Stefan

> Ok, how about Cenaclul Retro?
> It's about the music of our time,
> the kind we want to bring back.

Ligia

> That's actually... perfect

Sonia

> We have a winner! 🎉

Honestly, I think that simple explanation won the race for the new name.

And so, with the coming of spring, in March 2017, *Cenaclul Vox Maris* donned a new identity under the name *Cenaclul Retro*. Our friends from the Vox Maris Band came to many of our shows afterward, and we felt their presence—close in spirit, through art and culture. It is remarkable how art, in any form, brings people together and offers beautiful, unforgettable moments and connections.

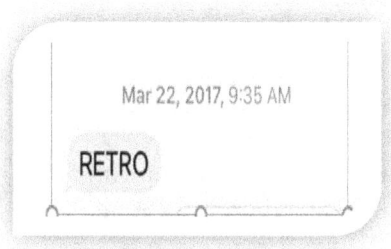

Mar 22, 2017, 9:35 AM

RETRO

February 2017 - **Alina**

A cold Saturday in winter. Ștefan suggests we go to Chicago for a protest. I tell him I've already made plans to attend an ice sculpture exhibit in Lake Geneva. He insists. I insist.
And so, for the first time, we decide to spend a Saturday apart — each following our own plans.

I head to Lake Geneva. He — of course, with his guitar on his back (because how could it be otherwise?) — heads to Chicago.

The ice sculptures, the cozy small-town atmosphere by the lake, the steam rising from hot tea, smiles, and conversations with dear friends fill my day with joy. Just two stylish moms and three mischievous kids — Raluca with her two, and me with my daughter, Sonia. We always enjoy spending time together.

On the way back, Ștefan calls.
We're driving home — Raluca at the wheel, the kids in the back, and I'm the co-pilot. It's already dark, though it's barely 5 PM.

"Can you come pick me up?" he asks.
"Where are you?"

"At some friends' place..."
(I realize he hasn't remembered the host's name.)

"How far are we from home?" I ask Raluca.
"About an hour," she says.

"Ștefan, it'll be another hour before I get home. How did you get there? Where's your car?"

So many questions, but he sounds calm and cheerful.
"Don't worry. I'll explain when you get here."

I smile. Once again, Ștefan has found himself some new friends...

I get home, drop off Sonia — I'm tired, but what can you do? I have to go get Ștefan, since I've only got one husband and I seem to have misplaced him among strangers.

That evening, I meet Alina. I didn't know her, but I find out she writes poetry and has a book launch in February. And so, on a lovely winter evening in 2017, we're invited to her event — with Ștefan adding music to a beautiful night of poetry.

End of February 2017 - **Traian**

It's winter. Snow covers everything. Alina's event is held at Stan Mansion. A large crowd. Warm, good people. A book launch: poetry, emotion, a theatrical scene... but something is missing — a hush, a yearning for music. Alina introduces the musical moment.

In my (admittedly subjective) opinion, it's the most beautiful part of the evening. Music gives wings to poetry.

At the end, there's joy, congratulations, lively conversation.
Ștefan calls me over:
"Come meet a gentleman who's really excited about the music."

Traian - You can read on his face how deeply he enjoyed the guitar's music.

On the way home, Ștefan says,
"We should organize another gathering. We already have so many lovers of music and poetry."

So we began planning.

March 2017 - **The Beginnings of Retro Muse Society**

On March 11, 2017, we hosted a roundtable of friendship, as Ligia later called it in her article *Beginnings*. We invited both old and new friends — lovers of art, music, and poetry.

Ștefan says, "I invited Traian too."
"Okay, but we barely know him," I reply.
"No problem — we'll get to know him."

We start preparing the April performance. The house is full — food, drinks, dear people, good energy... Actually, it's always like that when we gather with friends and family.

We sang, recited poetry, formed small committees (PR, technical, website...). We welcomed all those eager for such events — and there were many. Someone floated the idea of a name. Suggestions poured in, but with so many voices, nothing stuck.

Not long after, Ștefan simply wrote in the group chat:
"Retro."

And Retro was born.

April 2017 **The Turning Point**

We held the show *In Spring's Harmony*. Three new members made their Cenaclu debut: Alina, Traian, and Oana. The performance was a success — the bar was raised. It was a turning point, laying the foundation for new collaborations and future events.

Sorin

Word about us began to spread. Someone from Saint Mary's Church called, inviting us to perform. Ștefan invited the man to our next rehearsal to see what we do. The day comes. Ștefan, Traian, Corina, and Laura are already rehearsing when a well-dressed man arrives. I open the door, greet him, and invite him in.

He sits quietly, listening intently... I can tell he's itching to join in.
"Do you play an instrument?" Ștefan asks.
"Bass guitar," he says.

"Perfect! We have a bass guitar. Anda, can you grab it from Sonia's room?"

And just like that, a beautiful connection begins. The bass guitar sings in his hands. He fits right in with Cenaclul Retro.

After the rehearsal, when we were alone, Ștefan says,
"I'm so glad we met a good bassist. We really needed that."
And I reply,
"Just make sure our muse society doesn't turn into a band again..."

<u>And Then the Debates Began...</u>

There it was — that moment when you realize things are about to shift. New people bring new energy, new dynamics... but also new **questions**. What is Retro Muse Society really about? Where is it headed?

We weren't just gathering for fun anymore.
We were attracting **audiences, interest, expectations**.

And along with all that came something less charming:
debate. disagreement. ego. misunderstanding.

All of it natural — maybe even necessary — when a group starts growing.

Suddenly, we were no longer just a handful of dreamers singing and reciting in someone's living room.
We were becoming... something more.

Some began to wonder:
Are we a **band** or a **cenaclu**?
Who decides what we perform?
Who gets the spotlight?
Are we open to everyone... or should we be more selective?

Small things — at first.

A raised eyebrow.
A tension in a meeting.
A disagreement about a photo.
A quiet exit after rehearsal.

But the seeds had been planted.

And just like any family or creative circle, we had to navigate the **growing pains**.

The one thing that never changed?
The music.
The poetry.
And the feeling — that what we were creating **mattered**.

REBELS

There are moments in life that remain hidden in the corners of the soul — good moments, and not-so-good ones. That is how it is in Retro as well; nothing is perfect, yet I believe the beauty lies even in imperfection. How delicate the definition of beauty is...

We have overcome many moments together, and I like to think each of us has learned something along the way. I recall here the words of Nina Tărchilă, whose reflection appeared on Facebook precisely when one of those less-than-perfect moments unfolded in Retro. Coincidence? Perhaps.

Since then, we have weathered many similar storms, and her words have grown more and more relevant. Looking back, I realize that all those moments shared a common thread — the seed of discord.

"People reveal themselves not through what they say about themselves, nor through the noise they make on Facebook walls or elsewhere.
People always reveal themselves through what they do, through their gestures of care for others, through involvement, through beliefs proven by actions and confirmed over time, through the patience and naturalness with which they listen to others, through the respect shown in conversation, through discretion and decency, and also through the envy, pride, and frustrations they cannot contain even while loudly proclaiming a superiority they believe to be divinely bestowed.
Perhaps that is why I have never trusted those who speak too loudly

25

of their choices, their virtues, or their private lives.
My values stop at common decency, self-respect, kindness, and those
pure touches of the soul like snow — the kind not everyone is
capable of.
Whoever is meant to remain by your side will do so, through any
storm. Whoever truly wants to know you will look into your soul
with warmth and without judgment. Those who matter, surely
know who you are. Those who choose to peer at a life through the
keyhole only reveal their own limits.
And the applause? Just wind.
Fame? Fleeting trifles that feed empty egos.
Disciples? Perhaps tomorrow's fiercest enemies.
Generosity, integrity, and openness of the heart to friendship and
love will always set people apart — for these require self-giving,
and not everyone is capable of living beyond their own egocentrism.
Today I want to thank those of you who are dear to me. Not for any
particular reason. Simply... because you are." — Nina Tărchilă

I know many versions have circulated about the more tense
moments. This is mine — and therefore my perspective. I try to
be fair and creative at the same time. To those who recognize
themselves in these stories, please do not feel offended. Instead,
take it as a sign of attention. It means you left a mark in Retro. Do
not scold me, I ask — a gentle nudge will suffice.

In all these moments, I will preserve the anonymity of those
involved. I still believe in kindness, honesty, simplicity, and love.
Truly, I do not believe anyone acted with bad intentions in what
follows. I believe that everything that happened taught us to be
better — and helped us move forward.

Note on Characters:
To preserve a sense of privacy and mystery, certain dialogues in this
book use single capital letters (A, B, C, ...) to mark the voices in
conversation. These letters are not initials, but gentle placeholders

— symbols of real people whose essence lives through their words.

May 2017 - **Moment – Over Coffee...**

Preparations were underway for the June 4th, 2017 show
Summer Harmonies. Rehearsals, laughter, good cheer... something
beautiful was beginning to take shape.

After one rehearsal at Corina's, with many smiles and much joy,
photos and videos appeared almost instantly on Facebook —
many, perhaps too many. The PR Committee (publicity and
promotion) was at work. Most of the Retro members didn't mind
the posts; in fact, some even enjoyed that little taste of "fame" on
Facebook. All good.

But later that evening, Ştefan received a phone call — a complaint
that perhaps too many photos had been posted, some of them less
than ideal. He told me: *"Please be careful about what gets put on
FB..."* I was, of course, part of that committee.

The next day, coffee in hand, we held a PR meeting — three of us,
connected by phone. We began our discussion, and among other
things, I said: *"It was suggested that we be a little more careful
about what we make public on the group's page."* I mentioned no
names. That was all.

That was enough, apparently.

A, the person who had made the posts (perhaps she hadn't slept
well?), suddenly lashed out at me:
*"And what do you think, that you can control people however you
want? Let them appear publicly as much as they like!"*

I froze, speechless.

Fortunately, **B** was also in the committee, quietly listening on the
other end of the line. I could feel her stunned silence. Neither of

us expected such an outburst. The shouting was aimed at me, the fury striking without warning. I hadn't even said that, in fact, some of the very people closest to her — the ones she cherished most — had been unhappy with how she treated the Retro page as if it were her personal Facebook account.

I thought to myself: *Why do I need this kind of trouble?*

Later, **B** told me she still couldn't understand why or how that revolt had erupted. I was left shocked, with a bitter taste. It is not easy working with people.

And just like that, a beautiful spring morning of coffee and poetry was clouded, leaving me with the lingering question: *Why do I make things so complicated for myself?*

Yes, there have been unpleasant situations along the way, but Retro has always carried itself through them with grace and tact.

"And it seems so strange that there is still time
for so much hatred, when life is but a drop
between this fleeting moment and the next...
And it seems so sad, so hard to grasp,
that we don't look to the sky more often,
don't gather flowers, don't smile —
we, who die so very quickly." — Magda Isanos

Laura & Cătălin

I had met the actors Laura and Cătălin many years ago. They were, as far as we know, the very first to create a theatrical organization here in Chicago, so far away from home. Through their work, they managed to bring to life many plays—old and new—so needed and so cherished by the audience. I remember that whenever they had performances, Stefan and I often went more than once to the very same play... that's how much we enjoyed what they had accomplished. Laura and Cătălin found a way to bring Romania closer to our hearts. Respect and appreciation for what these two actors continue to bring to the Romanian community. I also remember hearing Laura sing at Vox Maris concerts.

How easily and beautifully they blended into the Retro Circle. Even though they could not always take part in every rehearsal or show, we always felt their presence, as though they were truly part of us: Laura conveys deep emotion whenever she steps on stage, while Cătălin radiates joy, humor, and good cheer. Actors of great talent, whom we are so fortunate to feel close to the heart of Retro.

Marius

We were preparing for the *"Summer Harmonies"* show in June 2017. One evening, Laura called to ask if she could bring Marius to a rehearsal (which was being held at her house). He was a true lover of the arts, had heard about us, and expressed his wish to recite from his own creations as part of the show.

Of course, we responded with enthusiasm, delighted by his desire to join our gatherings. And so, Marius first appeared on the Retro stage. From the very beginning, he impressed us with his modesty, calm demeanor, and genuine talent. I remember finding out then that Marius had acted in a very successful TV series, and I wanted to include that in his introduction. But he pulled me aside and asked me not to highlight it... Much later, I watched that series myself—and it was truly impressive.

The show that followed was a great success—photos, friends, new acquaintances... Now all have become cherished memories.

Marius's presence brought an added richness to our performances. His calmness, modesty, and characteristic humor always bring us joy.

Fall 2017 – **Moment**

There are many moments I don't know if they're worth writing about... and yet, I write. This is one of them.

We were preparing for the autumn show, rehearsing eagerly with joy and passion. But the evening before the performance, King Michael of Romania passed away. Discussions began during the final rehearsal – the dress rehearsal.

A proposed that we cancel or postpone the show. He was deeply shaken by this event. Other voices could be heard... some agreed, others did not. After a few moments, **C** took the microphone:

"Considering that Cenaclul Retro has no political affiliation, and that we all put great effort into creating this performance, and because what we will present is too uplifting and beautiful to be lost, I propose we continue with the show, but begin with a moment of silence for this sad event."

I saw relief on everyone's faces. Everyone except **A**, who remained agitated and unhappy. He announced that he would not participate... and so the discussions continued. Once again, we realized how difficult it is to work with a group of people—each different, each talented in their own way.

The show itself was a success. It stirred emotions, joy, and many beautiful feelings. Afterward, we gathered to celebrate and to plan future Retro events.

Then **B** asked:

"Did you see what **A** wrote? About how some groups canceled (or postponed) their shows and others didn't...?"

No, I hadn't seen it. Honestly, I don't spend much time on Facebook or other platforms. But others had read between the lines, and it seemed that **A** had "thrown mud" (as **B** put it) at

Cenaclul Retro. I read the post and indeed felt an "arrow of malice" directed at us. Subtle, yes—but malice, like kindness, is contagious.

And since we are many and diverse, some arrows hit their mark... and wound. I tried to ignore it, as did Ștefan—he doesn't even check Facebook. If we considered every bit of negativity in the world, we would never move forward. Better to keep going.

But **B** was inflamed (perhaps too upset—I wondered why...) and exclaimed:

"I propose we expel him from the Cenaclul."

I was taken aback. That reaction felt too harsh. If you ask me and Ștefan, there's room for everyone in the universe of music and poetry. But I also realized that there were voices saying otherwise.

C added:

"I feel that **A** isn't really part of Cenaclul Retro. He comes to the stage for exposure; he uses us, in fact. It's easy to enjoy applause, kind people, harmony—without giving much back."

I thought of certain situations, and I had to admit **C** was right. In the summer, when we were forming committees for the smooth running of things, I suggested that **A** join the committee managing our Facebook page. I wanted to give him the chance to be useful, to help, to feel included in Cenaclul Retro. He politely refused, saying he had no time, as he was already involved in several personal projects.

Then **D** said:

"Ever since I've known him, I could tell he's determined to succeed in life on his own. He doesn't need a group. Sure, he likes the exposure—but that's about it."

B insisted:

"So what do we do? Do we expel him?"

Ștefan replied:

"We're too many, and we all have different opinions. I suggest we vote."

And so we did. But I noticed that the loudest voices were the ones being heard most. Too much time was being spent debating this problem. A shame, really, for such a beautiful evening.

C continued:

"If we don't resolve this here and now, we'll waste too much rehearsal time discussing nonsense. We won't get anywhere, and it will keep affecting us."

It was a new situation. We didn't want it, and we didn't know how to handle it...

At the next rehearsal, we sang, practiced, and recited. At the end, **B** asked again:

"So, what do we do with **A**?"

And the discussions started once more. Honestly—much ado about nothing. I realized there had been texts exchanged in the past between **B** and **A**, maybe even feelings (on **B**'s side?), which explained the intensity of her frustration.

So we voted. The conclusion: **A** would be excluded from the Cenaclul. But then came the question: *Who will tell him?* It was decided that **E** would do it.

I'm not sure how or in what form the message was delivered, but when I later spoke briefly with **A**, he seemed confused. It seemed that **E** hadn't known how, or perhaps hadn't managed, to explain why things had reached this point. Although **A** surely understood what had happened, he still seemed eager to stir up some fuss.

Later, Ștefan called him, clarified everything calmly and elegantly—as only he can—and wished him success in the future. And indeed, success followed.

We still meet **A** at community events. He gladly comes to our shows, invites us to his own projects, and we remain friends in art. Honestly, his success in the cultural life of the community makes us happy.

September 2017 - **Lucian and Monica**

At the "Summer Harmonies" show (2017), Traian invited two friends, whom we later found out had once been professional musicians in Romania. That's when we first met Monica and Lucian. I had noticed them among the audience and could tell they truly enjoyed the summer performance.

Shortly after, Traian called Ștefan to ask when Lucian might join us for a rehearsal.

Monica and Lucian—two warm, gracious presences—brought real value to the cenacle, integrating with ease. We shared beautiful moments, fruitful rehearsals, and bright days together. With his distinct pedagogical tact, Lucian took his role seriously and gradually left a strong mark on the musical direction. Monica intervened delicately, naturally, with her nightingale-like voice, as Anișoara would later describe her.

In Romania, they had once enjoyed much recognition, and this closeness to the Retro Cenacle did them good—just as it did us.

Lucian once said with emotion:
"You don't know how long I've been waiting for a group like this..."

October 2017 - **Radu**

I first came to know Radu through the press. After one of our shows—*Autumn Harmonies* (2017)—the newspaper *Tribuna Românească* published an article about the performance. It was completely unexpected... what a beautiful surprise! Sorin brought the paper to one of our rehearsals. We read it, rejoiced, and read it again.

"It's so much better that it was written by someone outside the group," Ligia remarked. And she was right—it mattered to hear the perspective of someone in the audience.

"Who wrote the article?" we asked.
Sorin replied: "Radu."

And that is how Radu quietly and humbly appeared in the life of our circle.

Perhaps the best way to describe him is through his own words, written after the 2019 Christmas show, when he moved us deeply with a heartfelt message and a poem dedicated to Retro:

"As you know, there are two kinds of Romanian emigrants: those who try to completely break away from the country they left, and those who keep their ties. I was one of the first—I had lost all connection to Romania. Then, about two and a half years ago, I met these wonderful people, and I carry an immense joy in my heart for being able to take part in this show and other Retro performances. And now, for the very first time in my life, I tried to write a poem. I don't know if it turned out well, but I was inspired by the greatest Romanian poet—Mihai, please forgive me."

Gratitude for Retro
by Radu Russell Răcean, Chicago, December 2019

I never thought I'd learn to love again...
The song, the play, the poetry.
My eyes once lifted dreamily toward the capitalist star,
When suddenly you appeared before me—
This group of kind and dreaming souls,
A poetic, musical, and joyful blend,
Brilliant, spiritual, delightfully mad,
Creators of music and poetry.

You stirred within me the longing for my Romanian roots,
You awakened my Carpathian being,
You filled my heart with joy,
When I was lost in the American whirlwind.
You stopped me, you sang "Bade Ioane",
And to me, to myself—
You have RESTORED me!

Ligia
It's a beautiful message.
If anyone asks us
what our mission is,
this poetic confession
can be read.

That's why it's good not
to let memories gather
dust.

Moment – Centennial 2018

We were invited to take part in the Centennial 2018 show by Mr. Tavi Cojan, a remarkable gentleman and true lover of the arts, who has devoted much of his life to organizing cultural events for the diaspora. We felt flattered, honored, and pleasantly surprised. But we immediately ran into a problem: with so many of us in the circle and with so much to say, how could we possibly fit into just 15 minutes? What could we present in only 15 minutes? For us and our message, it didn't feel like enough.

The texts flowed in the chat—joy, excitement, but also a touch of stress. *What do we do with only 15 minutes???*

Ștefan spoke with the organizers, negotiated a bit more time, and came back with a proposal: for the musical part, Monica would represent us, and for the poetry, Marius. Everyone agreed. We prepared—or rather, we didn't have much to prepare, but those of us not directly involved were ready to stand behind those who would carry Retro's voice at such a significant event.

Just two weeks before the show, Monica received sad news; we shared in her grief... and as a result, she could no longer participate. The repertoire had to change again. We settled on two songs and two poems and began rehearsing intensively.

The show took place at the **Copernicus Center in Chicago**. We arrived in the morning. Things quickly became complicated—many guests, long sound checks, endless waiting. Our patience and nerves were tested, but we stayed calm, shifted the repertoire again, listened to comments from all sides, and kept reminding ourselves: *this is how it is in Retro—stay calm and enjoy the moment.*

By the time the show began, we were exhausted but excited. It was a beautiful event—talented artists, well organized. I only wished there had been more pieces directly tied to the theme of the Union; after all, we were celebrating a great national holiday.

Then it was our turn. In the wings, ready, an organizer rushed over to Ştefan:

"Please shorten your segment as much as possible—we're already out of time. The other artists have gone way over."

Ştefan simply said: *"All right, don't worry."*

As the organizer left, murmurs followed: *"Really? Us? Cut again? No…"*
Ştefan turned to us: *"Now's the moment. We'll do what we know best. Go Retro!"*

We went on stage together, carrying the Romanian flag, singing, reciting, celebrating. We reminded everyone why we were there—performers and audience alike. And the miracle happened: **we lifted the hall to its feet.** It was the only moment in the entire show when the audience stood and sang along with us. We were far from perfect, but what mattered was what we managed to transmit.

Afterward—emotions, joy, and even some disappointment. I was surprised to learn that **A** had been very upset… **B** whispered to me: *"It seems the presence of the Romanian flag on stage was the cause of his great disappointment."* **E** added: *"Hard to understand… I'm sure everyone can find their own reasons for joy or for being upset."*

As for me—and most of our group—I've kept in my heart that image of the hall rising to its feet, singing with us *"An historic song reminds us…"* That's the picture that nourishes my memories.

And I'll never forget what **Maestro Nicolae Feraru** remarked afterward:

"You can be a perfect artist and perform flawlessly, but if you don't connect with the audience, you transmit nothing—you've done nothing."

Hats off, Maestro. All our respect!

Moment – Pandora's Box – or – Too Much Silence...

The joy of the Centennial carried us forward, but not for long. Soon, a new trial arose—unexpected, painful, and much harder to navigate.

I was in the school parking lot, waiting to pick up Sonia from her extracurricular activities, when I called **A** with a simple question. Instead, his words tumbled out:

"Anda, forgive me, but I have to tell you what happened. If Retro falls apart, it will be only because of me."

I froze. I had no idea what he was talking about.
"Haven't you spoken with Ștefan?" he asked, realizing he'd rushed ahead.
"No," I replied.
"Then let me explain... and first of all, I want to apologize if what happened brings trouble to Retro. I'm very upset. I already spoke with Ștefan earlier. Here's what happened: I invited C, D, and E to our house—to talk, to play cards... and of course Retro came up again. At one point, C said once more: 'Do you think I can't live without Retro?'—as if this circle meant nothing to him. I just couldn't take it anymore. I exploded. I tore into him, because I couldn't imagine such hypocrisy. Retro changed all of our lives so beautifully—especially his. Before Retro, almost nobody in the community even knew him. He admitted that himself countless times. And now to hear him dismiss it like that? I lost it."

I listened, sitting in that empty parking lot. Sonia was still inside—and just as well, because **A** wasn't done. In the background I could hear **B** trying to calm him, and their kids arriving from school.

He went on: *"Believe me, I didn't mean for it to happen. But my patience finally broke. I've overlooked so many things **C** said or did, but this time I couldn't. **B** tried to calm me down. Later she told me: 'It was the only time anyone has ever left our house upset.' And she's right—nobody ever leaves their home without feeling lighter and happier. But this time was different."*

The next morning, full of regret, **A** had called **C** again and again to apologize, but got no answer. *"**B** scolded me a little,"* he admitted, *"but I think even she is shaken. I'm sorry, ashamed, and I beg your forgiveness too. I don't want this to destroy what we've built with so much love and dedication."*

I felt his pain deeply. *"Don't worry, **A**. You did what you could. You apologized. Whatever is between you and him won't affect Retro. With time, things will work out."*

And I meant it. Because to us, every single member was dear, each bringing their own charm to Retro.

Still, from that day a shadow fell. I didn't speak of it openly, but I could feel the harmony of our group unraveling bit by bit. Ștefan preferred to wait, hoping the fire would burn out on its own: *"The rest of Retro must be protected,"* he told me.

For months, tension lingered under the surface. We continued rehearsing, laughing, enjoying our time—but the air was different. Those involved said they forgave each other, but something in their relationship had soured and no longer brought joy.

The phone calls poured in—mostly to Ștefan. He was bombarded with messages, yet always calm, patient, advising, trying too hard perhaps to hold everyone close and keep everyone happy in a nearly impossible situation. His tact, his perseverance, showed once more that he was truly the leader of Retro.

Meanwhile, I listened to **A**'s grievances, then **C**'s, **D**'s, and occasionally **E**'s eternal questions: *"Why do we call it a cenaclu and not just a group? What's he doing on stage? Why is she singing? Who invited the sound guy?"* And so it went...

Moment – Harmony in Danger
A distancing began within the circle; the harmony between us started to fade.

We all noticed that the focus had shifted almost entirely to the musical side. Perhaps it was necessary... but hard to understand for those who did not sing. At rehearsals, poetry was completely ignored, as were the structure of the show, stage movement, and connection with the audience. Nothing else seemed to matter anymore. Only the music...

The muse society had begun to resemble a "band," something we had deliberately tried to avoid from the very beginning.

*I once read that every thing has cracks in it—so that light can find its way through...

You were not created to be evil,
You cannot be evil, Human!
Because to you,
To you alone,
Was given
The healing power
Of the word

Anda – November 3, 2020

A reflection inspired by the wise words of
Ana of Sighişoara: *"the healing power of the word"*

Note: *In this book, you will find a blend of narratives, reflections, and poems that have grown out of our shared Retro Muse Society journey. While most texts appear only in English, some poems are presented bilingually, with the original Romanian on one page and the English translation on another.*

This choice was intentional. The format preserves not only the meaning, but also the musicality, rhythm, and cultural essence of the original verses. I invite readers to experience the depth of Romanian language and the way it resonates in translation.

Tu nu ai fost creat să fi rău,
Nu ai cum să fi rău, Omule!
Pentru că ție,
Doar ție,
Ți-a fost dăruită
Puterea vindecătoare
A cuvântului

Anda- Noiembrie 3, 2020

Moment – Frustrations

It so happened that **D** left a dress rehearsal frustrated, because everything dragged on the musical side... while those not involved in music quietly waited their turn at the microphone... the problem was, their turn never came. I admire **D** for the patience she showed, and for the courage to withdraw from one of the shows just one night before going on stage. Of course, this dramatic situation created a wave of emotions and dissatisfaction. Even **B** and **C**, the ones responsible, were deeply "struck" by **D**'s attitude and immediately suggested that we expel her from the cenacle.

It also happened that whenever someone proposed something new and out of the ordinary—for example, for **E** to make her entrance from the back of the audience, so that we could bring something fresh and different—there was always an obstacle: no cables for microphones, or a problem with the sound, and so on. We had many ideas, but unfortunately, we ran up against preconceptions and couldn't move forward. As I've said before, HARMONY—the very thing that defines the Retro Cenacle—was on the verge of being completely lost.

Moment – Rehearsal at the Library

Rehearsal at the library. The tension in the air was palpable... The time came for **B** to rehearse his part.
D, who was supposed to accompany him, walked out of the room. The others saw it, felt that something was wrong, but didn't understand. Neither did we. It seemed as if they had made peace and left the past behind... but clearly, it wasn't so.

As soon as we got home, the phone rang. **B** told us he wasn't coming back to Retro, that he was giving up because he could no longer be around **D**, and it was clear that **D** had no intention of leaving. He believed it was his right to stay.

I admired **B** for the sincerity and calm he showed, and I understood him. I knew it was incredibly hard for him to leave Retro. Retro was a part of him—he had grown up in Retro, grown up with Retro—and his place was here.

We didn't like what was happening. We had hoped it wouldn't come to this. It seemed the smoldering fire had not been extinguished; on the contrary, it was burning stronger, destroying everything around. Of course, the rest of the members soon found out that something unpleasant was happening. A few were surprised, unsure what to believe—or rather, whom to believe. Discussions erupted, "cliques" formed... and we let everyone come to their own conclusions. It is true that there are always multiple sides and points of view.

An African proverb says: *Until the lion tells his story, the hunter will always be the hero.*

I won't dwell on it here, nor give further details—though I am sure many readers will be disappointed—but I can say it was difficult... for the entire circle. We had always enjoyed everyone's presence on stage, and we had always valued what each brought to the audience. But we had to move forward.

December 2019 – **Cătălin**

Christmas Show: "Carolers with Dreams"

In December 2020, I watched this show again on YouTube and relived the emotions all over. Even if the virus had forbidden us from gathering to sing carols together, I could at least recreate the Christmas atmosphere: sacred carols, snowflakes, icicles at the window.

I remember that show so dearly—the hall full, the corridors full (once again), that feeling of the "sacred": traditional Romanian carols, newer songs, poetry, a beautifully decorated tree, *The Little Match Girl*, the group of children... And I remember noticing Călina and Cătălin in the audience. After the performance, they stayed behind, and that's how we met them—simple and refined, filled with the joy and emotion of that Christmas show.

January 2020

We began preparing for a show dedicated to Mihai Eminescu. This, too, seems to have become a tradition. Many ideas were proposed, and we concluded it would be beautiful to give everyone the opportunity to bring a small "offering" to the one recognized as the greatest poet of our people. Said and done—but not so easy to put into practice.

We invited beloved people from the community, both adults and children. That complicated things logistically. Working with people is never simple. Even organizing just ourselves takes enormous effort; behind every show is so much unseen work. To "add" nearly as many new moments into the program, with people you don't know well, not knowing how serious they are or if they'll show up on time—it was a real challenge.

Ligia did an extraordinary job: patient, gracious, reshaping the program several times to accommodate everyone. We all strove, adapted, and supported those who joined in that special performance.

It was then that I came to know Cătălin better: timid, calm, warmhearted, and always helpful. **A** said to me, *"Now this is someone I'd love to keep working with."* I smiled and replied, *"Indeed, he brings an extra measure of harmony to the muse society."*

We let things unfold naturally. We invited him to rehearsals. He was quiet, thoughtful, doing his part without fuss. I had the sense he didn't want to disturb anyone, yet I was sure he was observing us, just as we were observing him.

His simplicity, kindness, and the sweet voice of his violin soon won us over. He brought a measure of peace and harmony. His vocal notes in the group chat were a delight—guiding us, teaching us in such a gentle, gracious way that it was a joy to listen. It was as if he had stepped straight out of a story to make the Retro story more beautiful.

"Through the enchanted grove let's go,
Hand in hand beneath the sky…"
—The sweet voice of the violin

"Thank you, Cătălin, for your professional lessons, explained with such talent and pedagogy, clear and understandable for all. Corinuța, you can put the wooden spoon back on its hook—our

Teddy Bear doesn't need it 😊 .
I'd like to insist on one important point you mentioned: it's very helpful for us to listen as much as possible to the original vocal lines, both melody and accents, so that when we meet, we are all prepared and on the same page. At the same time, let's also follow your exercises with vocalizations and sound modulations. For the mix to come together beautifully, each part must be in harmony with the others, otherwise it becomes harder.
I can't wait to see you all at work on Saturday, my friends! Go Retro!" —Ştefan, from bits and pieces of texts

---

= *The Value of a Man Lies in His Capacity to Love* =

Ştefan

A strange phenomenon sometimes occurs: the closer someone is to you, the more you take them for granted. You see them only through your own eyes and assume that everyone else sees them the same way. That was how it was with Ştefan—I didn't write about him for a long time. I thought it unnecessary; after all, everyone knows him, most people love him... he is the very heart and soul of our cenacle.

He brings countless good ideas, always listens to others, and carries within him a passion for music, family, friends, and above all, the joy of seeing those around him happy. That's where the beauty in everything he does comes from. Sometimes I think that many don't deserve to have him nearby. But I like to believe that together, when we created this cenacle, we drew in—like a magnet—many beautiful people.

"Let them come. Those who don't belong by our side will fall away. Life runs its course; we don't need to force anything." — Ştefan

The first song I ever played for him on guitar, many years ago, was *Dumbrava minunată* (The Enchanted Grove — a beloved Romanian cultural symbol of childhood wonder and natural

45

beauty). That melody, once tucked away among student memories, was reborn within Retro. It inspired not only a new arrangement, but also the title of an original song we created together. Later, it even became the theme of one of our shows that year, carrying with it the charm of a grove forever alive in our hearts.

For years it had rested quietly on the dusty shelf of memory. Then, one March evening in 2020, in a warm room with a fire in the fireplace and Retro gathered close, I picked up the guitar and played it again — timidly, gently, just as I remembered it. The reaction was unforgettable. Maybe the planets had aligned that night, but everyone loved it. Soon after, the suggestion came: we should rework it and bring it to the stage.

As I write these words, I know that the summer 2021 performance is titled *In the Enchanted Grove with Cenaclul Retro*. Ștefan had taken the song, shaken off the dust, given it a jazzy rhythm, and breathed new life into our grove.

Ștefan: a rare talent, passion in everything he does, and—above all—love, abundant love.

Biography of a Soul

Do not open my soul,
For inside there is still light,
That could... blind you.

Do not open my soul,
For the pain you will find there
Could bring you to your knees.

Do not open my soul,
For inside there is also darkness
That could frighten you.

Do not open my soul,
Let me be the one to show it to you...

Ștefan Cristolțean   *06/02/2001 – Chicago*

Biografia unui suflet

Nu-mi deschide sufletul,
În el mai există lumină,
Care te-ar putea ... orbi.

Nu-mi deschide sufletul,
Căci durerea pe care o vei
afla,
Te-ar putea îngenunchea.

Nu-mi deschide sufletul,
În el mai există şi întuneric
Care te-ar înspăimânta.

Nu-mi deschide sufletul,
Lasă-mă să ţi-l arăt eu...

Călin

A warm, simple, and sincere presence. When I think of Călin, my mind goes back to the very first Retro event in May 2011. He has the same stage presence, the same ease, and he still recites from the same author—his uncle, Florea Florescu... though sometimes he switches things up.

You can feel how much Retro means to him. Perhaps not quite as much as soccer—his true passion—but close enough. Not long ago, at one of our autumn shows, in fact the last show of 2021, *Together Again*, Călin surprised us with his preparation, the poetry he brought, and the effort he put in. It is admirable how we support and encourage one another. I remember before that show, chatting with Corina and Călin. I mentioned in passing that Retro would soon celebrate five years in March 2022. He corrected me with a smile:
"Actually, it's been 10 years this year."
I looked at him a bit surprised. So he remembered. That May 2011 truly mattered to him. And I was glad.

Some time earlier, on his birthday, we had a dress rehearsal. He brought food and champagne... As always, our rehearsals became moments of harmony and joy, made even brighter by a special reason to celebrate. He told me:

"I gave up my soccer match tonight just to be here. That doesn't happen often. In fact, it's only the second time—both times for Retro."

Another time, during a rehearsal at our place, everyone was ready. I noticed Călin leafing through his "verse notebook" from twenty years ago. Back then, it was usually the girls who kept notebooks of poems. I remember seeing one like it with Olezia on another occasion, and I felt nostalgic—transported for a moment into the past. Few still hold on to those notebooks from a world unimaginable today, a world without the internet, Facebook, or computers.

Back to that evening: he asked me,
"What do you think of this poem?"
I read:
'I would like to be a tree and grow by your window...' — Magda Isanos.
"Beautiful choice," I replied, "but we just performed it at another show. Maybe you don't remember, Călin. And besides, this one should really be recited by a woman."

Another moment. Călin confided:
"Do you know why I sometimes stumble on stage?... Actually, it happens on the soccer field too, even after playing for more than twenty years. It's because I'm full of emotion..."
Emotion. But if you feel and transmit it, then you've fulfilled your mission.

Moment – Winter on the Lane

We presented this poem at two Christmas shows in 2017. Its Romanian title, *Iarna pe uliță*—which means "Winter on the Lane"—comes from a beloved poem by George Coșbuc, who beautifully captured the sights and sounds of village life. Performing it always felt like stepping into a quiet, snowy lane myself, sharing that world with the audience. Wanting to involve as many people from the audience as possible—and, as Ștefan always said, to make as many people happy as we could—I thought of inviting them to recite a few verses this beautiful winter poem, watching with delight as their voices mingled with the magic of the season. this beautiful winter poem.

So, I got to work, arranging the verses and imagining how each voice would join the chorus of the poem. I selected only a few stanzas, reached out to those I knew wanted to take part, sent them their lines (divided into roles), asked them to rehearse at home, and then we met at the show. The most difficult part was technical: how would the microphone get from one to another when the participants were scattered among the spectators? Somehow, we solved the problem with two microphones.

Then came the unique moment. Delight, emotion... everything went beautifully. After the show, on my way home, Raluca called. I could hear the joy in her voice. She congratulated us once again and told me:
"Do you know what Adeline said? She said she wants to be in Retro when she grows up."

Adeline had already taken part in other events we organized. She once recited the poem *What I Wish for You, Sweet Romania* in a show dedicated to the great national poet. Her talent, candor, pride in being a little Romanian girl (born far from Romania), and her joy in reciting in her mother tongue—all of it enchanted the audience.

At the second winter show, during a rehearsal when we were discussing the program, I suggested again *Winter on the Lane*. A voice asked:
"Anda, why do you insist on complicating things? Why involve others from the audience?"

I was left with a bitter taste. Even within our own circle, the mission of the cenacle was understood very differently. But I continued the project and once more brought this wonderful poem to the stage, with the help of some amazing young people. Yes, I complicated things, but I also know I planted "seeds of creation" in the souls of the next generation. And for that, I am glad.

We've had such discussions before. The idea of creating opportunities for those who wanted to be on the Retro stage was not new. But often, I felt resistance from within the group. I remember one moment clearly:

A: "We're fine the way we are. We're doing our job, we can work on many new ideas, and there are enough of us. Why bring in others?"

That comment saddened me.

I replied:
"**A**, let me ask you a question. Think carefully. Has Retro changed your life?"
He paused, then admitted:
"Of course it has… and I am grateful."
"Then why not try to do the same for as many others as we can?"

And so, I would like to thank all those who, in one way or another, took part in our events, and through their talent and dedication helped us fulfill our mission:

Alexandru Grindeanu
Andreea and Dănel Haidău
Carmen, Ruxi, and Gina Griza
Andreea Bălan
Adeline Sîrbu
Stephanie Sălăjean
Geta Haţegan Pupek
Johnny and Lucas Raicu
Robert and Lucas Ciocan
Rebecca Răcean
Daniel Feraru

Bogdan Groza
Roxana Iacob
Olimpia Tudor
Florin Romoşan
Dana Ghiurcuţa
Adrian Donisa
Athena and Ana Mărincaş
Iulia Romoşan
Ionuţ and Marc Dima
Dana and Victor Lari

…and many more. You were—and remain—wonderful

ROMANTICS

From Gathered Performances

Note: This chapter presents actual excerpts from Retro Muse Society performances, blending Romanian songs, poetry, and cultural references. While all non-English content has been translated, some elements—such as traditional holidays, historic figures, famous artists, poets, authors, cities—may be unfamiliar to readers outside the Romanian community. These passages aim to convey the spirit, emotion, and shared experiences of the gatherings, inviting you to feel the music, poetry, and joy as if you were part of the circle.

Presentation: Retro Muse Society – "Armonii" *(Harmony)* Show, June 2017

Good evening and welcome to another Retro performance.
Now that you've opened the gates of your hearts to us, let us
continue with a short story—our story.

- *Summer 2010: Ştefan and Dan concerts*
- *May 2011: the first Vox Maris (as we were called then) performance at the Romanian Heritage Center*
- *December 2016: reunited again, still under the emotion of Romania's National Day*
- *January 2017: a show dedicated to Mihai Eminescu at the Holy Nativity Church in Chicago*
- *April 2017: "In the Chords of Spring," already under our new name, Retro*

Tonight, we greet with joy the presence of:
- Mrs. Consul Mihaela Deaconu
- The Consul General of Romania in Chicago, Mr. Tiberiu Trifan

Our story continues here and now, and we invite you to hum along to beloved songs, to feel Romanian at heart, and to dream together on this June evening.

Meet the Retro Family

Anda Cristolţean
From: Satu Mare
Two words that define me: Simple and complicated.
Passions: Fascinated by the order (or disorder?) of the Universe. I am overwhelmed by the beauty around me, and I believe it's within our power to see it, feel it, and turn it into a lifestyle.
Secrets: I feel a healing energy in nature and in art.

Laura Şişu
From: Brăila
Two words that define me: I love music and theater.
Passions: Actress and mother of three.
Secrets: None to share.

Călin Mărincaş
From: Cluj Napoca
Two words that define me: Charismatic and well-behaved.
Passions: Soccer and philosophy.
Secrets: NWO synthesis.

Ştefan Cristolţean
From: Cluj-Napoca, a stone's throw from Gelu's Fortress.
Two words that define me: I live life with the intensity of a hockey game.
Passions: Music, poetry, painting, and art in general - they relax me.
Secrets: I can't wait to get back on the ice.

Corina Vlad
From: Satu Mare
Two words that define me: Childlike soul.
Passions: Nature and traveling.
Secrets: She writes poetry.

Traian Bălan
From: Bucharest
Two words that define me: Laidback traveler.
Passions: Skiing (downhill), traveling, reading.
Secrets: What you see is what you get.

Marius Stan
From: Urziceni, Ialomița
Two words that define me: Creator, leader, and servant.
Passions: Writing, reading, observing.
Secrets: He's in love with AI—Artificial Intelligence, of course.
(And a secret he didn't reveal, but some of you might already know: Marius Stan played Bogdan in the TV series Breaking Bad.)

Decebal Sorin Griza
From: Banat (Reșița until after high school, Timișoara until before becoming American)
Two words that define me: Handsome, smart, talented, and above all, modest—an ordinary guy with the simplest of tastes: I'm satisfied only with what is best and most beautiful.
Passions: A ton of them—fishing, gardening, hiking, singing with friends and alone on the hills, and organizing Facebook movements (the most recent one: #numairezist—join in!).
Secrets: A few small ones, but for fear of revealing them to others, I haven't even confessed them to myself.
Another note: I climb mountains so I can have somewhere to descend, trade witty lines with my mother-in-law, and make poached eggs with a rock.

Cătălin Nicolae
From: [blank]
Two words that define me: [blank]
Passions: [blank]
Secrets: [blank]
(As you can see, some of us simply don't conform...)

Alina Celia Cumpan
From: Mercina, Caraș-Severin
Two words that define me: I can't be defined in just two words; I am myself an incomplete definition of my own lived words. For me, culture is a lifestyle and a form of therapy.
Passions: Since writing is only my sweet burden, I have made a passion of listening to silence and a hobby of studying people and their emotions.
Secrets: I live the moment turned inside of me.

Passing through...
Prof. univ. **Dr. Ion Berghia**
From: Basarabia, teaching at "Al. I. Cuza" University in Iași. Poet, prose writer, essayist, and satirist. President of the "Dor de Bucovina" magazine organization. Professor of Romanian language and literature.

Ligia Grindeanu
From: Sighișoara
Two words that define me: Have patience to speak my name, have patience—for the sake of the second that has already passed.
Passions: Nature, poetry, music—the music of the soul.
Secrets: She loves to dance.

That night, our "introductions" were not just lines on a page—they became brushstrokes in a portrait of Retro. Each person brought a different shade, a different rhythm, and together they painted the harmony of who we were.

Note: This presentation was my idea, created with a simple Google Form. I asked everyone to fill it out online... (This kind of idea is widely used in education when you want students to collaborate on a group project.) Applied to Retro, it worked wonders.

Harmony in Action

A Word About the Program

Or, as Ligia likes to call it: *the "Desfășurător."*

This script was crafted by Ligia and I, shaped through countless hours of listening to the thoughts, ideas, and suggestions of all those involved. Our goal was always the same: to bring to the public a performance of quality, woven with music, poetry, humor, and friendship.

It is in these long hours of planning together that RETRO's spirit of harmony is most visible: each member contributing a verse, a song, a gesture, until the performance becomes more than the sum of its parts.

And so, *On the Staff of Love* was born — not only a program, but an experience of collaboration, joy, and community.

On the Staff of Love - *Retro Muse Society – May 18, 2019*

Ștefan:
Good evening, friends, and welcome to the Retro Circle's show *"On the Staff of Love."*
We are so happy to see you here tonight in such large numbers, and we hope to warm your hearts after such a long winter.

Ligia:
The Key of Light – Ana of Sighișoara

On the staff of love,
The key of light appears,
In harmonies that awaken us—
On the staff of love!
A key opens the soul,
If it is stretched out by a hand,
And harmony will decide,
When flowers weave their crown.

Anda:
Minor and major scales
Entwine in embrace,
Seconds rounding into hours,
Songs of heaven's praise.

We invite you tonight to join us in this play of minor and major scales, *On the Staff of Love.*
Let us begin with a piece by Lucian Blaga.

Lucian Blaga: *Whispers of Love*
Ligia: *What Happens to Us* – Ligia Ana Grindeanu
Corina: *Two Hands* – Bosquito

Anda:
Winter has passed, spring is here, and it's time to see where love leads us.
I would say love is an ancient destiny—cherries dangling from our ears... Sorin, what do you say?

Sorin:
For me, love at first sight is real.

Sorin: *Love at First Sight* – Ilie Micolov
Ligia: *Sentimental Story* – Nichita Stănescu
Corina: *Rediscovery* – Traian Alex Bălan
Anda: *Nuances* – Anda Cristolțean

Ștefan:
For those from Cluj, and those who lived in this university city for a time, "U" is not just a letter.
It is the symbol of passionate hearts beating for the university sports club *"U" Cluj.*
This year marks its centennial, and the next piece is a tribute to its supporters and athletes.

Ștefan: *I Love You, But Not Like I Love "U"* – Ștefan Cristolțean
Anda: *Jealousy* – adaptation after George Topârceanu

Traian:
Hmm... come to think of it, I also have something to say.

Traian: *The Canadian* – Pasărea Colibri
Sorin: *I Like Tamara* – Alexandru Andrieș
Monica: *I Say Goodbye* – Monica and Lucian Blaga
Călin: *Bad Payer* – George Coșbuc

Intermission (10–15 minutes)

Scenette: *Around a Divorce* – George Topârceanu

Sorin:
And what can we do, if Zoe has brown eyes...?
As the old saying goes, "A woman's eyes speak louder than her words."

Radu: *Your Eyes* – Ștefan Hrușcă

Traian:
Ah, women's eyes... always a source of inspiration for artists.
I wonder whose eyes inspired Ștefan? Could they have been blue eyes?

Ștefan: *Your Brown Eyes* – Ștefan Cristolțean

Anda:
I wish I were a child, with a lilac branch,
Barefoot on the cobblestones,
To sit and quietly count
How much I love you.

Monica: *Who Made Me Grow Up* – Delia
Ligia: *The Crow and the Fox* – Florin Iordăchescu
Traian: *From Too Much or Too Little* – Vasile Şeicaru

Ligia (recites):
Stay where you are, don't move.
And if you love us—oh, if you truly love us—
Wait for us the same for just one more year...
One year... That's all... Only one more year...

Sorin:
Love, Porcelain Trinket... Recognize the words? I hope you'll recognize the song too.

Sorin: *Romance Without an Echo* – Mondial

Anda:
Romantics, nostalgics, with dreams and perfumes...
As long as we feed our souls with music and poetry, as long as we still hold hands—secretly or not—romanticism is not outdated. And yes, knights still exist... they're right here among us.

Corina: *Love Is an Ancient Destiny* – Vasile Şeicaru

Sorin (recites):
My love, one day, indeed,
In a restless late summer,
We will be like two apple halves
Forgotten on a bench at a train station...

Monica (with Retro): *My Love* – Holograf

Ligia (recites):
Twilight sketches the horizon
In charms of reverie,
A rainbow gently dances
On the staff of poetry...

Anda:
We slip heaven inside us,
At the meeting of eternity,
When we shine in unison,
In the charms of reverie.

Traian: *Neighborhood Story* – Traian Alex Bălan

Comic Interlude – Recipe for a Successful Relationship

Radu: Advice among friends:

Ştefan: 1. It's important to find a beautiful, smart woman who isn't jealous.
Călin: 2. It's important to find a woman who knows how to cook the most delicious food.
Sorin: 3. It's important to find a woman who doesn't get upset when you're late—on the contrary, she jumps into your arms and kisses you tenderly.
Traian: 4. But most important: these women must not know each other. Otherwise, this is what happens...

Ştefan: *I've Got Nothing in the Fridge* – Ştefan Cristolţean

Radu: Advice among girlfriends:

Anda: 1. It's important to find a man whose eyes don't wander when you're walking hand in hand.

Ligia: 2. It's important to find a man you can always rely on, romantic, who brings you flowers every day.

Anda: 3. It's important to find a man who thinks maturely, like a real grown-up.

Corina: 4. But most important is not to lose hope… and patience.

Closing

Anda & Ligia: Presentation of the Retro Circle members.

Ştefan: As you've seen, we in RETRO are intelligent, beautiful, young, perfect, and sublime.
All we have to do is snap our fingers, and spring instantly arrives!
Thank you for being with us tonight, and we hope to see you again next time!

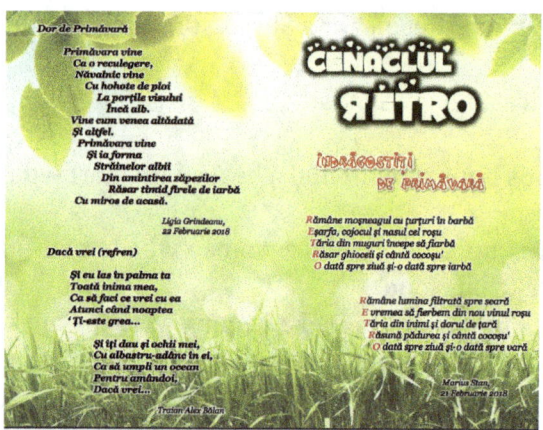

Note: This poster announces a Retro Muse Society performance titled *Îndrăgostiţi de Primăvară* (*In Love with Spring*). It features original verses by Ligia Grindeanu, Traian Alexandru Bălan, and Marius Stan, capturing the freshness of spring through poetry in the spirit of the Retro gatherings.

Harmony in Action - With the Contribution of Those Eager to Join Us

"Let Eminescu Judge Us…" *They Had to Have a Name…* Sunday, January 19, 2020

(Program devised largely by Ligia)

Note: The title *"They Had to Have a Name…"* is inspired by a poem of Nichita Stănescu, one of Romania's most beloved contemporary poets, dedicated to Mihai Eminescu. Eminescu, Romania's national poet, stands as a symbol of cultural identity and literary brilliance. In the Retro Muse Society show, we followed Stănescu's poem from beginning to end, weaving in songs and verses from Eminescu's works along the way—celebrating his legacy and keeping alive the tradition of honoring him as a guiding light of Romanian literature.

Anda, Radu, Retro: *Dor de Eminescu*
(On stage: Retro & Cătălin)

Anda: Opening remarks

Ligia *(reciting, over Cătălin's instrumental intro 0:00–0:32)*:
Eminescu never existed.
There only existed a beautiful country,
At the edge of a sea,
Where waves tied themselves into white knots
Like the uncombed beard of kings.

And waters flowed like tall trees,
Where the moon had its turning nest.

61

Anda *(reciting, over Cătălin's instrumental 0:33–1:33)*:
Evening on the Hill
Evening descends, the horn calls with sorrow,
The flocks climb, stars sparkle along the path,
The waters cry, springing clear into fountains;
Beneath an acacia, my love, you await me.

Ligia *(reciting, over Cătălin's instrumental 1:33–2:15)*:
The Unpaired Poplars
So many times I passed by the poplars,
The neighbors all knew me—
But you did not.

At your window, shining with light,
I gazed so often;
The whole world understood—
But you did not.

Cătălin: Instrumental — *Why Don't You Come to Me*

Radu *(reciting, over the same instrumental)*: *Ode in Ancient Meter*

Corina: *The Living Fire*

Ligia: And above all, there existed simple people.
People called Mircea the Elder, Ștefan the Great,
Or simply shepherds and ploughmen,
Who loved to tell, around the evening fire,
Poems like *Miorița*, *The Third Letter*, and *The Morning Star*.

Ana: *The Morning Star* (fragment)

Daniel: *Evening on the Hill* and *I Have But One Wish Left*

Geta: *Between Clouds and Between Seas*

Corina: *You Rise*

Ligia: And in the time left to them, between dangers,
These people carved flutes from wood,
Channels for the tears of softened stones.
And the doinas flowed down
From the mountains of Moldavia and Wallachia,
From Țara Bârsei and Țara Vrancei,
And from all the Romanian lands.

Sorin & Ligia: *Tear and Song*

Ligia: There also existed deep forests,
And a young man who spoke with them,
Asking why they swayed without wind.

Alexandru: *Why Do You Sway, O Forest?*

Ștefan: *Silver Nights*

Ligia: This young man, with eyes as vast as our history,
Walked, lost in thought,
From the Cyrillic book into the book of life,
Counting again and again
The poplars of light, of justice, of love—
And they always came out without number.

Roxana: *By The Unpaired Poplars*

Anda: *Poplars Without Him*

Olimpia: *Come Back, Beloved, to the Village* and *Doina*

Ligia: There also existed linden trees—
And two lovers,

Who knew how to bury all the blossoms
Into a single kiss.

Corina: *In the City with Linden Blossoms*

Ligia: *Longing for Eminescu*

Andreea: *The Birth of Eminescu*

Radu: *And If...*

Bogdan: *For Future Generations*

Ligia: There also existed birds and clouds,
Wandering above like moving plains.

Sorin: *For Her*

Ana: *The Morning Star of the Great Worlds*

Roxana: *If You Were a Willow by the Shore*

Ligia: And because all of this
Had to have a name,
One single name—
They called it **Eminescu**.

Ştefan, Roxana, Retro: *Eminescu*

Ligia: Cenaclul Retro thanks all who made this evening possible:
Florin Romoşan for photography,
Mr. Steven Bonica for hosting,
And our collaborators tonight:
Georgeta Haţegan, Olimpia Tudor, Roxana Iacob, Andreea Haidău, Daniel Feraru, Olimpiu Bodea, Bogdan Nicolae Groza, and Cătălin Lari.

And thousands of thanks to you, beautiful souls, thirsty for these emotions—
All of you here tonight with us and with Eminescu.
The Retro heart beats for Romanian poetry and music.
We need your help and support to continue our mission
And to create more evenings like this.

Anda: Don't forget our guestbook, website, and Facebook page for future events.

Anda & Ligia: Presentation of Cenaclul Retro members...

Returning to the thread of our story and to the moments that bring Retro to life...

RETRO MUSE SOCIETY

SIMPLY US

Autumn 2019 **Moment –Shades and Tones**

We were invited to organize a charity performance for one of the Romanian churches. We answered with joy and enthusiasm, as always. The money collected from ticket sales was donated to the church. A beautiful gesture, one that further defined our mission.

Then came preparations, rehearsals, and a lot of hard work. For those without instruments, cables, microphones, or amplifiers to carry, everything seemed much easier... even simple, I'd say. *"I just go on stage. I don't have to worry about anyone else, I don't have to sync with anyone."* Perhaps that's where some frustrations come from. Honestly, I might not fully grasp how much work goes into a performance either—if Ștefan weren't always beside me showing me how much unseen work a performance truly requires.

We arrived at the church well before the show, to set up and check the sound system. We were drenched, hungry, and tired. And yet, *"Shades and Tones"*—our autumn concert—was one where we gave everything we had, once again delighting everyone who came to watch, listen, and celebrate with us.

From bits and pieces of texts

"Dear Retro-ists,
As you know, at the end of Saturday's show on October 26, Roxana will bring her daughter to sing. I think it's an excellent idea, and

that's why I propose we take this opportunity to encourage the younger generation to participate in the cenacle's activities. Here's what I suggest: let's include a short moment with no more than three kids or young people, as the opening of the show. Instead of waiting 30–45 minutes for the audience to gather, we could begin at 7:10 with their moment—no more than 15–20 minutes.

I'm sure each of us knows at least one child or teen who'd love to join. The moment doesn't have to be perfect or complicated. I've raised this idea before, but that's where it stayed—at the discussion stage.

With this gesture, we don't just create beauty and awaken memories in the hearts of our audience; we also inspire the younger generation. I know there are many talented kids in the community. My thought is to vote on three for this show, while others will come another time. After their performance, we take a short break, and then we begin our program. And at the very end, we'll close with the voice of a child."—Anda

---

Moment – Thoughts and Emotions

"An unforgettable October evening!
With rain!
Yes! It rained that night!
It rained with applause! It rained with autumn emotions!
It rained with smiles, but also with sighs, with laughter, but also with tears of longing and pain!
Yes! This bundle of souls in love with beauty — Cenaclul Retro — lifted us once again to our feet and moved us to tears!
Thank you, Cenaclul Retro, for this wonderful evening!
Thank you for reminding us where we came from — we, the wandering sons and daughters!...
Bravo, Cenaclul Retro!"— Olezia Comşulea, October 26, 2019

May 2020 – **Moment Retro ZOOM**

A Zoom meeting, transcribed with much effort from the recording. Full of joyful, funny moments... Believe me, we laughed until we cried.

Anda and Ștefan are hosting. One by one, the Retro family begins to connect. Technical mishaps, inside jokes, and the warmth of friendship quickly set the tone.

Anda & Ștefan: Hello, hello Radu?
Ștefan: Can you hear us? You sound like a cyborg. Turn your volume up.
Anda: Who else just joined? Sorin? Since I didn't give out the password, now I have to accept each of you one by one.
Ștefan: I thought you said, "Since I didn't give out the password, you have to pay to get in."

(Laughter erupts.)

Sorin appears on screen, silent and enigmatic. We can't tell if he hears us or not.

Anda: Sorin, do you have audio?
Radu: "Unmute."
Ștefan: Now he's really turning into a cyborg.

Sorin puts in his earpieces.
Ștefan: Like in Star Trek: DATA. He's DATA. Hand on chest — like the emblem on those old Oltcit cars back home.

Radu bursts out laughing.
Sorin still doesn't react.
Ștefan: I think he's watching TV, not us.
Radu: Romanian TV.

For nearly five minutes, we all watch Sorin fumble with his setup. He doesn't hear us, but that doesn't stop the running commentary.

Anda: I don't think he can even see us.
Ștefan: Told you, he's watching YouTube instead.

(Everyone laughs harder.)

Ștefan: How's life treating you all in this strange time?

Ligia logs on next, bringing an instant burst of energy.

Anda: Servus, Ligia! (Our Romanian "hi!")
Ligia: Hi Retro! *(She shows off her Retro T-shirt full-screen. Everyone cheers, except Sorin who still looks serious.)*

We text Sorin. Suddenly, he disappears.
Radu: He gave up.
Sorin reappears: "Hello, hello… Now I hear you. I didn't at first."
Anda: We weren't even sure you could see us!

One by one, more familiar faces join: Iulian, Anişoara, then later Corina. Greetings, jokes, and memories flow easily.

Anişoara: Look, the mentors are here—Ștefan and Anda!
Sorin: An afternoon tea dance.
Anişoara: Or maybe… "Cenaclul Anytime."

(Applause and laughter.)

Anda: Keep it coming—we like this!
Anişoara: And sometimes, instead of a *muză*—our elegant muse—we get a *muzoi*—her clumsy, imaginary 'male' cousin!

Anişoara: Ladies and gentlemen… Happy Anniversary!

Yes—there's an art to making people feel good. And Retro seems to carry that seed within us all. Even virtually, harmony is present.

Sorin walks through his "Town Hall" (as Retro nicknamed his house), phone in hand, taking us with him. He shows us the basement "dungeons" and his impressive drink selection.

Anda: Who's missing? Corina? Călin? Cătălin?

Sorin sits awkwardly under a ceiling light, glaring into his camera.
Ștefan: Sorin, did you point a spotlight at us?
(Laughter. Sorin shows his beer.)
Ștefan: Like he's from security—"Confess everything!"

Twenty minutes have flown by, filled with laughter. Finally, talk turns to what really matters: music and poetry.

Anda: Ligia, what's the program?
Ligia: I thought we'd each sing or say something...
Ștefan: Let me grab my guitar—I'll sing first.
Ligia: Good. Then Anișoara with a poem.

Corina pops in, hood up.
Ștefan: OMG, you look so gangster!
Radu: From the hood!
Corina: Hi everyone. Just out of the shower. Did I miss anything?
Anda: Don't worry—we recorded it. We'll post it on the site.
Ștefan, alarmed: Don't you dare!

(More laughter.)

Corina: What's going on?
Ștefan: It's spring break, Corina.
Anda: Smile for the camera!

And so, with jokes and laughter, Retro's harmony flowed easily—
even across virtual space. We ended the evening the way we
always did: with music and poetry

July 2020 . **Moment – Adventures at Rock Cut State Park**
*Or - **Wandering through the Enchanted Grove***

It was time to plan another camping trip.
Even though many in Retro love nature, not all were inclined—or
let's say thrilled—to spend one or two nights in a tent. Recently,
Ștefan and I had bought a camper, and Corina and Sergiu had one
as well, so we could offer proper beds to those who couldn't sleep
outdoors. Campsites in beautiful parks are usually booked far in
advance, but we decided to take our chances.

Corina and I coordinated the planning and managed to find a few
scattered spots at **Rock Cut State Park**. It wasn't perfect, but it
would do. We spread the word and made our plans.

We arrived Friday, each settling into our spots before gathering at
Corina and Sergiu's site — our "tarla."
It was magical there. Nature greeted us joyfully; the clearing felt
like a *dumbrava minunată* — an "enchanted grove" straight out of
childhood memory. We cooked, played, laughed, and delighted in
each other's company.

The next day we headed to the small lake. Not knowing much
about the place, we set up camp at the forest's edge. It was hot,
and even though the water was murky, full of duckweed and who
knows what else, we couldn't resist jumping in. It didn't matter —
joy carried us through.

That evening we gathered around the fire, singing, taking photos,
and soaking in the moment. Some had to leave, but a few of us
stayed. The decision proved right — because the following

morning we discovered the park's true wonder: the great lake. We decided to walk its trail, wandering through one meadow after another, each more beautiful than the last. Hidden among them, grove after grove appeared before us.

And then, with her usual enthusiasm, Corina exclaimed: "*Dumbrava minunată!*" (Enchanted Grove)

We laughed, but in truth, her words stayed with us. What began as a playful remark in the middle of a summer outing became a seed — one that would later blossom into the title of a song we created and even the theme of a future Retro show. In that moment, though, it was simply joy in nature, joy in each other, and joy in discovering that even the smallest glades could carry the enchantment of childhood wonder. Retro's *Enchanted Grove* was born there, in that moment, among friends, in a glade where joy itself seemed to take root.

October 3, 2020 **Moment – The First Postponed Show...**

Today we should have been on stage at the Heritage Pavilion Park in Wheeling, performing a Retro show. Instead, the performance was postponed due to Covid-related restrictions.

Maybe it's for the best... After all, the weather is against us too — cold and rainy — certainly not the kind of evening for an outdoor concert.

Cenaclul Retro is feeling sad.

⭐ Favorites · October 2, 2020   •••

Ladies and Gentlemen,

Due to precautionary measures regarding the epidemic and the rules imposed by the Park District, we are forced to postpone our autumn show to a later date, wh we will announce.

We thank you for your understanding and wish you a beautiful autumn, filled with music and poetry in your hearts. 🎵🍁✨

We, your audience who love you, understand and are waiting for you with so much, so much love, and even more longing to see you live on stage!

You are always amazing! Because everything you do comes from the depths of your souls, with so much love and selfless passion.
A beautiful autumn tore coming soon!
May we hear only good news! 🧡

Moment – The Story Continues Indoors

But *the story in the park* continued at the Ro-Am Network library.

The messages began to flow from early morning. We were all a bit shaken and disappointed that the concert hadn't happened — but, more than anything, we missed each other, we missed Retro. (Even though we had just met for rehearsal the week before.) Sorin was the first to propose a weekend get-together. It took us a while to shake off the disappointment of not performing on stage... we were slow to start texting, but once the ideas began, there was no stopping us.

And so, by 4 PM, we gathered at the library — with instruments, speakers, amplifiers, microphones... and food. Was it a party? A rehearsal? With Retro you never really know. Everything blends together so beautifully that the answer to both questions is simply: does it even matter? Whether a rehearsal or a party, when we're together, positive energy sparks and lifts us all to give our very best.

Once we set up our "stage," Ștefan suggested:
"How about we livestream this on Facebook?"

If you haven't yet seen those first clips from our "live" debut on Facebook, they're worth searching out. Within hours they reached thousands of views — not because they were professional, but because they carried raw emotion. They radiated the joy of being together, of singing, reciting, and sharing time as one.

Around midnight, after packing up all the equipment, we lingered — chatting over a glass of wine, singing patriotic songs, laughing, and marveling at how many memories we shared from our teenage and university years in Romania. We remembered verses from childhood poems, from socialist-era songs. It's fascinating how certain lines learned as children stay with you forever — tucked away in memory like little porcelain figurines, gathering dust but never forgotten.

At last, reluctantly, we said our goodbyes — as if no one really wanted to head home. Meanwhile, Facebook was buzzing. I was glad we'd been able to give our friends and supporters a taste of Retro, a slice of performance. I even received notes from American friends who admitted the music had touched their hearts. That's the gift of music: it's universal; the language hardly matters.

The next day, we struggled to shake off the euphoria.
I missed Retro already.
And once again, the messages began to flow...

Unleashed – from collected texts (Oct 3 and Oct 4, 2020)

What's going on, dear ones?
I thought my phone was
resting... when suddenly I see
dozens of messages flooding
in... what organization!
As I was saying, we could put
on a show in just a few hours...
So, see you soon... 1:26 PM✓

Corina
Love u all sooo much!
See you at 4
I wonder if we should let Mrs.
Ana from Sighişoara know
so she's ready by the time
Ligia comes from work.
Do you have her number or
Iulian's 11:16 AM

Ligia
You are adorable! Mom is
already matching her scarf
with her purse.
We'll arrive a bit later, around
6 pm. We had an earlier
invitation from a family who
were supposed to come to

Radu Raceanu
It was all so beautiful!
Thank you from me a well, for not
giving up on the idea of the
Cenaclul, even while going through
darker days and months. The fact
that we do it with joy and as
volunteers is truly wonderful!

Catalin Lari
Go Retro!!!!
I, for one...haven't
finished my coffee...
Love you all and
see you soon!
1:37 PM

Indeed
Indeed!
It seems Retro
enthusiasm can
handle spontaneous
stuff! I realized we
are invincibile!
A little more focus
and we will be
immortal!
Already dreaming
about the next
moments
Thank you all!
❤️ u all! 11:27 AM

Anakin
Yet another
wonderful evening,
dear Rebels.
You were all so
warm and original.
12:08 PM

Ligia
We thank you too
for organization,
refreshments, and
technical support,
and of course for
the warmth we
have alongside you.
You are wonderful
and talented!
12:08 PM

The songs and lyrics
flowed as we
promised our
friends
12:08 AM

I think it was good that we released the videos; it seems quite a few people from all over are watching them, and at the next event, whenever that may be, we will have a sizeable audience. I hope we meet again and work just as efficiently in the meantime. 12:10 PM

I hope we meet again and work just as efficiently in the meantime.
Thank you, Radu, for mediating between us and Steve so we could go to the library. It's a great pity that everything will have to be moved from there, but who knows, maybe that will be another beginning, as the song says...

It would be good if we could also help, however we aca...
I think we've at least managed to cast a ray of light on these gray times we're going through. Love you aиi! 💕
Go RETRO! 😘 12:10 PM

📌 **Notes:**

- Sorin has the longest "epistles."
- Anakin is Ștefan.

November 1, 2020 **Moment – Rehearsal**

We were preparing a message-performance for December 1st. We gathered at the library, around the "round table of friendship." Those of us who don't usually sing — myself included — probably don't realize how much every detail matters. Some songs didn't sound quite right... Maybe that's why a bit of tension arose. Or maybe **A** just needed a little action — he tends to enjoy being "dramatic," even if he won't admit it in public.

To lighten the atmosphere, I picked up the microphone and made these dedications to the girls:

To Corina: *"If one day you feel like crying, look for me... I can't promise to make you laugh, but I can cry with you."*

To Anişoara: *"If one day you feel like running away, look for me... I can't promise to stop you, but I can run away with you."*

To Ligia: *"If one day you look for me and I don't answer... come quickly to see me. Maybe I'm the one who needs you."*
(lines by Marin Sorescu)

It worked — everyone relaxed, which was exactly the point.

Radu, smiling: *"Can we have dedications too?"*
Me: *"Of course! But I'll have to write them, since Marin Sorescu stopped here."*

We left that night "on fire," as Corina put it. It was a beautiful evening; one we learned a lot from. More than just a rehearsal — it was both an experience and an experiment.

Happy National Day, Romania! – 2020

EVEN MORE REBELLIOUS

The story of Retro continues with renewed energy, unexpected twists, and even bolder adventures. What follows are moments that capture the spirit of playfulness and resilience that define us—always together, always moving forward.

From Bits and Pieces of Texts - A Fruitful Rehearsal

My dear friends,

Here's a small selection of what we 'committed' today. Thank you for the recordings. I'm thinking we could use them as backing tracks — then each of us can record our own vocal and instrumental parts at home, and send them to me for mixing. This way, everyone can take their time and try multiple takes, and we can choose the best ones. Otherwise, it's really hard to balance all voices and instruments 'live' at the library.

If you agree, we could start with one song and see how it goes. Please, suggest which one.

*After listening to the recordings and to the advice from **Cătălin** and **Sorin**, I've realized again how much potential we have to grow. All we need is to keep polishing the Retro stone until it shines like a diamond. We've come such a long way since we first embarked on this journey into the Beautiful, and it's inspiring that we all want to keep growing.*

So — let's keep adding vocal warm-ups and other exercises at the beginning of rehearsals, even just ten minutes or so.

Sorin, I know how energized you get when you're working on mastering the sound, and I share your optimism that we can make the mixing work. The question is: when do we meet to start recording?

GO RETRO! — *in the voice of Ştefan*

December 29, 2020 **Moment – Year-End Emotions**

I find myself drifting into memories. Again...
It's been a hard year with this Covid crisis, and some of us have lost loved ones back in Romania. We try to rewind the film of our memories, to savor the good times—moments from long ago that feel as fresh as yesterday.

Facebook brought up *"Brother Ştefan's Carol"* from two years ago—a moment dedicated to Ştefan by Ana of Sighişoara during a Saint Stephen's Day gathering at our home. I watch the video and listen... how beautiful, simple, and pure it all was.

"When I think of this bond that Retro is, I realize I truly cannot live without it," confesses Ana.
"And who else can...?" another voice chimes in.
"Neither can we, neither can we..."

Frozen tears in winter
Remind us of sorrowful silences
Of Christmas reunions among the stars
White snowflakes turn back into pages

—Ana of Sighişoara

Moment – New Year's Emotions

from Facebook posts

Bogdan Adrian Toma — Cenaclul Retro
New Year's Message

"From Sandu Pop, a.k.a. *Văru' Săndel*, for Cenaclul Retro: hoping for a 2021 with less illness and more poetry, with less distancing and more performances, with less 'scientific' normality and more romantic delirium. And, after all, with more crystal-clear glasses of wine raised in honor of literature in all its forms. *Cenaclul Retro is the solution* Happy New Year!"

Anda and Ştefan: *"Cenaclul Retro is the solution."*
What a wonderful surprise! May we meet again soon, and in good health. Thank you for the message!

Nicole Bogdan Groza: *Anda and Ştefan: "The ending is great."*
There (at Retro) mind, soul, art, and the Romanian spirit all come together. *And that's the truth!*

Moment – A Carol in Falling Snow

Or – At the Ice Rink with Retro

We've been living through difficult years, a time in human history that we will always remember with sadness: Covid. In the beginning (2020), we met faithfully on Zoom every Saturday at 6 p.m. Each of us would prepare a little "moment," and despite the technical hurdles, we still managed to connect beautifully in the virtual space. During the summer we even met outdoors — in gardens, forests, and open air — and somehow we kept rehearsing with dedication and harmony.

Then autumn came, followed by winter. The year 2021 began, and... we couldn't take it anymore! We missed each other too much.

It was January, there was snow and ice, so we made plans. Corina came up with the idea: *"Let's all meet at the ice rink. Maybe we'll even build a snowman."* Not many were able to say yes — understandable in those times — but Corina, Sergiu, Sorin, Călin, and the two of us went.

We arrived at the park. The snow was slushy, but the rink was still frozen. The energy and harmony, as always, were at their highest. Before we left home, Ştefan had said: *"In this weather I'm not even putting skates in the trunk — it's not skating weather."* But, as the saying goes, *"there are few like Retro."* We ended up skating after all. Ştefan hadn't packed my skates, but Călin, as luck would have it, had a pair of women's skates in his trunk — and they happened to be my size.

The skating itself was... interesting. With the slushy ice, it felt dangerous. Brave as ever, Călin put on skates for the first time in his life. To everyone's surprise, he didn't fall once. Ştefan guided him a bit, he wobbled here and there, but he kept his balance. Clearly, all his years of passionate soccer training paid off.

Ştefan: *"So, Călin, how was your first experience on ice?"*
Călin: *"Well... let's just say, I can't describe what I can't remember. I don't feel a thing..."*

Corina and Sorin looked like naturals on skates. Ştefan, this time, stayed in the role of coach and cheerleader.

Back at the rink, I noticed Corina stubbornly trying to build — or in Retro slang, to *"construct"* — a snowman. The snow was far too wet, but seeing her determination, I joined in. And somehow, together, we ended up with a tiny little snowman. A small but beautiful reminder to never let the soul grow old — to remain children forever.

How we had missed each other! We sang, we joked, we laughed — the same good energy flowed, stronger than even the pandemic.

Corina began singing: *"Ninge cu vorbele tale / E iarnă fierbinte ca o rugăminte"* (Karma).
Sorin threw in a joke: *"So, at what temperature does a right angle boil?"*
Answer: *"At 90 degrees."* Smiles and banter all around.

It was a perfect snowy day with Retro. I only wished all of us could have been there.

March 13, 2021 **Moment – Coffee with Poetry**

A heartfelt reflection inspired by the volume of poems **Anotimpuri de Dor** *(Seasons of Longing), recently published by Ligia.*

I spent my morning having coffee with Poetry. I sat down with my longings and unraveled the seasons.
This morning I cherished *"Ploile de martie"* (The March Rains), *"Zăpada târzie"* (The Late Snow), and *"Întrebările fără răspuns"* (The Unanswered Questions) woven into *"O altă poveste"* (Another Story). Thank you, Ligia, for touching my longing with your infinite blue. Somehow, the coffee tasted better.

"Fotografiile nu mai ajung pe hârtie.
Dar oare amintirile unde se duc?"
"Photographs no longer make it onto paper.
But where do memories go?"

Dear reader, if you have patience, in this *"digital world"*, *"pe cerul inimii la poarta sărutului"* (on the sky of the heart, at the gate of a kiss) I invite you to *"te oprești să admiri infinitul"* (pause and admire infinity).

For a long time now, every Friday, Ligia calls me, smiling on the other end of the line: *"Dacă e vineri, e cafeaua cu Poezia, cu Anda şi Ligia."* *(If it's Friday, it's coffee with Poetry, with Anda and Ligia.)* It is our moment to disconnect from everything and wander together through the unseen world of words. And the ideas, the verses, they flow... and yes, the coffee truly tastes better.

April 10, 2021 **Moment – A Cultural Dialogue**

Our first rehearsal after a long period of isolation.
There is singing, reciting, and laughter—an unmistakable harmony in the joy of being reunited. Ştefan prepares a surprise for Anişoara: he composed a song using verses adapted from one of her poems. Anişoara is delighted—she has been waiting for such a moment for a long time. We had tried before to set her poetry to music, but somehow it never fully came together. Now it finally has.

She confides that the piece is very dear to her, and she is overjoyed that its message found life in this song. *"I'm going home to post it on Facebook, just to make the enemies die of envy!"* she teases. Everyone—especially the musicians—jumps in: *"No, not yet... not until we polish it!"* She looks a little disappointed, but she understands.

"A man without enemies is like a statue without a shadow," she says.

Ligia recites in response, quoting Adrian Păunescu:

„Nimeni nu e singur pe pământ
Cineva în grija lui îl are
Nici cei singuri, singuri nu mai sunt
Dacă are umbră fiecare"

"No one is ever truly alone on earth,
There is always someone watching over them.
Even the lonely are not truly lonely,
For everyone carries their own shadow."

The cultural dialogue flows so naturally. Afterward, Sorin plays the piece *"Singur" (Alone)*.

I am so used to this unique way of connecting—and in Retro, we connect so easily through music, poetry, and beautiful thoughts—that I feel compelled to share it. I want these pages to carry at least a spark of this energy to you, dear reader. If you are reading this book, it is because you love what we do. I feel your closeness, and I wish these good thoughts to travel with you—and why not, to inspire you too.

April 21, 2021

Among Retro's many voices, Sorin's stood out for his playful "Epistles." Written in jest, full of wit and exaggeration, these letters became a trademark of Retro's chats and gatherings. They show not only his humor, but also the affectionate bond that tied the group together.

Sorin – from the series "Epistles"

Dear Rebels,

On this quiet evening I'd like to hold your attention with a proposal about an event that's fast approaching next week—namely, as we all know, the birthday of our dear comrade in class and in mischief, captain of the crew, and on top of that, a saint—yes, I'm speaking directly and explicitly about Ştefan. 😛

Cătălin and I have been scheming (in absentia, while at church after Sunday's service) to surprise him with—well, a surprise. Hopefully a pleasant one! Perhaps fulfilling a wish, more or less burning, that he might secretly enjoy. For example, a gift from the Retro crew that would be both useful and a keepsake of our wild yet beautiful "school days."

I appeal to your unlimited imagination, but especially to the necessary suggestions of Anda, who is both his teacher and private tutor, and therefore knows best how he's doing in her subject—and what he might still need to boost his grade this year.

Of course, I'm counting on Anda to keep the secret—at least until the event itself—so the surprise won't be spoiled. To put it simply, we have 1–2 days to bring in proposals and ideas, leaving us just enough time afterward to go fishing on the Danube... or maybe even the Amazon.

Kisses to all, and of course—Go RETRO!

April 22, 2021

Wonderful, Ligia! In just a few words, chosen with inspiration, you managed to paint the pastel shades, the figures of speech, and the inner emotions that give birth to feelings ready to take flight toward the souls of those who love beauty. My opinion (but only this time) is that any additional stanza, even a single verse more, would become superfluous, risking dissonance in the harmonious unity so vividly cemented through the vibrations of the metaphor "doo-wop and la-la-la."   *Sorin – from bits and pieces of texts*

April 27, 2021 **Moment – Ștefan's Birthday**

Part One – Reporting live from the scene. It's April 27, and tonight wonderful things will unfold... It all started last Friday, when Sorin sent an "urgent" message to the Retro group —

conveniently leaving Ştefan out, of course — with the idea of planning a surprise for him. His birthday is tomorrow...

I am utterly exhausted, but I'm waiting with anticipation for something special to happen. There have been beautiful ideas shared in our group chat, but also a few frustrations... Still, tonight all the beauty of Retro will burst into life.

Ştefan's birthday always falls close to Orthodox Easter, which makes it difficult to plan. This year it lands on Holy Wednesday — right in the middle of the week. Saturday is out, since it's Holy Saturday, Sunday is Easter, and if I postpone for another week, we'll already be in May. That's why I decided to invite Retro on Tuesday, the eve of Ştefan's birthday.

It's never easy to gather during the week, but tonight, Tuesday, the Retro crowd will come together from 6:00 to about 8:30 to surprise Ştefan for his birthday. I'm waiting eagerly to celebrate him in true Retro style. Stay tuned for Part Two...

Anda – in the heat of preparation

April 28, 2021 **Moment – Part Two**

Joy, dance, laughter, HARMONY = Retro.

It's two in the morning — nobody wants to leave. We all have to work tomorrow, but no one feels like saying goodbye.

As we leave, Anişoara turns to us: *"You two are perfection. Read my poem; it's titled **Perfection.**"*

Here is her poem, written just a few days earlier:

PERFECTION

by Ana Munteanu Drăghici   April 24, 2021

Love is no mere artifact,
Carried through ages by a wonder.
Love is forever the unbroken voice
Of a sun that never sets!

It is not the chase for a summit,
Of a fleeting passing moment.
It is the gift that no flower's bloom
Shall ever come to end.

From beauty's corolla spring forth
Colors, offered in their giving,
With the brightness of youth's glow—
Passing on, yet never fading.

Love does not live in calendars,
Searching for a place to rest...
It is a garment of waiting,
An eternity among the hours.

Love is no artifact unearthed,
No discovery of archaeologists.
It is built of living souls,
Explored only by love itself.

Through seeking, through rediscovery
Within the sunrise of the soul,
It never strays nor loses way—
Love dwells in one single thought.

Mortals have given it names,
By time-forgotten, nameless voices.
Others have clothed it in decades,
Those who evoke it in their poems.

Yet the universe clothes it still
In harmony, ancient and true,
That shall never know reversal
Through the perfect, kindred soul

April 28, 2021 - Ştefan

My dear friends, thank you and I love you all with all my heart. You are that joining of souls for which the universe and time itself stand still. Forgive my delayed reply, but I've just woken up. I took the day off.

May 2021 **Moment – A Note of Seriousness – message from Corina, "The Forest Girl"**

My dear friends,

Any change on a large scale begins at the level of the individual. Each of us goes through experiences that shape us, and the decisions we make depend on many factors.

In my case, I take into account not only logic but also that gut feeling (explained, perhaps, by the laws of quantum physics), as well as personal experience. Whatever the decision, each person bears responsibility for it (or at least should).

This crisis, beginning last year, has led to a desensitization of the human spirit, often preventing us from taking the right actions or making sound decisions. I notice how people are increasingly divided according to beliefs, and more recently, by whether they are vaccinated or not. I do not believe humanity will truly evolve this way.

I do not side with either camp, but I do believe we are witnessing a phenomenon of mass brainwashing. Forgive me, but I cannot agree with someone walking alone through the forest with a muzzle on their face. And yet—I do believe in Covrig (for the curious).

We are witnessing various experiments that restrict human freedom, stir up fear, and push people toward hasty decisions.

Let us not forget the purpose for which we gathered: **Retro** *(Renaştem Elogiind Trăirile Româneşti Oriunde am fi – "We are reborn by honoring Romanian experiences wherever we may be"). Let us look at one another as a WHOLE, not as individuals separated by beliefs, rivalries, and differences. We all come from the same source (Love) and we all leave this world carrying nothing but the Light within us! That is true evolution.*

Love you all! Wishing you a healthy Easter and peace in your hearts! And may we also bring this "covrig" business to an end.

On my path through this life, I strive for an evolution that is as harmonious, honest, and positive as possible. I have valued the guidance and advice of those with more experience, and I will never forget the beautiful memories that made me truly vibrate with joy. But, alongside modesty, I carry another quality: I cannot fake feelings or give compliments out of mere politeness.

When someone you trusted, someone who once did things out of sheer passion and not for money or fame, later throws mud at you behind your back, it becomes difficult to move forward with the same feelings. To forgive is necessary if you want to evolve, but forgetting—it takes time. And when you no longer resonate, you simply go forward on your own wavelength.

I love stories with happy endings, but when someone cuts the branch out from under their own feet, they alone are responsible for their action.

I wanted to say this to the whole group—I don't like cliques or little circles. As far as I know, we gathered together freely, to revive Romanian feelings and experiences, and to offer soul-joys to those who open their hearts to them. (In American terms: voluntary work, not forced, and not for profit.)

I move on, hoping the good things will gather and that we will collaborate wherever our souls are called. And since we all admit that "once upon a time" stories are worth telling, let's not waste time and instead weave our story as beautifully as possible. In the end, you take nothing with you to the other world—not even "Retro's fame"—only what you gave, if you never took.

She closed her message with verses:

"And a corner of my life
Dared to stand before you,
To wipe away, if it could,
Another wrinkle from your brow.

I'm a fleeting shadow,
Like Puck, like Ariel.
If I've caused you any sorrow,
Be upset with me a little.

But if for a single moment
I've helped you dream again,
Give me each one feathered wing
And let's be brothers here on earth.

If you've paid a bit of heed,
If it brought you some delight,
Then I'll just say this, indeed:
Till next time — goodbye, goodnight!"

With respect,
Corina

Moment – "Ochii tăi căprui / Your Brown Eyes" – a Personal Project

Behind the Scenes (the long story)

It seems that Retro acts like a catalyst, especially when it comes to personal creations. Seeds sprout and blossom when they find fertile ground and a nurturing environment. *"Look at Corina, Traian, Sorin, and others,"* Ligia says. *"How much they've grown artistically."* In truth, all of us have "grown" and "borne fruit" since being together.

Ștefan's songs and poems are surfacing. It was about time. I've known some of them since the day we met. Each one is dear to him—and dear to me. I wouldn't want them to be lost. I remember, back in the reading room of our university dorm, we recorded all these songs on a stereo tape recorder. The hall had an incredible echo. I put that cassette away safely... maybe too safely.

The idea of making an official video belonged to Ștefan. He thought of two original pieces: *"N-am nimic în frigider"* (*"You're All I Have"*) and *"Ochii tăi căprui / Your Brown Eyes."*

"You know, this is going to cost us," he told me. I replied, *"What matters more? The joy of the soul or the money? I'm just glad we've reached a point where we can afford to make even one official video. What you've composed is too beautiful not to be shared with others."* And so, the work began.

Ștefan had ideas, contacted videographers, negotiated prices, weighed experiences—some positive, some less so. He said:

"I spoke with two people who've done this kind of work before. Both did a good job in the past, and honestly, I'd work with either. I'm thinking of doing one song with each. The price is slightly different, but that doesn't bother me." That was so typical of Ștefan—always trying not to upset anyone.

He began making calls to explain his decision. He wanted to start filming *"Your Brown Eyes"* first, then move on to *"I Have Nothing in the Fridge."* But one phone call quickly took an unexpected turn:

Ștefan: *"Here's what I've decided. For Your Brown Eyes I'll go with A, and..."* He didn't even get to finish before **B** exploded: *"What do you mean? You looked for someone else? Do you Romanians think others will do better work than us?"* and continued ranting, upset that Ștefan had dared to seek a second opinion.

B's impatience and attitude made the decision easier. Price was a factor, yes—but ultimately, what truly mattered was the creative concept behind the video.

August 2019 — filming begins. We needed two young people with brown eyes. We tried with our kids, but they were either shy or uninterested. In the end, Paul (our son) took the role more seriously. For the girl, after a few discussions, we chose Ruxi (Sorin daughter) And so, Paul and Ruxi became the protagonists of the video—young, in love, carefree, and joyful on the beach.

As a big fan of U-Cluj soccer team, Ștefan added small touches: the "U" jersey, passing a ball on the beach, then a guitar appears... and in a little detail, "Retro" was written in tiny letters on the ball. One day of filming on Evanston Beach turned into a wonderful experience.

Then came 2020. Work began on the instrumental track, but everything slowed down because of the global crisis. Ștefan dreamed of adding a second part to the video, one featuring us— Retro—performing together.

It was a beautiful late-summer day. *"Let's go to the lake. I want to show you some places and share my idea,"* he said. The winding road reminded me of Romania; my friend Aneta said it reminded her of Poland. Just a few serpentine bends were enough to stir homesickness

His idea: *"What if we brought the camper, parked it on the sand at the beach, and used it for filming? Each of us could step out one by one, playing, singing, smiling in the sun and by the water (Lake Michigan). Everyone from Retro could be in the video—it wouldn't be static. It would be something special."* I agreed—it was indeed something special.

We scouted locations, spoke with the district about permits, filled out forms, faced red tape. *"You know,"* I told him, *"What if we had just come here with the camper and filmed? Without all this bureaucracy..."*

Another idea Ștefan toyed with was filming Retro on a pontoon. We had rented pontoons many times with family and friends and carried fond memories of those days. But for a music video with the whole Retro group, things would have become complicated— too many people, instruments, filming logistics, and pandemic restrictions.

Eventually, we settled on a new vision: Retro in Chicago. Where could we film with the city skyline as a backdrop? That's when we thought of Mădălina, who lived downtown. From her rooftop, the view of Chicago was spectacular. Ștefan called her, explained the project. Mădălina—a dear friend we consider family—was delighted and offered her place without hesitation.

I left the orchestration decisions to Ștefan. *"I wish everyone from Retro could be there... but it's not possible. I don't have instruments for everyone,"* he said, uneasy. Decisions like this are hard for him. In the end, only part of Retro made it to the rooftop, each holding an instrument, thrilled to be part of this project.

Mădălina welcomed us warmly, helped, then stepped back to let the filming flow naturally. We played, we danced, we were cheered from neighboring rooftops. We kept going, over and over—at least twenty takes—until nobody applauded anymore. We grew tired too. Filming isn't easy.

A Journey through Music and Poetry

The sun set cheerfully, as if singing with us. The Chicago skyline lit up behind us—a dream scene. Cipri, our videographer, later said that the daytime shots were no match for the magic of those filmed after sunset.

Summer 2021 — the video was ready. In July, it was launched on Facebook and YouTube. We were at Pokagon State Park, surrounded by friends, when the countdown began. That was all that mattered—a dream fulfilled.

"I'd like to thank someone, but I don't know whom... for your brown eyes." (a line from the song's refrain)

"Dear ones, this is absolutely enchanting! Congratulations! Now let the album come!" — *Mihaela Deaconu*

The Story in a Nutshell (for when you just want the magic)

Retro has a way of sparking creativity, especially in personal projects. Seeds planted in friendship and trust soon blossomed into songs, poems, and dreams. Ligia once remarked: *"Look at Corina, Traian, Sorin, and the others—how much they've grown artistically."* Truly, all of us have "grown" and "borne fruit" since coming together.

For Ștefan, it was time for his songs to see the light. He had long cherished pieces like *"N-am nimic în frigider"* (*"You're All I Have"*) and *"Ochii tăi căprui / Your Brown Eyes."* One day he said: *"I want to make an official video."* It wasn't about money—it was about joy, and about sharing something beautiful.

After a few hurdles with videographers, the decision was made: filming would begin in August 2019. Two young people were needed to play the leads. Our children were shy, but Paul took the role, and Ruxi joined him. They became the young couple on Evanston Beach, playing ball, strumming a guitar, carefree and in love. Ștefan even slipped in a subtle Retro detail—our name written on the ball.

Plans for a second part of the video evolved: a camper on the beach, or Retro playing together on a pontoon. In the end, the perfect setting appeared: the rooftop of our dear friend Mădălina, with Chicago's skyline glittering behind us. On that summer evening we sang, we danced, we repeated the scene until the sun went down and the city lights rose. The magic was undeniable.

By July 2021 the video was finished. We launched it on Facebook and YouTube while camping at Pokagon State Park, surrounded by friends. That was all that mattered—a dream fulfilled.

"I'd like to thank someone, but I don't know whom... for your brown eyes." (a line from the song's refrain)

"Dear ones, this is absolutely enchanting! Congratulations! Now let the album come!" — *Mihaela Deaconu*

September 2021 **Moment – Poetry – Corina's Debut**

I believe all of us have been positively influenced by the creative atmosphere of this cenacle. Inspiration has followed us at every step. Some have already published volumes of poetry; others are preparing to publish... our original works are becoming more and more familiar to the public.

Corina, our "Forest Girl," continues to amaze us with her energy, her joy, and her creations.

In September 2021, she debuted with her first volume of poetry, *"Trăiri în focuri vii / Living Feelings in Living Flames."*

I lose myself in her verses. Suddenly, I find myself wandering through Vlad's forest, guitar slung over my shoulder, feeling the cool caress of a mountain stream and the warm breeze from that place where earth seems to touch the sky."

Reading Corina's poems, I rediscover the spirit of Retro in titles like *"Candor," "Depth," "Encouragement," "Let Me," "Chimeras," "Why?" "Today Is Everything," "Acrostic in Verse," "I Can't Sleep," "The Retro Plugușor," "Sometimes,"* and *"Why Do You Judge Me?"*

And then—suddenly—an idea came to me.

★ **Interview with Corina**

When did you start writing poetry, and what inspires you?
Or, put another way: Do you remember the first time you knocked at the gates of the soul?

From early childhood I began knocking at those gates, when my shyness made me retreat into the depths of my being, because I felt that something magical was hidden there.
I scribbled verses as a high school student, but only in 2016 did I truly begin to put them down on paper.
I am inspired by emotions in all their diversity, by nature, and by everyday life.

How did you decide to publish this volume? How long did it take you to complete it?
This book came about as a gentle nudge to share the treasures hidden in the drawers of my soul.
Since I already had much of the material written, the book itself took about three months to assemble.

Can you speak about your love for poetry and for music?
Through writing poetry, I step out of the everyday and enter another dimension—the dimension of emotional harmony.

Poetry is the distillation of my own inner experiences.
And when words are carried into music, they create a special
state of mind.

**How did you come up with the idea of dedicating an entire
chapter to "Acrostic Verse"?**
I adore word games. I wanted to set these acrostics apart from the
other chapters.

**And what about muses? It seems that even without a muse,
you find inspiration—as in your poem "Without a Muse."**
My muses are in fact my own emotions, kindled by the living fire
of the heart.

**How do these "living feelings in living flames" reveal
themselves in your daily life?**
Enthusiasm is my personal creed. I live by the laws of the soul.
I fall in love with the smile of every sunrise and sunset, I rest in
the hammock of optimism, and I embrace every moment as it
comes—as part of the greatest gift of all, LIFE.

**I found some poems inspired by unique Retro moments—
"The Retro Plugușor," "I Can't Sleep." Could you tell us the
story behind one of them?**
"The Retro Plugușor" was written, paradoxically, on a scorching
August day while I was perched on a mountain rock. I was in a
state of exaltation, fascinated by the beatitude of nature in all its
splendor, and for a few moments my thoughts turned to these
dear people of Retro—nature lovers themselves.

The Retro Plugușor *(August 2, 2018)*

Hark, hark, people and friends,
Stand with Retro, join our hands,
Gather near, lend an ear,
Hear the words we hold so dear!

Breathe the verses of longing,
Of love and hope, belonging.
Sing with us in joyful tone,
Songs that keep our spirits strong.

In this story ever turning,
Find yourselves in it, returning,
Your years, our years intertwined,
When at our shows you come each time.

From the youngest to the old,
Retro's gift is pure and bold.
What we give is candor bright,
Tears and laughter, shared delight.

We sing with hearts that overflow,
Emotions round us ebb and flow.
We recite warm lines of rhyme,
Through the winter's frosty time.

We jest a little, to keep awake,
When knees grow stiff, when dreams overtake,
In reveries of rediscovery,
As through time you drift so quietly.

Now, as evening shadows fall,
When carols knock on windows all,
We wish you peace, and blessings too,
And hearts made light with grace anew.

Thank you for standing close to art,
To beauty told as from the start.
For TOGETHER we renew,
A spirit eager, pure, and true.

May we pass the years with grace,
Hand in hand, in Retro's place.
Honoring feelings old and bright,

That shine on us like stars at night!

And what about "I Can't Sleep"?
That poem came after a Retro rehearsal—a session full of emotion, productive and lively. I even recited, despite the fact that oratory is not my comfort zone. It was all charged with feeling, and plenty of humor too.

What are your hopes for the future, Corina Vlad?
I want to continue BEING what I FEEL—to keep evolving as a human being, to remain energetic enough to savor every blessing. As for more detailed plans, I prefer to keep them wrapped in a veil of mystery...

Working with Corina on this interview was a joy. She lives in the moment, offering beauty simply and naturally, never tripping over egos or petty interests. She was among the first to receive news of this book's publication with unguarded enthusiasm. I can even imagine staging this interview at one of our future Retro shows. Thank you, Corina, for BEING. Never change—and never stop writing.

Moment – Money and Harmony

I sent a dear friend in Romania a video of a street artist somewhere in New York, singing reggae about Romania. What followed was this exchange:

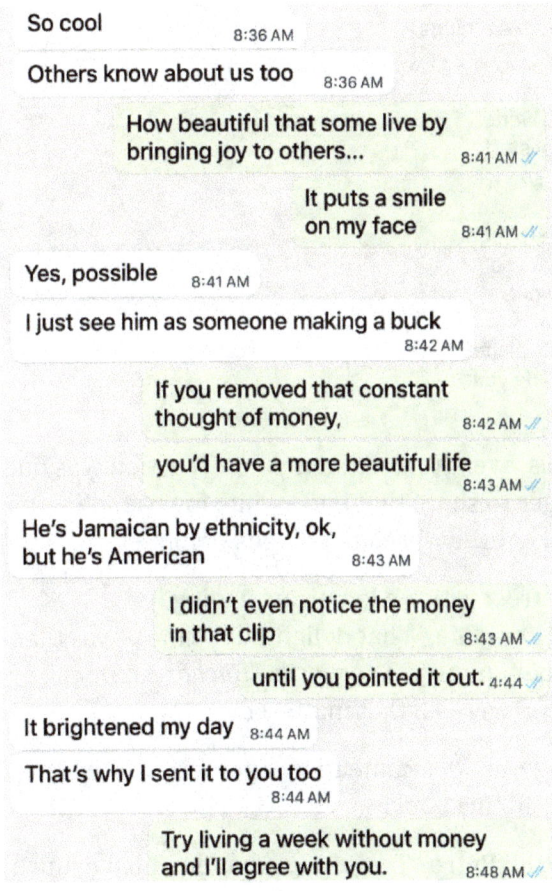

So cool 8:36 AM

Others know about us too 8:36 AM

How beautiful that some live by bringing joy to others... 8:41 AM

It puts a smile on my face 8:41 AM

Yes, possible 8:41 AM

I just see him as someone making a buck 8:42 AM

If you removed that constant thought of money, 8:42 AM

you'd have a more beautiful life 8:43 AM

He's Jamaican by ethnicity, ok, but he's American 8:43 AM

I didn't even notice the money in that clip 8:43 AM

until you pointed it out. 4:44

It brightened my day 8:44 AM

That's why I sent it to you too 8:44 AM

Try living a week without money and I'll agree with you. 8:48 AM

> Whatever you say, whatever you do, however much you philosophize,
> in this life everything,
> absolutely everything,
> comes down to money. 8:45 AM

> It's all in how you look at things. Perspective. 8:45 AM ✓✓

> Didn't you say that you work, and that you do cultural stuff besides? 8:46 AM

> I said remove the thought of money, not that you shouldn't go to work.
> Work is part of life,
> and money has its place...
> but don't let it guide your thoughts. ❤️ 8:48 AM

It struck me as curious, even ironic, that my first reaction was one of joy and pride—eager to share that joy—while my friend's response was filtered entirely through the lens of money.

In that video I saw a street artist, a Jamaican singing spontaneously about Romania. What delighted me most was that he even knew about our country. The words *"Bucharest, Hagi, Transylvania, Te iubesc"* were all that mattered.

And after this exchange, an idea came to me: perhaps I should also talk about money in this book.

So—money and Cenaclul Retro? Two things that don't have much in common. Yes, money is necessary, but when art is a passion, when it doesn't matter whether you earn an income from it, money takes a back seat. Of course, this is not the path of professional artists, but for Retro it was always different.

The little money we managed to gather came through sponsorships—the classic way of involving companies (mostly belonging to acquaintances, friends, or family). Ștefan was the one who took this on: knocking on doors, meeting with friends, talking to them about our mission. Sometimes he succeeded, sometimes not. Whatever funds we collected were entrusted to a committee, and all expenses were discussed in meetings. When it comes to money, transparency is essential—even when everything is done out of passion.

With those funds we managed to buy a sound system, reward ourselves at the end of the year with T-shirts and mugs, gift mugs or shirts to sponsors, and order a banner with the Retro logo. That was about it. The committee that handles money keeps an eye on the account—and worries. Every few months the receipts and financial situation are discussed and reviewed. The problem is... there's not much to review.

More recently (September 2021), I tried engaging the audience directly, encouraging them to make even a small donation through a "Google" form that ensured anonymity and could be accessed by anyone who appreciated our work. Naturally, there were debates about this in Retro as well.

Most of the expenses, however, are personal. Ștefan comes home with a new guitar and tells me how much it cost. My response: *"At that price, it should play by itself."* Then he replaces an amplifier because the old one no longer works. Sorin buys a wireless connection system so we won't be tied down with cables. Radu buys speakers. Each of us bought our own microphone. And so it goes.

We would need proper stage lights, reflectors, wireless microphones, stage decorations, and volunteers to handle sound and lighting... all hard to find. The fact that we try to handle the sound, the lighting, and everything behind the curtain—while at the same time being the artists the audience expects to see on stage—is a challenge. And yet, we seem to be handling it better and better. Still, we would need an entire support team around us, and I hope one day we will get there.

Back to money... a few experiences. At first, we had an entry system based on donations. It was a headache to organize. At the end of each show, after paying for the hall, parking, and other expenses, we were left with—or without—a minimal sum in the account.

One story still makes me smile, bittersweet as it is. After long negotiations for a certain hall, well known in the community, we held an exceptional show. It took a lot of work, many rehearsals, but in the end it exploded in applause and emotion.

Before the show, Ştefan announced: *"Friends, what do you say we celebrate at the pizzeria across the street? I think we deserve at least that. We'll use whatever money we collect tonight to pay the bill."*

That was the first and last time we ever tried celebrating at a restaurant and paying from the Retro account. Why? Because, at the end of the night—even though the hall had been full—after covering hall rental, sound, cleaning, and the many fees that venue imposed, we were left with around 80 dollars.

Still, that didn't stop us from enjoying ourselves, or from continuing to bring joy to those around us.

Later, we asked ourselves whether it was worth all the trouble with "donation tickets." Someone suggested: *"I recommend always putting tickets, even if only symbolic. Spectators don't take you seriously if the shows are free."*

Many times, though, we organized charity concerts. We left ticket sales entirely to the hosts of the venue, and all proceeds went to a noble cause.

And after the long months of isolation—we simply offered free shows.

Moment – Quarrel – or "Much Ado About Nothing"

The idea of turning this little story into a skit belonged to Ligia. I can still hear her saying: *"This could be a play..."*

Honestly, I wasn't feeling very inspired. I was exhausted from rehearsals, ideas, debates, and so much energy poured into things we shouldn't have been worrying about before a show.

How did it all start? With an invitation.

We were at a rehearsal when **A** announced that we were invited to perform. *When?* Soon...

My first impression: delight. Finally, our first show after this long "hibernation."
My second impression: joy. We had so many songs (old and new) waiting to be shared with the public.
My third: worry. How would we organize it? Who should we invite? A hundred questions filled my head, while **A** wasn't very clear. What exactly was expected from Cenaclul Retro? Were we to make the invitations? It seemed like a private event. How many people? We couldn't just post the address on Facebook...

I suggested a method I had already used at Equivox Multicultural (a cultural organization founded in 2019). We could announce the event publicly without revealing the address. Once a certain number of people signed up, we could close the list. Simple.

C then said: *"I think we should invite only certain people—important people."*
I raised an eyebrow. "Important?" To me, everyone matters.

Nothing concrete was decided. Ştefan stayed rather absent from the discussion. Time passed, and suddenly it was May. We were rehearsing like crazy, but nobody was talking about how to

107

organize it. To be honest, that's never been our strong suit. We even discussed postponing the show…

D: *"What are we doing about invitations?"*
B: *"I don't know. Nothing's been decided."*

Were we really going to invite only "important" people? The one who suggested it had now gone silent. Personally, I wish that when someone brings ideas to the group, they'd also carry them through. That would make everything so much simpler.

Then came another suggestion:
A: "We should bring wine, beer, mici—grilled Romanian sausages—and other things…"
B: (laughing) "Why not sarmale too? You know, those cabbage rolls stuffed with meat and rice."
C: "Wine, beer?"
D: "We'll nibble on mici, recite a poem, and toss in a sarmală for good measure."

I smiled bitterly and made a mental note: the mission of the cenacle needs to be reviewed.

E: *"Why should we bring food at all? What kind of show is this—performance or party?"*

Time went by, nothing moved forward, and those who had proposed inviting only select people stayed completely silent. We were confused. What exactly made someone "important" enough to be invited?

E: *"If that's how you want to do it, fine, but don't count me in for grilling mici."*

Weekend arrived. We were at the lake, enjoying the forest, the water, the people. **B** came over with his laptop, sat beside me, and asked innocently:
"Sonia, we've got almost a thousand friends on Facebook. Who do we invite?"

I looked at him, a bit shocked, and I'll admit—I was wicked. Yes, wicked.
*"Call **D** and **C**. Put them to work. This was their idea."*

Then **A** appeared, so I stood up and walked toward the lake, leaving them to sort it out. And sort it out they did. Later I found out they had invited almost all of our friends—most of them in Romania.

Honestly, I'm not sure they really knew how to handle Evite or Facebook, because many friends later told us they had never received any invitation at all.

The show date grew closer, and the chat started filling up with messages.

Then **D** called me: *"I can't believe we're doing a show with mici and beer. What is this?"*
I told him: *"Write what you think in the chat."*

But I knew him well—he was more comfortable telling me directly, while steering clear of the quarrel. And so once again, verses appeared to change the subject.

I'll share them here.

A full-blown Retro party is shaping up!
9:20 AM

Life—it's almost a melody,
With verses of poetry,
And Retro in a waltz,
Even the mosquitoes will
join the dance!
10:11 AM

Hai iu iu
Luiuiu itchy (from the mici)
Tonight we'll grill the mici!
Hai iu iu
Luiuiu itchy,
Let's escap e from work!
10:00 PM

Friends, I'll post the
program tonight.
1:38 PM

Yes, we'd like to know
what the program is.
Hopefully it won't be
too "timed" but will
flow as each sees fit.
We'll handle the
singing and reciting
as you say
10:36 AM

Let's put work aside—
If the mici are on the grill,
We'll call in the violln,
And life won't taste so bitter!
10:02 PM

Sorin
A full-on Retro cookout is
shaping up!
11:11 PM

Life—it's even a ballad
Over poetry we'll spin
While we have Retro dance
a waltz
And mosquitoes will thin!
11:11 PM

Hey ee-oo itchy ooh
(from the mosquitoes) 😂)
Cause tonight we'll grill the
fries
Hey ee-oo itchy ooh
Let's flee from the flies!
10:00 PM

Let's leave work now since
we'll be grilling the fries, I say.
10:59 PM

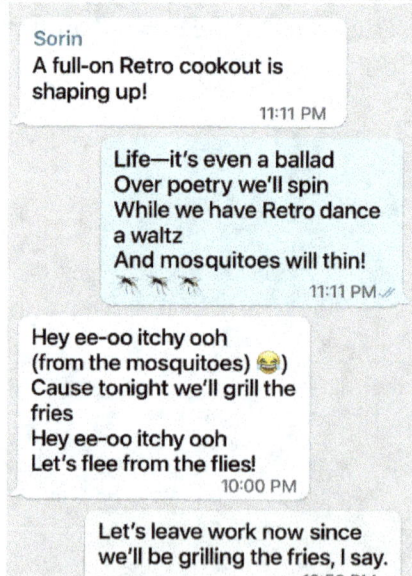

When we go to concerts at Millennium Park, we take a snack and a bottle of wine, like Ravinia—it's served before or during intermission. People sit close to the stage, almost picnicking on the grass. I love being near the stage and listening to music. 11:36 AM

I don't think they expect us to serve dinner, but Romanian hospitality has its way... and we want everyone to feel at home. We could prepare some drinks: water, juice, coffee, maybe an aperitif, and maybe some mici for those coming from far. 11:37 AM

I say let's not smoke ourselves out at the grill. Let's just order from Pita Inn, eat well before, then toast with guests over a glass of wine and some veggie chips—done! 11:40 AM

Sorry, but everywhere else you go, a portion of mici costs $15, plus entry, and drinks are separate. 11:40

Anakin
Beautiful and talented rebels,
The fault is all mine—so don't be upset with each other.
Pour your frustration on me,
And I'll answer with *Harmony*,
the way we know best.
And make it a show to remember.
10:36 AM

If all that energy had been used to shape new creations, it would have turned into something wonderful.

August 2021 **Moment – Tour in Cedar Rapids, Iowa**

The Iowa tour is becoming a tradition. Ligia—organizer and promoter of this tour—works with dedication and love to find the best date on the calendar, the best conditions, and the best and most beautiful people.

There aren't many Romanians in the Iowa community, but for those who are—hats off! Respect to them! Warm-hearted, generous people, with a love for beauty, art, and culture.

I remember how, before the first tour (two years ago), Ligia told us: *"You should know, I don't think there will be more than about twenty people in the audience."* But if those people were happy to have us among them and shared with us the joy of Romanian song and poetry, then that was all that mattered—not the number.

And so it was. What joy and beauty we carried to them and brought back from that tour!

Now, once again, we were to present our show at the same place, the Cedar Rapids Public Library—this time *In the Enchanted Grove.* The performance would take place on Sunday.

Ligia sent us the schedule of the tour. She deserves all the admiration; she planned everything from start to finish. I only helped her with renting a pontoon. Saturday morning, we swung by their place to pick them up; Ștefan said it wasn't much of a detour, so off we went toward Iowa City. The car rang with stories, memories, poetry, and laughter. No surprise there, with Anișoara, Ligia, and Iulian along for the ride.

Our first stop: **IOWA 80**, the largest truck stop in America—or so Iulian says. There's even a museum there. Truly something I had never seen before: a parking lot with hundreds of vehicles, mostly trucks. A little mall of sorts. We were impressed, and Iulian was happy to have impressed us. Anişoara delighted in the experience, living every moment with enviable intensity.

Then we reached the meeting point in Iowa City, at Café ZingZang—the same place as last time. That café has a special charm. The air practically hums with university students. And as for the delicacies served... what can I say?" We waited for everyone to arrive, and soon the group was complete. Ioana and Dan showed up too—they had offered to host us, though in the end it wasn't needed. Still, they came joyfully to greet us: *"Welcome!"*

Next stop: the dock. We hopped on the pontoon with guitars, food, and cold drinks. Stories, songs, poems, smiles—all mixed with the heat of a summer's day—seemed endless. Oh, how we wanted to jump into the water! But apparently it wasn't allowed. We were tempted to break the rules...
*"Go ahead and jump! If we get arrested, I'll call **M** to bail us out,"* Ligia joked. We could almost picture it—maybe too many movies in our heads...

Later, we did make it into the water, following the rules, of course, and using the designated beach. What a joy! In the parking lot, we shared a little more food before heading to our hosts.

Our meeting point: Gabi and Bogdan's home. They welcomed us with warmth and joy, as though they had known us forever. The joy on everyone's faces, the songs and poems by the fire, the lively atmosphere stretching late into the night—all experiences I wish I could describe fully.

Morning came with great coffee. I found everyone already deep in conversation—ah, those endless stories. Ştefan entertained them with tales of our RV adventures. I stepped outside: fresh air, a wide-open field, a beautifully kept garden adorned with artistic touches, an outdoor shower with beads that looked like something from a Jamaican vacation, and horses running free in the neighbor's yard across the lake. I asked Corina if she wanted to walk with me around the lake. Off we went, talking as the fire inside us kept burning bright. When we reached the horses, they seemed to speak back to us—coming closer to the fence. Whispers, strokes, and more whispers...

When we returned, the group was ready to head to Ioana and Dan's for breakfast. What a beautiful, well-organized little Romanian community. Truly admirable.

After breakfast, we strolled through the park to visit Ligia and Iulian's old house. We gladly accompanied them on this trip down memory lane. We all know how powerful the memories tied to your first home can be. We had all been there before.

After a morning full of activities and wonderful people, we headed to the Cedar Rapids library, where Alina had once again reserved the same room as two years earlier. A truly beautiful room with excellent acoustics. I read the event description prepared for the American audience—*"Summer Ballads with Cenaclul Retro"*—and thought how far we had come, literally and figuratively.

The audience began arriving—we expected maybe 20+, but to our surprise, more and more came until the room was full.

The rest was the story of *In the Enchanted Grove*—our story, kept close in our hearts.

It was the most successful show of that summer: in sound, stage movement, interpretation, everything. We felt and shared our joy with everyone in the hall. There was singing, dancing, reciting... We left for Chicago with hearts full.

Ligia Grindeanu 🙂 ···
Feeling inspired with
Cenaclul Retro
in Iowa City, Iowa.
Aug 6, 2021 · 🌐

Notes of longing in Iowa City, where we lived and wrote many of the poems included in this book.

Thank you, Alina Dinescu and Anda & Ștefan for the heartfelt presentation, thank you Cenaclul Retro and everyone who was there with us in the atmosphere of music and poetry.

Alina Dinescu
With pleasure, my dear poet friend, and indeed we go—further toward destiny, with poetry and song within us. We carry the cenacles in our hearts!

Anda & Stefan
To get lost across Iowa, among beautiful people and notes of longing—it is a great honor and joy for us to be part of this event.

 Cenaclul Retro
⭐ August 6, 2021 • Cedar Rapids, IA

The stage became the Enchanted Grove at the Cenaclul Retro show from Chicago. An event organized in collaboration with Cenaclul Dor and the Romanian Cultural Organization of Iowa City.
Many thanks for the warm welcome!

Cassy Casian •••

Anda & Stefan, the artistic and heartfelt act completes the pride of being Romanian, in a natural, respectful, and warm form. Continued success and we look forward to welcoming you home.

🎵 **Anda & Ștefan**

Cassy Casian, it was a wonderful concert, in a small Romanian community, but with a very big Romanian heart...

November 2021 **Moment – In Vlad's Forest**

We are at Corina and Sergiu's place in Indiana. It's never easy to gather everyone together, especially so far from home, but Corina had the idea of spending a weekend at their estate - part retreat, part meeting - to talk about future plans, changes, improvements. Ștefan had sent the agenda ahead of time, with the points we needed to discuss.

We arrived first, even though we live the farthest away — we had left early in the morning. Corina and Sergiu welcomed us with joy and with a *cui* of peach brandy and blueberry liqueur... tasty, so very Romanian. We parked the camper in a dreamlike setting. Though it was November, the weather seemed to smile upon us — sunshine warming our faces and our hearts. Nature itself reflected the rays of light in the dance of multicolored leaves.

We set out for a walk through Vlad's forest, carried by good energy that seeped into us. We breathed in light. Their cat Bobby followed us — until we lost him. That turned into a new mission: searching for the little rascal. After a few moments of panic, we gave up and headed back toward the fire. Just then, Bobby appeared, strolling nonchalantly along the path, as if to ask, "What's all the fuss about?" Clearly, he had found a sunny spot in a clearing while we were searching in vain. Bobby, Bobby...

We lit the fire for the *ceaun* —a big Romanian pot— peeled potatoes, and Corina took care of the rest. They were pros at this. Soon Călin, Steliana, and their girls arrived — full of delight. The children sang, jumped, and ran around; what joy to see them. Later Carmen, Sorin, Radu, and Cătălin showed up with trumpets and laughter, though they couldn't stay overnight. By then the food was ready, the fire burned with violet sparks, and we were starving. Perfect timing.

Still to come were Ligia, Anișoara, and Iulian. They had said they would arrive later. The fire roared, the wine foamed in glasses. Radu brought speakers, put on music, and I suggested he search for Cenaclul Retro on YouTube. How our faces lit up when our own past performances filled the clearing — poetry and song interwoven. Radu even surprised us by singing *Bal la Apahida*, a lively Romanian folk tune, in his own style — charming and joyful as always.

Night fell. We gathered around the fire and began the meeting. Problems were discussed, frustrations aired. The original idea had always been simple: we do what we do to awaken feelings and bring joy, not to be perfect.

Still, at one point **A** raised his voice. That was not good.
A: *"It seems we're losing fans. People won't come anymore if we act as though we're perfect and smart, while still making mistakes."*

We all knew where this seed of discord came from — easy to recognize. Voices rose to explain that this was never our mission.

B: *"Yes, we need to improve and find solutions. But we must separate the problem from the person. Raising voices and pointing fingers leads nowhere."*

I've known **A** for a long time — a good, warm soul, a person of great value. I could feel his words carried frustrations and outside influences. And **B** — admirable, calm, steady. It's rare to see such composure in heated moments.

G: *"Let's not forget what we've done for the community all these years. We do this to give, and people appreciate it."*
A: *"Friends come only out of politeness. At the last show, a fan told me we sounded bad."*
L: *"But so many gave positive feedback! Someone even suggested we book the Heritage Pavilion for next year."*
J: *"Why let one negative comment overshadow all our joy?"*

Examples were shared, energy wasted on past grievances. Voices grew louder. A release, perhaps needed.

118

Anişoara: *"In the beginning was the word. And words can lift you up, or tear you down."*
L: *"I don't agree with 'telling people to their face.' I color that green a little. I don't like confrontations."*
Me: *"Who does?"*

We talked about inviting others onto our stage while remaining the core. Nothing new — it had always been the idea. But reciprocity was needed. We could not allow ourselves to be used as a launch pad again.

A grew louder, no longer able to hear anyone else. His wall was built. **C** tried to break through: *"Do you realize what a beautiful song you wrote on **L**'s verses? It would have fit perfectly at **M**'s celebration. But we weren't invited…"*
Me: *"No matter. He lost out."*

C: *"The Retro train has run for many years. Many have boarded, some have stepped off. Everyone is free to do so."*
L: *"Here's the truth: we can go on without them, but they cannot go on without us."*

Powerful comments. Time to close the meeting. But voices still lingered. Finally, I said: *"We must take care of ourselves, and of the harmony between us."*

We ended with a bitter taste. No more songs or poems at the fire that night, only a few chords.

Morning came with sunshine inviting us on a hike.
I told Ligia: *"I'd like to use what happened last night as an opportunity — to grow, to create, to keep moving forward."*

She answered: *"You are too good. And yes, I believe it's in our power to channel all this energy onto the right path, so it blossoms and bears fruit. If everyone did this, we'd live in a better world."*

November 4, 2021

Good morning, Rebels,
A beautiful Retro Retreat is ahead.
Besides metaphors and music, I'd like us
to discuss a few topics:
1) What can we improve in our activity
to have more success: sound,
rehearsals, etc.
2) Where and how many shows should
we prepare for next year.
3) I found a theater in Bufffalo Grove,
but we need to have other alternatives
as well. We are in discussions with the
manager about the price
4) We've had a few *"open mics"* in the
past. How do we integrate those
moments into the next shows? 10:15 AM

...continued:

4) We've had a few 'open mics' in
the past. How do we integrate those
moments into the next shows?
Let's not forget that the vision with
which we started this activity was
to give those with talent the chance
to present it. We are the nucleus of
the Cenacle, and...

5) Financial situation.
6) What is our position toward the
Community Center.
10:16 AM

Well, I think we are already "in" and we should be "in". This is a Romanian Community Center and we are Romanians and this is our community. We are "in" because many of Cenaclul Retro members are "in" and involved already to some extend and care about the mission

leadership or experience or past participation to RUF events or zoom meetings. The question is how are we "in" and we can use the model of other organizations that are supporting the center as well. Successful project at the community level are possible with collaboration and people

should not loose our energy and identity in this debate, but rather help with we can, mainly with our art. We can decide for a donation (after a show for instance) as a group and the monthly membership pledge can be an individual decision.

4:20 PM

Great points!
Let's not lose our identity and uniqueness! And let's not forget that in 2022 we celebrate 5 years of Retro, and this year 10 years of Vox Maris!
During these years we've done so much for the community.

121

Retro Encouragement – OR – How We Support Each Other...

> **Sorin, the answer about merit lies within you, not in those who throw their own frustrations in your eyes with opinions that don't resonate with who you truly are.** 4·29 PM
>
> **Try to look from below but feel from above... the rest is chasing the wind!**

Inspiration is found where you least expect it. An intense evening carried on its wings the following verses...

EPIGRAMS IN SCENES

CHARM
The orchard's vault at dawn,
Its colors send a shiver on.
The distant leaves begin to fly,
As words take wing across the sky...
Thanks for this heaven, sweet and spry,
To our hosts — lords of this land nearby!

MENU
The meat is boiling in the pot,
Ideas, too, are cooking hot.
Harmonies, from inside out,
Flare like fire, without a doubt...

TO AN ACTOR
In Hollywood, a famous name,
Ştefan, actor of true acclaim.
But his greatest fortune came,
With Anda walking at his side.
Fame never led his heart astray,
Yet still an artist, day by day.

HOSPITALITY
Corina and her Puiuţu, too,
So welcoming, their kindness true.
Such gracious hosts, all is complete,
Until the cat jumps in to eat!

TO A POET RECITER
Ligia, gentle as a doe,
Would recite a poem, aglow,
Quite fitting for the grove that night,
But her turn never came in sight...

TO A MELANCHOLIC REALIST
Iulian, with science in tone,
Blends his being with the known.
He calculates, as if by fate,
According to the stars' estate.

TO A FAN
Carmen, always in accord,
Says: "On stage, I can't afford!
I'll remain a fan for life,
Never stepping in the spotlight!"

TO A SINGER-SONGWRITER
Striving hard for pure perfection,
In your voice and song's direction,
There is always room to grow,
Sorin, this you surely know!

TO A VIOLINIST
Stars and notes together weave,
For the evening's sweet reprieve.
Moonbeams spread in bars of light,
Sheet music glowing through the night.
With serene soul, so genuine,
Cătălin contemplates within.

TO TWO LITTLE FAIRIES
The two small doll-like sprites,
Still glued to internet nights...
They barely went off to bed,
Though mischief pulled the cat instead!

TO AN ELVIS
Elvis ended unemployed,
Time itself seemed null, a void.
Still waiting in his stage attire,
To sing without a word required...

"CĂLIN, PAGES OF A STORY"
A poem from an uncle dear,
Is poetry's trunk, sincere.
"Călin, Pages of a Story,"
Holds the truth in all its glory.
Călin, your wine is strong and fine,
Refreshing, joyful, just like you — divine.
It brings us inspiration's flame,
For creation, for the stage, for fame.

THERAPY
From "Retro" comes therapy,
Healing even poetry.
Too many pills can harm the art,
But Retro cures the poet's heart.

TO THE LAWYER LADY
We know that justice took our part,
Thanks to the lawyer, wise and smart.

124

Lovely Steliana, so bright,
Praised our efforts all the night.

THE FLYING LANTERN
From creative souls took flight,
Even the lantern burning bright.
Through song it pierced the darkened skies,
With poetry and mystery's ties.

TO THE CENACLUL FRIENDS
Beneath the starry, endless dome,
Retro gathered, far from home.
Not to count the stars above,
But to share proposals, joy, and love.
I offered epigrams this time,
With irony, and gentle rhyme.
I hope to turn back toward lyric streams,
After this evening of quakes and dreams…

Ana of Sighişoara
Indiana, November 7, 2021

A witty recollection.
Thank you, Ana
Munteanu Draghici.
Greetings, dear friends!

12h Love Reply   2

Anda & Štefan
A 16 mm smile 🤭
Beautifully captured by
the immense talent of
Anişoara!

November 21, 2021 **Moment – Vox Maris Band,**
10 Years – Anniversary Concert

"Are we going, are we not going to the concert?" — we had asked ourselves this question some time ago. Sometimes I said no, other times yes... I was undecided, but Ştefan wanted to go. And so, last night we ended up at the anniversary concert.

I can still hear **C** saying: *"I can't believe Ştefan wasn't invited to at least present his own song, I just can't believe it..."*

I notice that after all the discussions in Retro, **C** — who is usually calm and reserved — has found her voice and now expresses her emotions a little more strongly, even with some frustration about the conversations we had two weeks ago in Vlad's Forest.

"It's such a shame about that beautiful evening around the fire, which should have been sprinkled with guitar chords interwoven with verses. I still can't get over it. It left a stone on my heart."

I can feel how that weighs on her even during this concert.

The music is loud, the whole hall vibrates. The soloist's voice isn't heard well (a common problem when all instruments are at maximum volume); the lyrics are hard to make out. Still, the energy improves in the second half of the show when the atmosphere heats up with older songs (from the album *Travelers with Dreams*) and the well-known anthems of the Phoenix band. The audience is on their feet, people are dancing, those who want to sing along are searching for lyrics on their phones — and I think again of the PowerPoint slides with lyrics that I had worked on so lovingly for our first shows.

Ştefan is called on stage for the final piece: *Andrii Popa.* The difference in voice, in energy, is instantly felt throughout the hall. **C** can't contain herself — two seats to our left, she jumps up, dances toward us, singing and radiating energy (she, who is usually so calm). She had been upset that Ştefan hadn't been called on stage until then; I could read it in her eyes, in her posture. Now her face is glowing with joy.

And what a difference... Ionel, Adi's brother—Adi being the current leader of the Vox Maris Band—and a devoted admirer of Ştefan, is genuinely delighted. Later, he tells Ştefan: *"Your place is on stage. My heart overflowed with joy when I saw you up there, Ştefan—the Founder "*

As we leave, a voice from the audience shouts: *"Congratulations, Ştefan, for laying a brick in the V.M. Band!"*

Another voice replies: *"The first one!"*

C is overjoyed: *"You had to get up there on stage — that's where you belong."*

M, when asked about the beginnings of the band, replied: *"One evening we were rehearsing/playing with **D**, when a good friend called to tell us about an event in the community, and that's how it happened — we were in the right place at the right time!"*

Hmm. **C** says: *"Right time, right place? I was there! He could have mentioned Vox Maris Cenacle."*

A: *"Yes, he could have said it... That event they were invited to was the result of a year and a half of work by Ştefan and Dan P, starting with Cireşarii. It would have done him credit to acknowledge that. Nobody would have taken away their aura or their years of hard work. In fact, it would have been greatly appreciated that they hadn't forgotten their roots."*

C, with sadness in her voice: *"I was there..."*

Later, more comments from **C**: *"At the song where Ştefan came in, you can clearly hear that another voice entered. And I'm not saying this lightly — just watch the video. It was a beautiful concert. Vox*

Maris has opportunities and knows how to make the most of its potential."

I'm surprised by the passion and determination she shows whenever Vox Maris Band is mentioned. I believe it stems from the fact that she is herself a founding member of the Vox Maris Cenacle.

"I was there..." — I can still hear her say it.

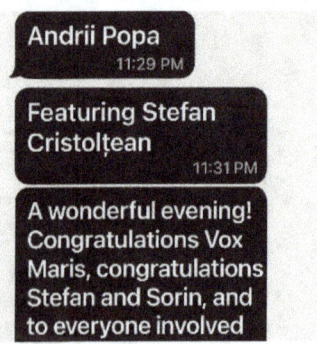

We thank you, Ștefan, for stepping away from the Vox Maris Band five years ago and daring to begin a new adventure called **Cenaclul Retro**. Without that choice, this book would never have taken shape, and all the moments, joys, craziness, emotions, and beauty that we have shared with the community would have been scattered and forgotten.

And this is how one ending became a new beginning.

December 2021 **Moment – *Mi-e dor de tine / I Miss You***

It's Saturday and I'm very busy. Finals week is approaching, and I'm caught up in work, grading nonstop. I tell Ştefan that I don't have time for much; he busies himself, takes Charley for a walk... he keeps pacing around the house. It's as if he can't find his place. He comes upstairs to my desk and says: *"Here's what I was thinking. Let's take the camper into Chicago to see the Mi-e dor de tine / I Miss You sign (a temporary installation along the Chicago River that winter of 2021). Let's invite Retro, too."* Lost in my thoughts, I nod and continue working.

The messages start to "pour in." When I finally glance at my phone, there are already about 15. I'm surprised — I didn't expect Ştefan to actually invite Retro, much less stir up such a buzz. Positive responses come in quickly for this impromptu outing. Sometimes it's good to break out of the monotony.

So a meeting spot and time are chosen, and we gather — full of enthusiasm, with guitars, violins, and a few snacks. We're not many, but the energy is right... just like Retro. The city lights smile noisily at us. It's a unique experience to see Chicago at night from the comfort of your own little home on wheels.

First stop: Adler Planetarium. From here you get the most beautiful view of the city. We step out of the camper and are greeted by a mild winter evening. It's not too cold, and there's no snow — though how wonderful it would have been to have a few playful flakes fall around us. We laugh, joke, and take pictures, so many pictures. At one point I hear Cătălin quip: *"The mayor lost control of us."* He smiles, and I find myself smiling too. Later, Ligia posts some of these pictures in our group chat with that same comment. Jokes and teasing that make me raise my eyebrows in amusement.

How good it feels to step into a warm home, even if it's only on wheels.

Verses spring to mind:

"How warm it is here in your home,
And all things inside feel sacred.
Look how December's snow is falling —
Don't laugh, keep reading on..."
— from *Decembre* by George Bacovia"

Until the next stop, I grab a guitar. We sing carols, play music, share stories, and simply enjoy being together on the eve of the holidays, roaming through Chicago in our camper. A more beautiful evening couldn't be imagined.

"This night carries something rare,
A grace that feels beyond the norm.
So let us all be kinder now,
And believe in miracles —
At least at Christmas..."
— from the Christmas carol *A Carol Like No Other*"

We reach the "Mi-e dor de tine / I Miss You" sign. Ştefan finds a parking spot — 30 minutes with hazard lights on — we can hardly believe our luck. We step out, cross the street against the rules like rebellious children, and take in the view. Nostalgia washes over us — longing for people, for places, for you. Ligia's voice drifts through the air as she recites from her own poem, *La Taifas*:

"'I long for snowfall back home,
With fir trees bent over branches of dreams.
So close to that magical moment
As the sky meets the mountain peak.
That's where I'd go — to forget, to weep,
To search for icons on my knees among the leaves,
To have it be noon, to forget to eat,
While tears guide my way across my cheeks...'"

Romanian original:
"Mi-e dor de-o ninsoare la mine acasă,
Cu brazi aplecați peste ramuri de vis.
Atât de aproape de clipa măiastră
Cum cerul, la munte de pisc,
Acolo m-aș duce să uit și să plâng
Icoane să caut în genunchi printre frunze,
Să fie amiază, să uit să mănânc
Cu lacrimi pe-obrazi călăuze…"

How wonderful and fitting this moment is.

We take more photos; we even receive one from Corina, who couldn't join us but asks that we include her picture if we post on Facebook. Sweet and thoughtful — just like her.

We return to our starting point, tired but full of joy and gratitude. Thank you, Ștefan, for this magical evening and for knowing how to bring joy to those around you. Thank you, Ligia, Iulian, Cătălin, and Călin, for joining us on this adventure and for caroling with us in our little home on wheels. **Go Retro!**

Anakin
Dear friends, after such a sunny day I had an "epiphany": what if we took a ride by the "Mi-e dor de tine" sign, boarded in our RV and armed with guitar, poetry, and violin.
We could meet in a central location for everyone at 6PM. Who's in? 4:34 PM ✓

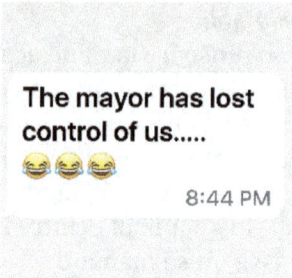

The phrase *"The mayor has lost control of us"* was uttered in jest — a playful rebellion within our circle. *The mayor* is Sorin, so nicknamed because his house is large enough to host our gatherings, a kind of informal town hall for our spirited meetings. Whenever the laughter rises and the evening drifts into delightful chaos, we tease that *the mayor has lost control* — meaning that order has given way to joy, and spontaneity now rules the room, as it so often does among us.

THE RETRO EFFECT

Decembrie 2019 **Moment – "Mission Accomplished"**

Good morning!
I woke up before 8. I would've liked to sleep more, but an avalanche of feelings burst out of my heart: joy, emotion, dreaming... I smiled, I laughed, I cried... tears of happiness!

We are so amazing that we don't even realize it ourselves!
May God give us fiery days, to keep vibrating and to keep this Flame alive. Oh, how wonderful you all were!

Radu, I reread your poem of gratitude. This time I let my tears flow and clear the eyes still clouded from last night—clouded by so much life!

Ligia, we missed your gentle presence, but "Miss Ana of Sighișoara" ended up kneeling as if before an altar, on the dancing scarf (she'll tell you the details herself).

Călin, only in the morning did I realize that you actually spoke well last night—and maybe that's why I forgot to check your jaw (sorry).

I won't go on and on, so I'll just say: thank you and I love you—even if in person I'm not always the best at expressing it!
And here I am crying again 🥹 *Have a blessed day—you deserve it more than words could ever say!* ❤️ ❤️ ❤️ ❤️ ❤️ ❤️ ❤️ ❤️

Corina – from bits and pieces of texts

Texts/Impressions after the shows

Friend

All day I've had in my head only "If you want, only if you want"...

> You're so sweet
> You make me smile
> Shall we sing it together sometime?

If no one else can hear us and you volunteer yourself...

8:44 PM

Ştefan
Good morning, Retro,
Congratulations on another beautiful show.
Have a blessed day!
Go Retro!
8:37 AM

Corina
Vivid moments for late memories!
It was a beaut'iful experience!
I already miss you all

I didn't get to hug you all before leaving!
Woke up with cheeks bronzed by the wild wind!
9:14 AM

Lucian Muresanu
You are wonderful!
Thank you for existing—without you, we wouldn't have lived so many beautiful momente...
Go Retro! 😊
8:14 AM

Moment – At the End of the Show
Stephanie – In the Enchanted Grove

"I'm so happy to be here with you…" I heard the delight in her voice. I've known her for a long time—a young lady of extraordinary talent and of a sincerity you can only still find in the soul of a child. After the show she handed me flowers, visibly moved. "These flowers are for you," she said, "a great STAR."

Later, I sat at the table with Corina, both of us exhausted yet filled with joy. Stephanie came over, calm and radiant. "I came to see what it's like between two stars," she said. Corina lifted her gaze toward the sky, and so did I. But we didn't catch her meaning at first. Where were the stars Stephanie was seeing?

I wish I could glimpse the world through Stephanie's eyes— where joy, innocence, wonder, and truth shine so brightly.

Christmas Montage 2021- Feedback

"Thank you for the montage you shared during the holidays.
It filled our hearts with joy, with memories, and with hope for a good and happy life alongside family and true friends.
We wish you to keep the same energy and inspiration in your creations, and to continue sharing them with us."

Thoughts… from Near and Far

Happy
Thanksgiving! ♥
♥ 🍁 🔥

Happy Thanksgiving, dear ones!
Another year has passeed,
We've had sunshine, and we've had rain,
But it's important that we're together!   10:16 AM

Sorin
Happy Thanksgiving, dear friends! I've just had a long chat with poets and was inspired in the moment to share this message with you all from the bottom of my heart, just as you give me so many wonderful moments, for which I thank you from my soul. ❤️

Cătălin Lari
My dear friends, thank you for existing in my life... I have a whole list I'm grateful for.

9:33 AM

Cătălin Lari
The beautiful clip *Your Brown Eyes*
The most wonderful *Mocirita* I sang together with you
The most beautiful song-greeting on my birthday

A memorable 4th of July weekend
A tour in Iowa with a concert

A

Thank you all for your voices, your talent, and your desire to walk this path together 😍 Love you all

---

Impressions from Across the Ocean.

Ana Dănuț – Sun, Nov 12, 2017

"You were superb!!! Bravo!!
I have no words to describe the joy I felt listening to such beautiful songs, seeing you once more, as artists, so close again... You are a wonderful group... I'm only sorry we don't live nearer."
Sending you a warm embrace, --Ana"

Our reply:

"Thank you for your kind words, Ana. We bring joy to so many people through the cenacle, and that is our own joy as well. Now

you know what we are doing here—out of passion and love for people. Soon (December 16) we'll have an evening of carols. How nice it would be if you could be closer; but know that we keep you close anyway..."

Autumn 2020

You're doing something beautiful.
9:43 PM

Touch people's hearts with your melodies.
9:44 PM ✓

As best as we know how.
9:44 PM

I don't know if it's really you, but the video and the song are superb. And that girl's voice is divine. Congratulations! 12:08 AM

It is you! 12:10 AM

Congratulations for the melody. And the lyrics are really... 12:10 AM

Yes, I was truly enchanted by her voice.
8:38 AM

Thank you, Radu. I'll pass along what you wrote. 8:38 AM ✓✓

If you want, you can also leave a comment on YouTube.

I can't. You've disabled the comments. I don't know why... otherwise I would have for sure.

Happy National Day to all Romanians everywhere! 🇷🇴 ❤️
www.cenaclulretro.org

8:11 AM ✓

RO - Nadina
How beautiful! Thank you, Anda, for everything you all are doing there! 🥹🥰

8:20 AM

A top-notch video, beyond perfect. What a wonderful surprise, dear friend! Beautiful images, lyrics, interpretation— everything is superb. A total harmony!

1:04 PM ✓

Impressive

I watch your videos on YouTube

1:04 PM

I am fascinated by them

1:04 PM

I'll buy a ticket to your next show

1:05 PM

A true celebration! Happy National Day, motherland! Happy day, brothers and sisters!

Confessions – a Personal Note

12:17 PM

Anda, look at the picture featured on my phone today and the movie. Wow, good timing: everything you touch is beautiful

12:18 PM

Hi Anda and Stefan. Just saw the pic of you two from last weekend and wanted to say how great you both look ... and happy. When I think about a great couple you two are the only ones that I think of and I wanted to let you know what great role models you've been over the years. You've been part of the reason I've tried again many times. Your relationship has truly been an inspiration. I think it's rare and wonderful and I hope we all live to

hope we all live to be really old and quirky :)... I dont know that I want all of Facebook to read this so texting you directly. I miss you both and would love to see you more often.

I'm happy and proud that I am a drop in this sea of Romanian spirituality created with much love and devotion by Anda and Stefan.

9:59 AM

 2 People

Ana, I got chills. Thank you for touching our souls with these kind thoughts. It's possible—but everything is possible with love... without love, nothing is possible. We must have done something right if the Universe has...

1:18 PM

 2 People

The Universe has sent us so much love... We want to share it with all those around us, and you and your family are first on the list ❤️ We hope to see each other more often.

11:31 AM

You are beautiful and kind, and more adventurous and wise than I ever guessed! I loved the slide show! And I'm so happy that I was

show! And I'm so happy that I was able to be part of your surprise party! Hope we celebrate many many more birthdays!!! 🎉 ❤️ 🥳 🎊

"Tradition, beauty, optimism - they shine through your eyes and can be found in everything you do, Anda and Ștefan."-Ligia

---

April 9, 2022 **At a rehearsal**

We had just finished rehearsing Ștefan's song *"On My Street"*, a song about longing for *home*. The chorus rose together, carried by all our voices—

"And how I wish   *If only I could*
To be back home,   *Be on my street..."*

Ligia answered gently, with a smile:
"For me, Retro means ACASA (HOME)!"

Translator's note: *In Romanian, the word **acasă** conveys more than just "house"—it means home, with all the depth of belonging, warmth, and emotional roots attached.*

March 22, 2022   **Moment – Five Beautiful and Harmonious Years with Retro**

We are on a ski trip, spring break... when the morning messages begin to arrive.
I am surprised by the first one—from Iva, who has been coming to our shows for a long time, even though she doesn't understand Romanian. The harmony and joy of Retro have reached her heart.

Iva ›

Good morning Anda ☀️
I hope all is good with you guys :)
I just have a reminder that it is Retro's birthday today 😄 is that correct?
Do you guys have any concerts planned?

Iva ›

So good to hear from you Iva!
Yes, it is right. 5 years of Retro
Thank you for remembering this date. You are the 1st one to remember
We will have a show this spring

HAPPY ANNIVERSARY, RETRO!
Today marks 5 years since we began this cultural journey.
We're celebrating it at great heights (12,000 ft.) ✈️
Love you all! 💗 😍

HAPPY ANNIVERSARY RETRO! 🎶🎻🥁🎹🎼
Today marks 5 years since we started on this cultural journey.
We're celebrating it at high altitude (12,000 ft.).
Love you all!
Love you all! 🥳

8:34 AM

Corina
Happy birthday Retro wherever you are!
A blessing to be part of this SOUL!
Enjoy the heights Anda and Stefan!
🌲 ❤️

9:59 AM

May the living fire burn forever in Retro hearts. ❤️

10:42 AM

Cálin
Happy Anniversary RETRO

11:04 AM

Sorin
If I were to express what I wish for all of us still in RETRO, now, 5 years since this project that 'stuck to me like a postage stamp' started, I would randomly choose: inspiration, health, and peace.

11:04 AM

Catalin Lari
O Retro.... 😌

2:27 PM

HAPPY BEAUTIFUL YEARS!!@

2:28 PM

Ligia
How beautiful! Happy anniversary Cenaclul Retro and to many wonderful events!

9:04 AM

Congratulations, Retro, on turning 5! 🎉
I think back to how it all began and how far we've come. What beautiful memories we've created together, what friendships have been strengthened, and what joy we've brought to the community.
May Retro always remain a beacon of poetry, music, and harmony, wherever we may be. 🎵

July 2022 **Moment – Facebook spoils us sometimes – OR – Why did you put me on Facebook again...**

A comment appeared marking ten years since the Vox Maris Cenaclu's event (back in 2011).

"It has been ten years since that Festival in the Romanian community, organized by the Romanian Heritage Center NFP – Chicago area. A beautiful memory with congratulations for Ștefan Cristolțean, Anda and Ștefan, who continue the tradition with passion and enthusiasm alongside the Retro Muse Society."

We rejoice at this moment brought back by Facebook, and at the comments that followed. How beautiful life is alongside Retro.

Ana Munteanu Drăghici: Admiration for your kindness and your art!

Mihai Lehene: That's it! As a Romanian in Chicago, I'm proud you exist.

Stana Dragoș: Congratulations on carrying the tradition forward! May God always guide your steps in life, filling the souls of those who listen to you with joy. Deep respect for everything you do!

Marina Grindeanu: Congratulations! Much continued success!!!

Roxana Iacob: Many more years filled with song and poetry ahead!!

Anda & Ștefan: So many beautiful memories created throughout these years...

Biserica Sfântul Andrei: Congratulations and thank you for everything you have done and continue to do for the continuity of a beautiful Romanian tradition! May the Lord Jesus Christ protect you!

Adrian Nechiti: Truly wonderful memories! Much success, Cenaclul Retro. May God grant us another 10 years together from here on.

$$\oint$$

September 2022 **Moment – The Retro Cottage – OR – What Happens in Wisconsin, Stays in Wisconsin**

A picnic at the farm for the Romanian-American community in Wisconsin.

We prepared with diligence and excitement. Not everyone could make it—some were in Romania, others had different plans for Labor Day. But those of us who gathered were determined and unstoppable. Two weeks earlier we had already begun working on the program. The list of songs and poems grew longer and longer, meaning... a mountain of work! I tried to "calm" them down, but how could anyone suppress such an explosion of joy?

The show was scheduled for Sunday, September 4, with the final rehearsal the day before. The list had at least fifty moments— songs and poems to review. Strangely, the energy was low. At Retro rehearsals, especially final ones, joy and enthusiasm usually overflow. But this time, only fatigue. Maybe it was the low barometric pressure—rain was in the forecast. We had carried all the instruments indoors, microphones, amplifiers... and in the end, it never rained.

As expected, with such a long list, we couldn't get through everything.

Ligia: *"I think it would've been better if we had the program written out like we used to, but we'll let Ștefan try his method this time—an Excel list."*

We discussed, sang, and laughed. At one point, both Ligia and I said in unison: *"I feel totally unprepared."*

Yes, it's a challenge to hold a performance outdoors, on grass. *How will the sound carry? Will poetry work in this setting—one, two, three poems?* We decided to adjust on the spot, even skip some poems or songs if it felt right.

Ligia smiled: *"I'm just happy I get to sing. The rest doesn't matter."*

Ştefan had the idea: *"Let's all go in our RV. There's room for everyone, plus the instruments."*
Said and done. On Sunday morning we loaded everything, climbed aboard, and set off. Perfect: Corina, Ligia, Carmen, Sorin, Cătălin, Iulian, Ştefan... all of us fit. We sang all the way, like students on a road trip. That's how the RV became the *Retro Cottage.*

At the farm, the organizers greeted us warmly. It was our first time meeting them, but I felt they understood Retro's mission. We unpacked, set up, and... realized there was no electricity. Suspense for a few minutes. Then, the power came on. We tested microphones, adjusted the sound, and got ready. Dressed in traditional blouses (the girls) and cowboy hats, we stepped into harmony with the farm.

Ştefan: *"Let's all sing something to test the sound before we start."*
What to sing? Something not even on the list: *Romanţă cu parfum. (A Scented Romance)*

We leaned toward the microphones and began:

"Late at your window, I see a light,
And I cannot tell
Whether you are awake or dreaming..."
These lines are from the popular song *A Scented Romance*

Romanian original
"Văd la fereastra ta târziu,
O lumină şi nu ştiu
De eşti trează sau visezi..."

Chills ran through me—it sounded so beautiful. Later, Cătălin, one of the organizers, who had sat silently in front of us, confessed: *"When I heard you, a flood of emotions and memories washed over me so strongly, I had to get up and walk into the woods."*

And so, we sang, recited, danced *horă* — the traditional Romanian circle dance — laughed, and played. A whirlwind of joy, beauty, and harmony. An unforgettable picnic

We even made a new admirer, Matilda, a sweet, fearless four- or five-year-old who sat right in the middle of the stage with her toy maracas, keeping rhythm. She wore a beautiful Romanian blouse and didn't speak the language yet, but I'm convinced she will, because her heart is Romanian. At the end, after nearly forty songs and poems, she was upset. She didn't understand why we had to stop — she simply didn't want it to end. We have a photo of her with us on stage, a little spark of that joyful evening frozen in time, and we'll keep that memory close. Who knows? Maybe we'll meet her again someday.

Of course, we made many other friends that day—kind people who appreciated the joy and beauty Retro brings.

The organizers told us afterward: *"You've raised the bar. We don't know how we'll manage next year."*

One lady said: *"Thank you for teaching me the Romanian dance steps."* I remembered she had joined the horă when the circle formed. Strangely, many Americans seem to appreciate these events even more than some of us Romanians.

Ligia remarked: *"See? We should think about this more seriously, and be more open outside the Chicago community."*

Impressions, harmony, joy. At one point, I caught a unique moment: Ligia and Cătălin slipped into a poetic dialogue called *'A Simple, Wandering Life...'* Once again confirming: poetry is woven into Retro's soul, giving us wings—even outdoors on the grass. This fluid merging of poetry and song, alongside the harmony between us, is what makes Retro unique in the cultural landscape.

Now we're seriously considering Retro's next Cultural Workshop.

We headed home in the *Retro Cottage,* hearts overflowing... and...

Catalin Lari
😍 me. Thank you Iulian for the pictures Stefan & Anda for hosting, and poetry. Ligia for presentation and poetry. Sorin for artistic performance. U rock Retro!
8:57 AI

Let's not forget that Carmen encouraged us by her simple and warm presenta!
8:58 AM

❤️   🤭
8:58 AM   8:58 A

What about me? Thank you for the pictures! See you on Saturday with cheerfulness and good will!
9:20 AM

❤️

Catalin Lari
😂😂😂 You are the star Corina!
9:28 AM

❤️

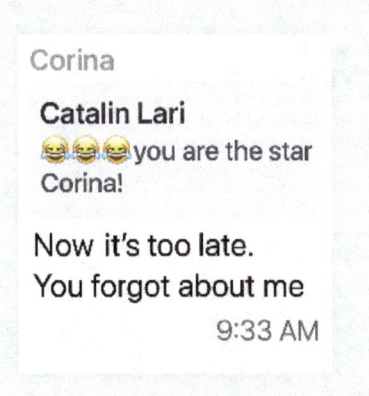

Corina

Catalin Lari
😂😂😂 you are the star Corina!

Now it's too late. You forgot about me
9:33 AM

SORIN

Thank you Julian, the pictures are wonderful, as usual. 👑 Corina, you were at heights and you transmitted your optimism and exuberance to everyone, new and those who have listened to us. We were all a united team, as a family, and we succeeded in ʍing this to everyone, in spite.

fatigue and the short time for rehearsals. This adventure has shown us that we can no longer be caught unprepared, and we have our bags ready to go whenever and wherever we are called. 🤗 🥰 💕

Prelude to the Next Chapter...

Corina's Reply, showing how many situations in Retro are solved through verse and song.

Corina

Corinuta, talkative but with good intentions! Love u all! 🤭

9:37 AM

Catalin Lari

The living fire...

9:39 AM

Corina

I'm small but brave,
Lively like a
spinning top,
In my thoughts
I'm still awake
And at times
I lament.

Nowhere long in fire,
I do a bit of everything,
Nor stagnate in desire,
From nothing build a castle.

Playful since I was small
And energetic in strife,
But mature, even quiet,
Often feel a premonition.

I burst with joy,
Fireworks burst from
my chest,
Like the sun I rise early,

If I err, I want to correct.

9:41 AM

I work and depend
on myself,
To be a pillar when
storms come,
Hope sustains me
And I still believe in
miracles.

9:41 AM

Among longings I walk
my steps,
In other worlds I lose
my way,
I return to my own stars
And with verses
I caress them.

9:41 AM

At times I scold but
you need not fear,
It's only my own
opinion.
Advice is the winged key
That opens up a solace.

9:41 AM

In nature I revive,
I cling to branches
like the wind
And like birds I rise up,
From my muse I write
the word.

9:41 AM

> All in heart I return
> To rediscover myself
> For from divine grace
> I take nourishment and
> living water
> 9:40 AM
>
> Catalin Lari
> Living water for the fire
> in the little heart. 9:49 AM

December 10, 2022 **Moment – How to Get into a Sold-Out Show**

Our 2022 Christmas concert sold out the very day it was announced on Facebook. Even for us (the Retro family), with so many members, families, and close friends, it became a real problem to reserve seats. In the end, from our own family, Sonia (our daughter) had to stay home.

Phones kept ringing, texts kept pouring in, and we had to explain again and again: it's not possible... there are simply no seats left. It hurt to be in that position, having to say no to so many friends who had always been in the front rows at all our shows.

So, I avoided the topic even with close family. With friends, I stayed quiet too.

The day of the show arrived. Scrolling through Facebook, my eyes fell on Raluca's reply: *"Coming to the show."* I froze. I hadn't seen her name on the registration list. Maybe she just wrote that today for appearance's sake, I thought. We had met recently—she hadn't said anything, nor had I.

A battle of thoughts began: Should I call her and tell her there are no seats left? I didn't want her to come all the way to Chicago for nothing. Or should I let things unfold as fate decided? Maybe she *had* registered, and I had missed it. A film scene: me with the phone in hand, suspense in the air—then I set it aside...

At ROCO: rehearsals, preparations, sound check, costumes—the usual pre-show madness. I forgot all about Raluca. Guests began arriving. I hid backstage; I couldn't bear to watch as some friends, who risked showing up without a reservation, were turned away. The girls at the entrance did an excellent job, but they had to be strict.

I paraphrase Cristina: *"With so many requests, we would have needed a hall three times bigger."*

As we got ready to start, I stepped out of the wings. The hall was full, buzzing with anticipation. In the crowd I spotted Andrei, Paul, and Vivian (Paul's girlfriend)—our dear kids—and not far from them, Raluca and Marian. I couldn't believe it! They were here. They must have been registered after all (good thing I hadn't called...).

I rushed to them: *"I'm so glad you came... I didn't know you were registered."*
Raluca looked at me, puzzled: *"Registered? I didn't know we had to... I just saw you had a show, so we came. First, we went to the hall across the street (where we've been together to a concert, recently), then we checked Facebook again and found the address."*
"And how did you manage to get in?"
Raluca smiled, realizing: *"Ah, so that's what that girl at the door was talking about... Well, I just walked in."*

I glanced toward the entrance. Ştefan was talking with Marian— and with Onița and Paula, the cheerful volunteers stationed at the door like border patrol. Later I learned what had actually happened.

Raluca and Marian had arrived at the exact moment Ştefan was heading over to speak with Oana, who was guarding the guest list with the intensity of a customs officer. He spotted them instantly—and noticed the girls getting ready to deny them entry with total professionalism. Without a second of hesitation, he marched over, shook Marian's hand, hugged Raluca, and announced to Onița:

"These are our dearest friends. There's no universe in which they get left outside."

Oana shot him a glare sharp enough to cut glass. Ștefan, unfazed, continued:

"Marian brought bronze home for Romania at the World Kayak Championships, and Raluca won bronze at the Sydney Olympics—also in kayak. You're really going to turn away two champions? … Come on."

The girls softened. Between surprise and the joy of meeting two exceptional athletes who had brought such honor to Romania, there was room enough for a Retro concert too.

Was it just coincidence that Ștefan happened to be at the right place at the right time? We can each believe what we will… but we will smile warmly every time we remember this story.

CREATIONS

A chapter dedicated to the sparks of imagination, the poems, songs, and moments born from our gatherings. Here, words and music intertwine, voices rise, and every line carries the unique fingerprint of Retro.

February 29, 2020 **Corina – after a Retro-style rehearsal**

I'd like to sleep,
But sleep won't come,
For just an hour ago,
A moment swept me up... 😊

It was so beautiful,
We sang again 🎻 *and,*
Like never before, I recited... 😚 😚 😚 😚

Emotions caught us
By surprise...
And tears we shed 🥹
But it's all right,
We cleared them away,
Our eyes full of calm and light.

The spontaneous is always welcome
When your soul is open wide,
And you give all you can—
For there is nothing to lose,
And to gain?
Does it even matter,

When to be HUMAN
Means to be made whole
By everything you are... 🔥 ❤️

I'll go to bed,
Perhaps I'll sleep,
If only a little,
To recover—
So I may rejoice
Completely
In a new day
That waits at dawn
For me to smile,
And to live it!

Thank you, beautiful people,
Who paint my life in colors...

I'll go to bed,
Perhaps I'll sleep...

Poem also published in Corina's volume of poetry.

December 2018 **Diplomas in Verse**

A project initiated by Ligia and completed by Anişoara

Corina Vlad — Across the strings' meridian, a sweet voice carries over the ocean.
Monica Topârceanu — A nightingale on the branch of the soul.
Lucian Blaga — The perfectionist professor, at the keys of artistic nature.
Sorin Griza — Renowned doctor of humans, artist embraced by fans.

154

Laura Sisu — The actress who holds the art of sound, with a melodious voice that surrounds us.
Marius Stan — Distinguished creator, captivating reciter.
Călin Mărincaş — The poet's nephew, carrying his legacy in verse.
Radu Răcean — Patriot in his song, always accompanied by the Tricolor of Romania.
Traian Bălan — With a Roman emperor's name, when you listen, you become a melomaniac.
Ligia Grindeanu — Messenger of the muses, through the tear of poems.
Cătălin Nicolae — The loving actor, bearer of humor.
Iulian Grindeanu — A discreet mediator, a bearer of the arts.
Anda Cristolţean — Lady in Red, the Enchanting Little Ant.
Ana Munteanu Drăghici — Ana of Sighişoara, carrying the muses' treasure.
Ştefan Cristolţean — The talented little cricket, cherished by us all.

The Cricket and the Ant – In Paris

Winter's here, the snowflakes twirl, playful dancers in the air,
After autumn's fruitful harvest, grains are stored with utmost care.
Sparkling wine now fills the glasses, fireside embers warmly glow,
While the little busy Ant has lost herself in wardrobe's show...

Her friend the Bumblebee is pacing, shuffling softly through the room,
With a scarf of silky shimmer, and a glass of wine to bloom.

"My dear, we must be going—let's not miss our Paris flight!
Hurry now, I've grabbed your coat, the plane is boarding tonight!
"

"What a splendor, what a marvel, everything just feels like bliss!"
The Ant was thrilled and wide-eyed when at last they reached Paris.

"Wait till you see the bars, the shows, the museums, every sight—
And tonight we'll go to Retro, oh, it will be pure delight..."

Down a lane lit dimly only by a single lantern's flame,
Shivered there a lonely Cricket, paper tucked inside his frame.
"Yes, it's me, your neighbor Cricket—I set out from Cluj in song,
Hoping here in Paris' winter, Moulin Rouge would take me on.

I auditioned once at Retro, sang so sweet, with all my heart,
But they paid me little notice—said I looked too rough, too tart.
So I sell tickets, sell the papers—do you want some, freshly read?
Only week-old, good for lining, keep your hands warm there
instead."

"Oh... the Ant and Bumblebee? Could it be? Or are my eyes deceived?
Better hide before they spot me, mock the life I once believed..."

He turned quickly, bent in silence, tried to slip away unseen,
But the Ant had caught him squarely, pinned him fast upon the
scene.
"Good evening, neighbor Cricket—what a marvel, what a chance!
In the middle of Paris' street, I should see you in a glance?"

"Good evening, dear neighbor lady, looks like you have company—
Brother, care for her with caution, or she'll flunk you, wait and see.
As you know, I'm here in Paris, with a life of great acclaim,
Such success, I am an artist—Retro now exalts my name.
I've just stepped outside a moment, needed pause, a cigarette,
For the stress is oh so heavy, being star of Retro's set."

"Oh, is that so?" the Ant replied, with irony and twinkling eyes,
"What about that crumpled paper, and the ticket in disguise?
And the lady Crickets—where are they? Did they leave you here
alone,
With your guitar in the shadows, on this cold Parisian stone?

I was just now at the Retro, saw no trace of you, my friend—
Cricket, Cricket, dearest Cricket, did you think I'd miss the end?"

As the fable's pages tell us—yes, La Fontaine was so aware,
With guitars and flashy Ferraris, you won't get too far out there...

Anda & Ştefan, December 2018
Sketch performed in the show "A Christmas Evening,"

And There Aren't Many Like RETRO

The sun is shining in the skies,
Retro weaves new verses, lets them rise,
Thoughts take wing, they fly so high—
Come along with us, give it a try!
To the dreamland once again we go,
Carrying the love we long to show,
Joy and kindness we will always share,
Songs on open wings float through the air.

Refrain:
Joyfully we live each fleeting day we meet,
Singing loud though bridges shake our feet.
That's the way it is, no one else can take our place,
Few like us were born of time and grace.
Joyfully we live each fleeting day we meet,
Reciting still though bridges test our feet.
That's the way it is, no one else can take our place,
And like Retro—there are none to trace.

Green leaf, evergreen branch of pine,
Though outside it's cold, inside we shine,
Romanian longing carries us at dawn,
Toward harmonies where white blooms are drawn.
When nostalgic moods make us serene,
We laugh, we play, step outside routine.
The living fire always burns anew,
Kindled memories that flow to you.

Where there's Retro—there's Harmony,
There is Music, there is Poetry,
And like Retro—there aren't many, you see.

The Sin (or The Commandment)

Let me tell you the story,
Of a song with quite a fate,
For this little situation
Truly made me narrate.

One fine morning, brave we were,
Both of us, hand in hand—
I with verses, he with rhymes,
Shaping music, song unplanned.

With one hand upon the guitar,
He cast his eyes to see,
At the title of the poem:
Commandment—clear as could be.

It spoke of youth, of burning soul,
Of longing, restless art,
And yet somehow the audience
Kept calling it The Sin—by heart.

Perhaps that very opening line
Sounded strange, a touch askew—
So every time we sang it live,
Sin is what they all construed!

And so upon the Retro stage,
We had no choice, no doubt,
The song once known as Commandment
As Sin they'd sing and shout.

But now that I have told the tale,
I pause and wonder still—
Was it Commandment from the start,
Or Sin against our will?

And if by chance my little joke
Has made you frown or pout,
Forgive me—soon I'll sing again,
And laughter will win out.

—Anda, April 2022

Note: This poem reflects a playful Retro anecdote. The song *Poruncă* (*Commandment*)—composed on verses by Licuţa Pântia—never seemed to resonate under its solemn title. Each time rehearsals began, someone would inevitably call out: *"Let's do The Sin!"* And so, within Retro, the piece was affectionately renamed.

April 2, 2022 **Moment – Creative Workshop**

At Corina's invitation, on a chilly April weekend, we warmed our souls by playing at spring—through verse, music, hikes, and yoga.

This little pause along the pathways of the soul unfolded in Vlad's Forest. We took in our dose of health and inspiration, so we could carry on our Retro journey with renewed strength.

Spring in Verse

A bud on the branch of my soul—spring!
Opened by the sun's warm ray,
Light floods into my being,
Eternity hides within a moment...
— Ana

From memories a longing is born,
The hope of a dreamed-of season.
I clothed you in a body of nothingness,
And serenity returns once more to my doorstep.
— *Ligia*

A white mantle of stars
Wraps around my being,
The tender green of spring
Revives my helplessness.
— *Corina*

I feel like a shower of dew at dawn,
Gathering fresh sunlight from the grass.
I would laugh, I would cry, I would dance with you—
This longing I would never want to lose.
— *Anda*

The following acrostic is the result of everyone's collaboration… including our talented boys…

Aprilie / April

A surge of ours at springtime's gate
Pervades the air and surrounds our state
Raindrops of morning smile so bright
In love our souls are wrapped in light
Lachrymal joy on branches of yearning
Inner song reflects, discerning
Emotions of this scene returning…

Creative Workshop, Poetry retreat

BACKSTAGE WHISPERS

Or – Verse Among Friends

What follows is a full chapter from the cycle "When Talent Haunts Us" — a whole collection of creations born from all of us, though some of us were clearly haunted by talent more often (and more dramatically) than others. In these pages, you'll find little snapshots of our crew — our stories, our laughter, and those late-night musings we definitely thought were brilliant at the time... and you know what? Some of them still are.

Many of these pieces first appeared on the Retro Muse Society website (cenaclulretro.org), basically as love notes to our own youth — the kind you reread years later and think, "Ah yes, this is what happens when you mix nostalgia with too much enthusiasm and not enough sleep."

Going through them now feels like opening a box of old treasures — the kind that makes you smile, tear up, and snort-laugh all at once. Sure, time has gone by (we'll graciously accept the idea that we're wiser now), but we're still collecting moments that make life sparkle — new songs, new memories, and yes, the occasional mischief. Some things, thankfully, never change.

So here's to everyone who's been part of this journey — those still here, those who've wandered on to new chapters, and all the beautiful, joyful, "delightfully unruly" souls who keep the Retro spirit alive and kicking.

With Love on a Bicycle (*a Rom-English poem*)

Ștefan:
As RETRO rolls along the lane,
It's pure delight, it can't be plain.
All on bicycles, so cool,
I forget about each rule. 🫢
I've a bike that's kinda old,
But it's chic, unique, and bold.
I ride no-hands, that's my style,
'Cause it looks much cooler while.

Anda:
I have a bright red bike instead,
Cuz' in poetry I tread.
I love sunshine, love the trees,
And adventure rides with ease. 🚴

Cătălin (aka Little Bear):
With my violin in tow,
Biking's harder, that I know...
But in Retro's crazy vibe,
I hit rhythms that just fly!

Iulian:
Well, I got myself a ride,
With a very special side.
Soon as I had heard the call,
That a Retro hike was all.

Anișoara:
And from early dawn, you see,
I prepare my bike with glee.
Rain or shine, through every test,
I'm in style, young and blessed.

Ligia:
And Iulian hurries, true,
'Cause he wants to catch the view.
But it's hard, no joke, my friend—
Even sunshine makes him bend. 🌞

Traian:
Bike or car? Not quite my thing,
I'm a Retro star, a king!
So of course, what fits my face—
Is a limo, full of grace!

Lucian:
A bike with sidecar, slow but neat,
Carried Radu off his seat.
From the mixing desk, oh dear,
Now he pedals, gears in gear! 😜

Radu:
I've got lofty, bright ideals,
Long prepared with all my zeal.
Over valleys, hills, I'll sing,
Launch a hit—an awesome thing! 🎤

Sorin:
I see Călin on his ride,
Scales and notes all at his side.
With no doubt, he hits the gas,
Pedals wild—alas, alas! 🤯

Călin:
Bikes, my friends, are not for me,
Doesn't suit me, don't you see?
But somehow I still feel free—
Like *The One* from history. 📖

Corina:
I like people bright and kind,
Light within their hearts and mind.
On the Retro bike I go,
Sing in techno's lively flow!

Narrator:
Sergiu's stuck inside his van,
Clients chase him—poor young man.
Free or busy, here or gone,
Calls keep pressing, on and on.

Narrator (aside):
Anda, teacher dressed in red,
With her fiery nails ahead...
Throws a look, a grade to jot,
Straight into the catalog.

Narrator:
Little Ant, as is her way,
While the Cricket starts to play:
"I adore you endlessly,
Join us at the Retro spree!"

Cătălin:
Laura, if I play some tricks,
Please don't go and act dramatic!
Look me in the eyes, relax—
Drop the fuss and skip the acts. 👀

Laura:
I'm surprised, and that's my tone,
Like the dusk when day has flown.
Even if I'm not to blame,
He just plays his little game. 🎭

Ligia:
To conclude this poem ride,
From my bike I'll say with pride:
Fear no fire, don't be shook,
It's just Retro in the book.

Ştefan:
Whoever hears Retro in May,
Joy will follow all the way.
Whoever hears us sing at night,
Summer days will shine so bright.

Monica:
Retro's clock has struck the call,
So together gathered all.
With our talent, strength, and cheer,
On American land—right here!

Retro at Work, April 18, 2019 – Adapted December 13, 2019 –
Adapted again, December 2022

Iaca Aşa: Urda şi Leurda

(title left untranslatable — a playful rhyme on fresh cheese and
wild garlic leaves, a traditional spring dish in Romanian villages)

If it's really about fresh cheese,
The old village kind, no less,
We'll add some leurda on the side,
Like in a pie — Romanian style. 🥔 🌱

If you sit and listen well,
We'll sing with sweet eyes as we tell —
But be prepared, don't you forget,
Else nettles might be what you get! 🌿

So early in the morning light,
We ready bikes, our gear held tight,
And off we go through woods so green,
To gather leurda — a springtime scene. 🚴

There's Traian upon his steed,
Stretching his saddle as he speeds,
His Pegas bike takes him with zest,
Toward the leurda, on his quest.

Ștefan's caught the call as well,
His bike all tuned, he rides pell-mell,
Over hills and valleys wide,
Where Sorin pedals side by side.

The girls all bustle, chatter, run,
They're first in line — the race begun!
And that's exactly why, you'll see,
They don't need bikes for victory. 😊

Corina lags a bit behind,
Checking all with her watchful mind,
Every five minutes, 'carefully,'
She inspects the crew with glee:

"If it rains and rains and rains,
And the clock strikes past nine chains,
Through the muddy woods, no way,
I won't go out for you today!

Put your craving on the shelf,
Ramble, rebels, by yourself!
Eat your powders from the mart,
Those will grow you big and smart.

But if you want sweet Corinuța
To gather leurda with her hands,
Then kiss those hands and thank her duly —
For you have no other plans!" 💐

At the Green Meadow – September 6, 2020

Why did this rain have to come?
To ruin all our plans,
To keep us from the blue beach,
From feeling the waves in our hands?

Ştefan

Until we stock the pantry,
Let's all head out already,
For a barbecue in the park,
At Rock Cut State Park.
We'll bring a BBQ,
Some sausages and some
beer too.
The rain that's on its way,

Will surely pass us by today.
We're getting ready, it's true,
And in an hour, we'll leave
with you.

We'll be waiting, Retro!

August 29, 2019 **Moment – The First Retro Tour**

We owe thanks to everyone who played a part in organizing and
making this event a success. Ligia was the heart of this tour, and I
can truly say she did an extraordinary job from every point of
view. She was supported by a small Romanian community with a
big heart.

As proof of that bond, we were invited back to Iowa two years
later, in August 2021, with the show *"In the Enchanted Grove."*

What follows is a lighthearted piece, born out of the joy and
success of our very first tour.

Emergency Communication – after the extraordinary Retro concert in Iowa, held at the Cedar Rapids Library Hall...

Ștefan to the Gang – OR – When Inspiration Hits Ștefan – OR – A Journey through Retro Chatter

Ștefan turns, his guitar rings,
The beloved gang together clings.
Autumn starts again, the heat has eased,
Our scribbled lines... not our best, at least! 🤪

My battle horse looked more like a nag,
I sold it quick and bought a shabby "drag."
And now, of course, while counting my money,
I poured myself an Armani cognac—funny.

Let me confess my little crime:
Though I had a treat to share this time,
I left them high and dry, no ale,
No chips, no sarmale, all did fail.
If only coins had filled my hand,
This thirst they'd surely understand.

So here I bow and make amends,
Apologies, my dearest friends.
Yes, I've pulled off mischief before,
But this outdoes them all and more—
To keep the whole crew parched that night,
Now *that* was never in my sight!

Epistle to the Treasurer
(to be read in rap rhythm)

My dear Treasurer,
I haven't neglected you at all,
I've got receipts and all the slips,
But you were off on trips—
To Riga or to Bucharest,

I couldn't guess where you might rest!
But now you've reappeared at last,
I'll bring them to your palace, fast.

Go RETRO! 🎵

The IRS does not much care
That we're fine poets everywhere!
Minstrels with a noble name,
However far we spread our fame.
But when it comes to money talk,
It's receipts they want in stock!
Be it Chicago, Bucharest,
Iowa or by the seaside rest,
Euphoria's good and true,
If the paperwork's in view!

So I look ahead, delighted,
With music, words, we stay united.
Let joy return, and cash as well,
To fill our chest—oh, can't you tell? 🤣

August 31, 2019

This Is How We Talk Finances...

Morning, gang,
Right near Labor Day,
I stopped by the bank,
We've got a thousand lei.
To be precise—a thousand one,
Like stories from Arabian nights.
Anda told me, half in fun:
"Careful now with what you write,
Throw an emoji in the mix,
Or you'll drive them nuts with tricks."

So for the second time,
In just a single week,
I do my MEA CULPA,
With Armani glass at peak.
No new card was opened,
It was just a joke to speak.

This year in total,
We're on the positive side,
Donations also trickled in,
Though a little late they arrived.

The purse is full,
As I've already told you,
We're ready, all together,
To climb even higher—shall we?

God bless you guys! Go RETRO! 🎶

Ștefan – Reply to a Holiday Greeting

And now I just can't refrain,
To reply in kind again,
To all of you who sweetly tease,
Preparing sarmale just to please.

But don't you think I'm all about food,
Forget the cabbage rolls for good! 😄
With a song and poetry too,
May life be lively, bright, and true.

May harmony always guide your way,
Happy New Year, with joy each day!

Greeting for Sorin

Sorin, you, with such a great soul,
And modest like no other role,
May Santa grant you health anew,
So back pains never trouble you.
May you climb the mountain trail,
With sunshine kissing, never frail,
And sing with Retro, joy immense,
Even crossing a thousand fence! 🎶

Holiday wishes were written for each Retro member, but only the one dedicated to Sorin found its way into this book...

May 14, 2020 **Gone Fishing**

Oh, what a big fish you've caught!
Luck was surely on your side,
We all know how skilled you are—
But I still must ask:

When the rain had finally stopped,
Did you throw it on the grill?
And was that the end of it?

Yet with all your careful watch,
The poor fish had no escape,
And as the waters slipped away,
You helped it not to drown!

Fishing dialogue – Ligia

February 2020 **Moment – Anniversary of *Tribuna Românească***

The next pages include our two event prompters — filmed especially for the February 2020 celebration. First comes our playful exchange, followed by Sorin's cameo.

Ştefan: Greetings to the "generation in jeans" ...
Anda: ...and with a key around the neck.

Ştefan: I've always been in love with the guitar. My parents would have preferred that I play a more "serious" instrument, but as a bit of a rebel, the guitar was closer to my heart.

Anda: I've always been passionate about art and culture, about people and nature. Something interesting about us?

Ştefan: The Retro Muse Society—unique in the diaspora, and growing with each passing year in our lives.

Anda: Retro is, at its essence, a simple conversation of souls, through music and poetry, song and verse.

Ştefan: Picasso said that the meaning of life is to find the talent you've been given, and the purpose of life is to share it with others.

Anda: I would add that it's equally important to find wonderful people to walk alongside you and help you move forward. That's what Retro Muse Society has given us—we are surrounded by talented people, and the joy they bring, along with the support of those who follow us, fills us with energy. It makes us better, more creative, more loving.

Ştefan: Because where there is no love, there is nothing.

Anda: The same spirit continues in the community thanks to *Tribuna Românească*. Our collaboration with Steven Bonica and the newspaper began many years ago.

Ştefan: Steven supported us from the beginning—first with the children's group *Cireşarii* in 2009, then with the Vox Maris Circle in 2010–2011, and later as we evolved into the Retro Muse Society.

Anda: We were also honored to join *Tribuna* at the *Romanian Origins Festival*, across all four editions from 2009 to 2013. *Tribuna Românească* brings Romanians closer to one another, and closer to home.

Ştefan: *Tribuna* is a magnet for the community. Without it, we would be poorer.

Anda: And so, we are glad to celebrate this special anniversary together.

Ştefan: Eighteen years is no small thing.

Anda: Indeed. That's why we invite everyone to join us in supporting the continuity and growth of this newspaper.

Ştefan: And, by following *Tribuna Românească*, you'll also hear about our future events—where you will always be warmly welcomed.

Sorin – Prompter

When I first arrived in America, I learned about *Tribuna Românească* from the few Romanian friends I had at the time. Though it was only a year old, the paper already carried news of every community event and all the services needed to make a life in a new land.

Not long after, I met Steven Bonica, the founder of this publication that has now been in print for eighteen years. Later, in the spring of 2017, when Ştefan called the roll (which he had "borrowed" from Anda), the Retro Muse Society was born. I happened to be there with a bass guitar in hand. I don't know how I passed the test, but since then, the roll call has remained open—for us and for anyone who wants to join us on this journey.

"The most important thing is to try and inspire people so they can be great in whatever they want to do." —Kobe Bryant

Gala Anniversary – *Tribuna Românească*
Fragment from the Presentation

The Retro Muse Society greets you warmly on this anniversary occasion. We are honored to take part in this special celebration—eighteen years since the founding of *Tribuna Românească*. Behind each issue stands an entire team, and today we applaud and celebrate them.

At the heart of it all is Steven Bonica. And as the saying goes, behind every strong man there is a strong woman—without Simona Bonica, today's celebration would not have been possible. Congratulations, Simona!

We are the Retro Muse Society, and in our journey, we bring shades and colors through song and verse.

Steven has always encouraged us. His genuine joy and enthusiasm are contagious. He is among the very few who still remember Cireşarii. It was Steven who, noticing Ştefan's hesitation, said to him: "Take credit for what you have done for the community, including the Retro Muse Society. No one will acknowledge your merits for you—people are people, they simply enjoy what you give them, and that's that. So don't be afraid to take credit for all that you've given the community over the years."

February 2022 – Retro's Last-Minute Creations – OR – A Winter Day in Verse

Note: *Inspired by Ștefan's WhatsApp "provocation" to the group: let's write a few playful stanzas and make some wind on WhatsApp.*

Good morning, Rebels,
I challenge you to write a
quatrain, just to shake off the
winter blues. Let's stir up some
wind on WhatsApp. 8.23 AM

The sun breaks through
the frozen branches,
and I wait for the flowers
on my window to fade. 8.25 AM

Catalin Lari
Ah, yes,
tum-tiddly-tum
The flowers won't
wither, but look,
Valentine's is coming
and we'll put new
flowers....
in the vase! 🌹 8:10 AM

Corina
And smiles will blossom
once more upon
the branches of hearts 💕
8:10 AM

Corina
And smiles will bloom 😊
Again on the boughs of
hearts
And everything will start to
grow again 🌱
Staring down January's chill!
8:43 AM

Radu Raceanu
Oh green leaf rich and 🌿
lata,
Let's leave this winter
behind! 10:08 AM

Anda
Just what I needed
most ❄️
A prompt that calls
on me
The snow outside.. 🍂
Makes me long for
Skiing, snowmen ⛄
And friends, of all I'll
see.

175

Anda
And I find you all again.
Some holding a
snowflake in their
palms, Trying to protect
it. Others with cups
held high, Knowing well
what comes next...

Catalin Lari
😂Stefan asked for
one stanza, and the
wifey wrote two...
Keep it going just like
that!
😍
10:37 AM

What began as playful WhatsApp messages soon took on a life of their own.
Laughter and emojis turned into rhymes and verses, flowing one after another.
Here is how that winter day unfolded...

🟩 Călin
Even if the winter is so hard,
It's always better with RETRO.

🟦 Corina
With one hand for a client,
And another for words,
I'll remake this tense body,
And a soul with many longings!

🟦 Corina
Because with Retro you're never stuck,
Life is a challenge,
The fire of the heart strikes,
Snowflakes make you lose your mind!

🟪 Sorin
This morning, at dawn,
I awoke from a dream,
Tormented by verses...
But alas,
The rhymes were still under the sheets...

Corina
Leave rhyme, be a rebel,
Don't anchor yourself in doctrines,
Like a bass, improvise
So that everything will turn out fine!

Ligia
And so it is, this morning,
Retro gathers once again,
With poems and quatrains,
May inspiration call us in.

April 2022

Moment – "Another Year Has Passed Through Us..."–Stefan's Birthday

Anda We are so grateful, Ștefan, for your creative spark, for the way you gather us all around music, poetry, and joy. Your birthday reminds us of the gift you are to Retro Muse Society.

Ligia Happy birthday, Ștefan! You are proof that harmony and kindness can truly change the world around us.

Corina Another year has passed through us, indeed... and it has left us richer. Thank you, Stefan, for sharing your journey with us.

Sorin Happy birthday, my friend! May your music always echo in our hearts and your path always be bright.

🟦 Corina

Then let us all shout together:
"Long live Your Highness,   (*Să trăiești, Maria Ta*)
Health and love,
May they be your eternal nourishment!
The Retro army stands by your side,
Just like Anda, Your Highness!"

And may your children carry on
Your fame, like stars across the sky.
Wherever life takes you,
May your solos bring smiles.
And though salt may sometimes taste bitter,
Don't let it weigh you down.
Happy Birthday! May joy and peace always find you! 💕

Note: *"Să trăiești, Maria Ta" is a playful Romanian phrase that mimics a formal courtly address — literally "Long live Your Highness" — used here in jest, as part of Retro's humorous and affectionate tone.*

🟩 Anakin

I keep reading your poem, Corina,
And I like it more and more.
Thank you for the warmth,
For hosting us and
For the delicious food.

Cătălin Lari

With such a lady poet,
What more could you
expect...
You bow with modesty

Anakin

Thank you, Cătălin,
Yesterday you
charmed me
with your violin,
And today,
With your poetry.

After so many colorful greetings, playful verses, and heartfelt wishes lighting up our WhatsApp screens, it felt as if the celebration had turned into a digital stage of its own. Every message carried a piece of Retro's soul—humor, warmth, poetry, and music. And yet, beyond the emojis and rhymes, there was something deeper binding us: the joy of being together, even at a distance, and of celebrating life through words. From here, the voices that once danced in chat bubbles now gather into a flowing chorus—ready to carry the story forward in a new rhythm, the block style of our shared Retro journey.

Corina
And so, without modesty,
Your talent speaks for itself.
From early dawn, you've lit the fire,
With wishes full of good cheer! 🔥

Ligia
Such beautiful wishes
For a dear and talented friend like you, Ștefan!
Happy Birthday! 🎂 ❤️ 🎉

Sorin
Happy Birthday with good health, Ștefan,
From all of us Grizescu family:
Carmen, Lavinia, Mom, and the girls!
May you stay forever loved and loving!
Kisses to Anda and the kids,
May your home be filled with joy! 💜

Corina
Fly to the Moon, Ștefan :) 🌙 ✦

Dedication for Ștefan – *Family Is Everything*
(to the tune of "Money, Money, Money" – ABBA)

🎸 *[guitar intro – upbeat]*

[All voices together]
Another year has passed,
And again, it's your day, Ștefan,
How wonderful...
In this fine, bright weather,
We are all together,
Healthy, joyful still.

[Solo voice – warm tone]
From childhood, you were an artist,
Ștefăniță, loved by all,
By those with hearts so rich,
Who admired your gift and soul...

🎵 **Refrain – [All voices, clapping in rhythm]**
It's your day, hooray!
We all sing, we all sing with joy,
Happy Birthday, Ștefan!
Blessings, happiness, good fortune too,
In all you dream,
And for others too,
May it all come true,
Love forever in your life! 🎵

[Spoken aside, playful]
Back at the dorm one evening,
You came to ask me for a guitar—
What a beginning!

[Duet – Anda & Ștefan, half-singing, half-speaking]
With folk dances and with song,
We roamed mountains, seas along,
Never giving up.

[All voices, softly]
Now we have three children, proud,
Guided by your gentle voice,
To chase their dreams with heart,
Not to leave them unfulfilled.

🎶 **Refrain – [All voices, louder, with handclaps]**

[Narrator voice – dramatic]
You, the talented artist,
Even in Hollywood you played,
In a film...

[Spoken chorus, teasing]
Then you formed your bands with flair,
Music always in the air,
For rhythm lives in you.

[Group voices, chanting]
Vox Maris! Cireşarii first!
And now Retro has its place!
The guitar in your hands
Brings us magic, brings us joy!

🎶 **Refrain – [All voices, stronger, the crowd joins in]**

[Spoken, rhythmic]
Sports as well, you play with talent,
That is surely true,
Indeed!
With a ball at your feet, or not,
There's no team like U—
Your team forevermore!

[Chorus building]
And to the world we'll shout it loud,
No soul is fuller than yours,

Joyful, smiling, giving love,
To all who cross your way.

🎶 **Final Refrain – [All voices, with cheers]**
It's your day, hooray!
We all sing, we all sing with joy,
Happy Birthday, Ștefan!
Blessings, happiness, good fortune too,
In all you dream,
And for others too,
May it all come true,
Love forever in your life! 🎶

🎂 🥂 *[guitar flourish – everyone cheers, Retro Muse Society bow]*

Happy Birthday, Ștefan! 🎉 🎶 💝 *—Anda, April 28, 2022*

June 2022 **Moment – *"Today is your day, your day, your daaay..."* OR – On My Birthday...**

🟦 **Corina**
Happy Birthday, dear Anduța,
Today I send you good thoughts.
Whoever wants to understand,
Should pick up the strings and play.

Isn't it too early, Corina?
Nooo, you remember it well!
If you're from Satu Mare,
The bags are already packed,
Potatoes and sausages roasted,

The camper and all the joy—
Those are true values of time.

Seventeen or nineteen—
It's all the same, don't you think?
Add up the reduced years,
Stop at eight if you wish,
Take whichever math you like—
Anda, trust this:
Recite a poem, and it's yours!

If you're from Satu Mare,
Celebrate when the time comes.
Even if today's not the big day,
Any day is a gift from the sun!

Two days before, arm in arm,
Two nights long,
We gather in clusters,
Like grapes for the must at dawn.
The bags are already packed—
If you recite a poem,
Surely, it will conquer her!

May health and love
Overflow into the years,
May song and poetry
Be your daily sweet.
May you shine with every day
And be reborn with every night.
Celebrate life itself,
Even if it's not Christmas or Easter!

I hope I managed, for a moment,
To make you smile again.
I'd even lend you a wing,
So you'd never fall apart.

So come on—strings and drums,
With great cheer, all for Anda! 🎵 💙

🟦 **Anda**
I feel that I'm truly living
A wonderful life when, with Retro,
I celebrate today's thoughts.
It's as if our lives
Bloom together.
Yes, with those from Satu-Mare,
Whenever it's someone's birthday,
It's still all under the sun,
So we rejoice with longing.

I'll stop here now,
Thank you for this gift,
But Corina, you really managed
To dot the "i," it's clear. ❤️

A wonderful weekend to everyone! 😊

🟧 **Cătălin Lari**
😍 Happy Birthday and joy, says the violin of the heart 🎻
Blending in harmony with the strings of the guitar…
All say, whispering in one voice:
Today is a great day!
Even the flowers in the garden stand taller in bloom…
"What could it be? What could it be?" shouts a cricket on a blade
of grass…
"Don't you tell me that now has arrived Old Man Autumn-Beard?"
That fell right out of the sky…
But nature replies with a gentle breeze, soft and soothing:
TODAY WE CELEBRATE A LADY!!! 🎉

184

Summer 2022 **Moment – Celebrating Retro-Style...**

What I've captured here is only a small part of the joy brought by celebrating our loved ones... The phone conversations, unfortunately, can't be reproduced, though there were many — and they were beautiful.

> **Corina**
> Cătáline, Cátáline
> The day begins wiith you.
> Dawn sings out with the violin
> Love surrounds you.
>
> 7:13 AM

Corina - *continued*
On the threshold of the years to come,
A cart of riches I would lay,
With health and love to guide your steps,
And grant you life that never fades away. 🌟

> **Corina**
> Cătăline, Cătaline
> Stay calm above your worries
> Don't be troubled in the storms
>
> Cătăline, Cătaline
> May everything go well for you!
>
> 8:07 PM

🟦 **Corina** - *continued*
Happy Birthday, live long and well,
With Retro may you always dwell,
Keep smiling, laughing, joy in sight—
Your song will make the whole world bright! 🎵

🟩 **Anda**
Our dear Cătălin,
May your days be full of clear skies,
Joy and fulfillment,
Health and love
Always be in your heart—
Both in good times and in hard.

🟦 **Sonia**
And on the strings of the violin,
May life flow lightly for you.
May Vic, Dănuța, and Calina
Always shine around you with light.

And with Retro, years from now,
We'll sing to you again:
Happy Birthday! 🎵

> Sorine, Sorine.
> You play the bass o fine,
> From afar we wish you
> Health divine.
>
> May all you do prosper,
> And don't forget — we
> love you!
>
> Happy Birthday, Sorin!
> 1:43 PM ✓

Sorin
Thank you, dear friends!
We'll keep you in our
thoughts and in our song.
1:50 PM

> Catalin Lari
> Who else, who else,
> Who else should we celebrate:
> The mayor of mayors,
> Loved by the world!
>
> And Carmen, to adore him,
> His daughters, to cherish him,
> We love him too, and we wish
> him well,
> Out loud we all praise him!
> 1:28 PM

🟨 **Cătălin Lari** - *continued*
The most handsome and talented,
Strong and respected,
And in Retro's joyful band,
He's always lending a helping hand!

With laughter, song, and so much cheer,
We shout together, far and near:
Long may you live, dear friend,
May happiness never end! 🎉

Catalin Lari
The most handsome
and talented
A *rebel*, but also a man!
And truly a son of the
Dacians—
An authentïc Romanian
at heart.
💖💖💖💖💖   1:51 PM

Sorin
Thank you for the
wonderful poem,
master of verse, Catalin!
It's like I can already hear
a violin in the background.
We'll be missing you
tonight
🥰   2:46 PM

🟦 **Corina**
Today, on your birthday, Sorin,
We think of you with love,
From afar we wish you
All that your heart desires.

And when we meet again,
We'll kiss your cheek,
Until then, live every moment to the fullest!
Happy Birthday! 💙 💋💋

September 23, 2022   **Moment**

Virtual Cultural Workshop initiated by Ligia... OR Sing with us to the tune of "Azi am să-mi crestez în grindă..."

Before diving into the verses, it's worth pausing for a smile. The inspiration for this playful creation came from a song every Romanian seems to carry in their memory: "*Azi am să-mi crestez în grindă...*". It's a folkloric tune, simple, funny, and almost impossible not to hum once it starts. The kind of melody that instantly lightens the mood and pulls people together.

In the Retro Muse Society's style, this familiar rhythm became a canvas for new lines—our own mix of humor and camaraderie. Just like at a village gathering where the laughter grows louder with every verse, this workshop flowed with words and music, bringing us closer across the screen.

Here we are again, so chic,
Five years on, such lovely tricks,
Life with Retro we have spun,
And that's how far we've all come.
And what charming, charming girls Retro has...

Lady Ana made her way,
Flying in without delay,
From afar she came with cheer,
To see Retro once again, so dear.

Lovely women, gracious friends,
Eager for the joy that blends
Verses, poems, songs at night,
Moments filled with pure delight.

Five years?
Hard to say—
Among the flowers, stones, and clay,

Still so young, so bright, so fair,
Smiles like bouquets everywhere.
Unique, unmatched, with grace anew,
Longing for a serenade too,
Soon, I'm sure, she'll take her turn,
Ana speaks—though time zones burn.

Time itself begins to bend,
European nights, American blend,
But when poetry calls our name,
Sleep will never win the game.
Only words will keep the key,
Unlocking tender reverie.
So I wait, with heart alight,
To meet you all—it feels so right.

Just be mindful, pay attention,
When longing stirs with pure intention.
Coachman, drive us, let's not wait—
The ladies are ready to celebrate!

December 10, 2022

What follows is adapted from an article I originally wrote for the Romanian-American newspaper Tribuna Românească, *published in Chicago in December 2022. The same piece later appeared in the cultural magazine* Creneluri Sighişorene *in February 2023. I have reworked it here so it finds its place in the story of the Retro Muse Society, just as it was lived — with music, poetry, and the spirit of Christmas.*

Whispers of Carols and the Scent of Baked Apples
Retro Muse Society Christmas Concert at ROCO, Chicago

I almost don't want to wake up from the euphoria brought on by this concert. And I think I share this feeling with everyone who had the joy of being with the Retro Muse Society on Saturday evening, at our Christmas concert so beautifully titled *Whispers of Carols and the Scent of Baked Apples.*

189

Even though admission was free (the space generously offered by Mihai Lehene – ROCO, and the gift of song and poetry offered by all of us), every seat was filled the very day the event was announced. We felt truly sorry that we could not accommodate everyone who wished to come — but we hope the emotions carried by the carols reached across the virtual space to those who held us in their thoughts.

Our Christmas concert, which we offer year after year to the community, has now become a tradition. We were honored to welcome in the audience the Consul General of Romania, Tiberiu Trifan, and his distinguished wife Gabriela Trifan. Their heartfelt message, left in the *Retro Memory Box*, touched us deeply.

I will let the impressions of those present speak for themselves, gathered from Facebook and from our Treasure Chest of Memories.

Tiberiu Trifan, Consul General of Romania in Chicago
Congratulations, Retro, for a wonderful evening full of sensitivity and holiday spirit. You reminded us of our childhood, of the beautiful Romanian carols that accompany us and define us as Romanians, wherever life may carry us in this world. Special moments that will remain beautiful memories in the hourglass of time. We will always remember Chicago and the Romanian community that gathers so beautifully around symbols such as Retro and ROCO. Happy Holidays!

Raicu Family – Lucas, Johny, Daniela, and Ionel
Dear Retro Circle,
An evening like a dream, as special as all of you are. Thank you for filling our souls with warmth, love, friendship, and the hope to be kinder, more forgiving, and closer in spirit to Romania and our faith.
Merry Christmas and good health.
Happy New Year! We love you!

Ana, Marius, Sergiu
Thank you for existing! It was the first time we saw you, and you offered us a wonderful evening. Happy Holidays!

Raluca Ioniță
You are wonderful! Thank you for giving us such magical moments and for making us feel closer to home!

Retro Muse Society
We are the whisper of carols, the dance of snowflakes, the footsteps of joy in the blue light of hope — we are together! The story of this winter evening will remain with us forever. Thank you, ROCO Chicago, the Romanian Community Center, for hosting this event. Merry Christmas!

Elisa Fedorca
We felt like we were in a fairytale: we sang carols, recited poetry, and performed alongside the Retro Muse Society. A wonderful evening that reminded us of the carols and festive atmosphere of "our street," of our grandmother preparing holiday treats, of our parents doing everything they could to make sure Santa fulfilled our wishes. We felt the emotions of the past, and you carried us back into another dimension — the world of childhood   !
THANK YOU, RETRO!

Geta Hațegan
A magical December evening with the Retro Muse Society in the "whispers of carols, the scent of baked apples, the taste of mulled wine, and stories of winter and Christmas" — all wrapped in warmth, festivity, and joy. Thank you.
"When you warm the hearts of others, you warm yourself as well."

BRAVO!! BRAVO!! BRAVO!!! Retro Muse Society!!!
An extraordinary performance!

You were amazing tonight — all of you, along with your wonderful guests, gifting us a superb holiday show with so much love! Our souls vibrated, tears of emotion streamed down our faces. Truly! And we thank you!

Thank you for carrying our thoughts and hearts back home to our beloved Romania — to the street of our childhood, with the scent of baked apples and basil, with the snowfalls of home, and with carols, carols, beautiful carols!

Thank you from the bottom of our hearts, Retro Muse Society! You are beautiful people, simple people, happy to be together, to sing, to delight us with music and poetry in perfect harmony. And we resonated with every bit of it!

We received your message — to be kinder, more forgiving, warmer... to cherish every moment and never forget where we came from. Proud to be Romanians!! Our hearts welcomed the beauty you gifted us.

And we, the audience,
THANK YOU!
WE LOVE YOU!
AND WE WISH YOU,
MANY YEARS AHEAD!
MERRY CHRISTMAS!!! — *Olezia Comşulea*

What can I say?
I left for home with a soul overflowing... overflowing with the joy of emotions lived through song and verse. Snow fell beautifully, like in a carol...The carolers came just as they used to long ago (*leru-i ler*), Jesus was born — the wondrous news brought by the Magi — all of it sank deep into the souls of those present. Audience and artists together created emotion, and for a moment (or more — the show lasted about two hours), we were wrapped in the hum of carols and the scent of baked apples.

Thank you to ROCO for helping organize this concert.
— *Cristina Haidău, Oniţa Cârcu, Cosmina Ungur, Georgiana Merdariu, Oana Dobrean Urzica, Paula Telcianu, Dan Cosma*

We thank everyone who accepted our invitation to join us. Through you, we felt that our mission was fulfilled.

"Wonderful! Wonderful! Wonderful!
Talents carrying the blood of our people!
So very moving!
Thanks to the invited guests of Retro Muse Society:
Athena and Ana Marincaş, Iulia Romoşan, Lucas and Johny Raicu,
Geta Haţegan Pupek, Traian Alexandru Bălan, Ionuţ and Marc
Dima, Dana and Victor Lari."
— *Olezia Comşulea (Facebook)*

We thank the members of the Retro Muse Society who so
generously offer art to all who wish to receive it:
Sorin Griza, Radu Răcean, Corina Vlad, Cătălin Lari, Ligia
Grindeanu, Ana of Sighişoara, Călin Mărincaş, Anda Cristolţean,
Ştefan Cristolţean

Video & Photography: Iulian Grindeanu
Technical Team: Adrian Nechiti, Carmen Griza
Sponsors: Sorin & Olezia Comşulea, Dan & Mariana Torz, Rodica
Bărănescu, Radu Mihalcea, Joselito Reyes

And not least, we thank all those who come to see us, listen to us,
and share with us the joy and harmony of being together.

In the hope that we have opened wide the gates of a storybook
Christmas 2022, and walked gently in the footsteps of the Magi,
filled with joy and emotion, we wish you a Merry Christmas!

And we thank you —
For inspiring us.
Through you we relive
Moments of longing that give us chills...

—Sonia Maria *Anda Cristolţean, Co-Founder, Retro Muse Society*

DEDICATIONS

The Retro Muse Society got involved — young and old alike — in what follows. The verses (and in some cases even the music) are ours, created within the circle. I hope these dedications bring you joy and a good laugh.

Since the verses were originally written in Romanian and translated here into English, a little of their original rhythm or nuance may have taken on a new shape. But the emotion is still ours, and the smile is still meant for you.

Here's a small glimpse "behind the curtain." The tunes are well-known, but if you're curious, just ask any of us. With a bit of luck, you might even get the right answer. 😊

🎵 *Dedication for Călin* 🎵

Oh, Călin, dear Călin,
Traveler through lands afar,
Today we've gathered here for you
To wish you days serene,
And filled with joy and cheer.

Oh, Călin, dear Călin,
As is fitting, we unite,
Year by year, weaving destinies,
Good people at tables full,
Raising a toast in your honor:

For your health,
Happy Birthday, many years, Călin!

Together with your shining stars,
We'll sing with laughter and delight,
And your handsome boys,
May they live in health and joy,
May your days be full of blessings—
Happy Birthday, many years, Călin!

Forever young, forever rich,
Inspired by the autumn's charm.

Oh, Călin, dear Călin,
We just cannot hold it back,
We must sing this just for you—
Happy Birthday, many years, Călin!

🎵 *Dedication for Ana and Ligia* 🎵

(on the tune of "Felicità" by Al Bano & Romina Power)

Congratulations!
For Ligia and Ana,
Daughter and Mother,
Who write their poetry,
We send them a kiss,
And an embrace, wherever they are.
In a shout or a whisper,
We tell them by night
Or in broad daylight:

Ligia, never stop
Writing in verses,
Never grow weary!
And Ana, with Retro you'll be—
By night or by day!

Congratulations!
For Ana and Ligia,
Two graceful ladies,
196

With no equal.
The blue of the sky,
On their gifted faces, they wear with calm.
Tenderness is the gateway,
That rocks their fate
All the way to the end:

Ana, never stop
Writing in verses,
Never grow weary!
And Ligia, with Retro you'll be—
By night or by day!

🎵 *Dedication for Radu* 🎵

Through the forest, dark and tall,
Radu's mother walks withal,
From her black eyes tears do fall,
As for Radu she does call:
Radu, darling, Radu mine,
Hear your mother's weary cry,
Radu, darling, Radu mine,
Hear your mother's weary cry.

"Have you seen my Radu dear?
He's at Retro, still he's near—
Sings and tells his tales with cheer,
Braves the sound without a fear.
Radu, darling, Radu mine,
Sings and tells his tales with cheer,
Radu, darling, Radu mine,
Braves the sound without a fear.

Diana listened, heart awake,
To the songs that Radu'd make,
Rebecca too was held in sway,
Loved the music's tender play.
Radu, darling, Radu mine,

Karaoke, strings that shine,
Radu, darling, Radu mine,
Talent circles us in line.

Radu, we give thanks to you,
For the Retro songs you drew,
Every word and every line,
Keep the spirit's flame divine.
Radu, darling, Radu mine,
With your pen and with your song,
Radu, darling, Radu mine,
Retro's heart beats loud and strong.

♫ *Dedication for Sergiu* ♫

We with you and you with us, we love to joke and play,
With RETRO near, we never tire, we laugh the hours away.
You may dream of fishing trips, but I doubt you'd dare
To leave us all and not be there.

Come now, Sergiu, speak a while, don't be silent so,
Sing a verse or hum a tune, let your music flow.
And perhaps inside your RV, you'll take us all along,
On jet skis we'll be riding strong!

Refrain:
Oh try it, ah, ah—oh try it, dear Sergiu,
Try not to run, to run away to waters blue.
You know too well we're not keen on pike or roe,
With RETRO life is better so! (x2)

Corina surely with her guitar will strum a song,
And later in the evening dance, the night won't feel too long.
With boats and snowmobiles and toys that make us spin,
Ah Sergiu, you draw us in!

We with you and you with us, we love to joke and play,
With RETRO near, we never tire, we laugh the hours away.

You may dream of fishing trips, but I doubt you'd dare
To leave us all and not be there.

Refrain:
Oh try it, ah, ah—oh try it, dear Sergiu,
Try not to run, to run away to waters blue.
You know too well we're not keen on pike or roe,
With RETRO life is better so! (x...)

🎵 *Dedication for Sorin* 🎵

Sorin, oh Sorin,
On the bass you're keen,
And we all adore you still,
For you're "cool," Sorin,
Retro sings within—
A little song we wrote with will.

Verse I
In Sorin's own garden fair,
There is wine and beer to share,
Laughter rising everywhere,
For Sorin has three girls so fine,
Who show patience all the time—
Ruxi, Carmen, Gina shine.

Chorus
Sorin, oh Sorin,
When we're here with you,
Songs come out so rich, sublime.
Sorin, oh Sorin,
Not just anyone,
We love you true, through every rhyme!

Verse II
With acoustic or with bass,
You keep steady, set the pace.
Dearest Sorin, night and day,

With the tunes by tens you play,
All night long you make them stay,
Rehearsals take our breath away!

Chorus
Sorin, oh Sorin,
When we're here with you,
Songs come out so rich, sublime.
Sorin, oh Sorin,
Not just anyone,
We love you true, through every rhyme!

Verse III
Faithful as in student days,
Through the night you film our ways,
Give us Retro's brightest praise.
On the website, strong you stand,
Keeping Retro's soul in hand,
Making life so sweet and grand.

Final Chorus
Sorin, oh Sorin,
On the bass you're keen,
And we all adore you still.
For you're "cool," Sorin,
Retro sings within—
A little song we wrote with will.

🎵 *Dedication for Ştefan* 🎵

Chorus:
Rise up, Ştefan, go chase your dreaming,
Music's heavy, strong today.
Faith forever to the Retro Circle,
We swear it, Your Majesty!

Raise your glasses, aim them higher,
Like we're striking battle goals.

Come and join the celebration,
Winter's fire warms our souls.

Ştefan and the Lady Anda,
Songs of praise we sing for you.
Hear our hearts, they call together,
Guide our dreams and make them new.

Chorus:
Rise up, Ştefan, and see your people,
Music's heavy, strong today.
Faith forever to the Retro Circle,
We swear it, Your Majesty!

🎵 *Happy Birthday, Corina!* 🎵

Corina dear, our wish today
Finds you just the same old way –
A gentle heart, a playful mind,
With clear blue skies within your eyes. (Repeat)

Your smile, it lights the world around,
You turn to song each sight and sound –
The orchards, flowers, mountains high,
The waterfalls through passing time. (Repeat)

Chorus:
Happy day, happy day, Corina!
Retro wishes you a happy day!
Happy day, many more, Corina,
Stay with us 'til a hundred years away!

Your love for nature is your crown,
The "living fire" is burning now,
With Retro's joy we celebrate,
Together on this special day. (Repeat)

Corina dear, our wish today
Finds you just the same old way –
A gentle heart, a playful mind,
With clear blue skies within your eyes. (Repeat)

Chorus:
Happy day, happy day, Corina!
Retro wishes you a happy day!
Happy day, many more, Corina,
Stay with us 'til a hundred years away!

Lyrics: Ligia Grindeanu
Music: Anda Cristolțean

🎵 *Hello, Traian!* 🎵

Verse 1
Traian, you are our shining star,
Always loving just who we are.
With sweet Iva there by your side,
You light up the night, our hearts open wide.

Chorus:
Hello, hello, Traian, hello!
Hello, we love you, Traian!
Hello, hello, Traian, hello!
Hello, we love you, Traian!

Verse 2
When the snowy hills come in view,
You prepare your gear like you do.
Even with your knee feeling sore,
You still hit the slopes, you're ready for more.

With your heart forever so young,
You still climb where mountains are strong.
Only you, dear Traian, can play
With love and with life in such a bright way.

Bridge:
Hello, hello, many years!
Hello, hello, Traian!

Refrain:
Retro sings this song for you today,
This is what you truly earn on your day.
Keep on writing music, year by year,
And we'll always sing you loud and clear.
Keep the jokes and laughter going strong,
With Retro you'll celebrate all along.
Retro sings this song for you today,
This is what you truly earn on your day.

Verse 3
When you sing on stage, Retro shines,
All your songs turn moments to rhymes.
Victor and your girls by your side,
Clap and cheer for you, their hearts full of pride.

With the hall all singing as one,
We recall the joy you have spun.
Every song you've made through the years
Has become a chorus we hold so dear.

Bridge (repeat):
Hello, hello, many years!
Hello, hello, Traian!

🎵 *Dedication for Iulian* 🎵

You delight us with your smile,
Like the sunshine for a while,
With that twinkle in your eye,
Bringing joy to all nearby.

You record us all the time,
Make our moments more sublime,
Maybe you have made a vow
To be loved by all somehow.

Chorus:
We are all around you now, Iulian,
Singing loud and clear for you: Happy Birthday!
Let us all stay joyful through the years,
Today with Retroooo – Happy Birthday! (x2)

And at volleyball you shine,
Guide the ball as if by sign,
Send it flying through the air,
Engineer with skill to spare!

Engineer of highest class,
Solar panels on your house,
Watt by watt you've stored away,
Ligia's heart you've swept away!

Chorus:
We are all around you now, Iulian,
Singing loud and clear for you: Happy Birthday!
Let us all stay joyful through the years,
Today with Retroooo – Happy Birthday! (x2)

♬ *Happy Birthday, Monica!* ♬

We all are gathered here at Monica's,
Who works all day, as busy as she is.
And like a cricket, music by her side,
She plays the piano with a happy stride:

Chorus:
Monica, Monica, Monica,
We all wish you "Happy Birthday!"
Monica, Monica, Monica,
Stay just like this through all the years!

The Retro Circle sings this song for you,
We wish you well in all the things you do.
Through mountain trips and seaside days we share,
Happy birthday, Monica — we'll always care!

Since '89, when first you met Lucian,
You won his heart — oh yes, you had a plan.
And ever since, you write him lines so sweet,
And he wins prizes (without missing a beat!)

SOLO (Lucian):
"My dearest Monica, I must confess,
I tease you much — but you deserve the best.
Today I say it truly, plain and clear:
Without you, love, I'd never make it here.

Let's not forget that day down by the sea,
Ursulescu gave you a new name with glee —
But here with Retro, always every year,
We call you Monica Topârceanu dear!"

♬ *Serenade for Anda* ♬
(to the tune of "Serenata" by Toto Cutugno)

The little cricket woke so early,
On his paper laid his poems surely,
With emotions like a bouquet made,
For Anda.
With the chords of gentle guitar playing,
"Happy birthday, good morning" saying,
From the first bright light of day,
For Anda.

She loves ballads, lyrical, inspired,
Epigrams with meaning, never tired,
Every moment shines so bright—
With Anda.
On the stage of life she plays so neatly,
Solving all equations so completely,
Life itself is beautiful—
With Anda.

Refrain:
We can feel your spirit close beside us, dearest Anda,
May your life be filled with love and light forever.
Two fine sons and one bright daughter, dearest Anda,
Show you every day how deeply they adore you.

The little cricket went to rest so early,
In his dreams still writing poems surely,
All his thoughts a starry sky—
For Anda.
With the chords of gentle guitar ringing,
"Happy birthday, and for the countless bringing—
This sweet song is always sung—
For Anda.

Refrain:
We can feel your spirit close beside us, dearest Anda,
May your life be filled with love and light forever.
Two fine sons and one bright daughter, dearest Anda,
Show you every day how deeply they adore you.

We can feel your spirit close beside us, dearest Anda,
May your life be filled with love and light forever.

Serenade, when the moon is shining,
Serenade, for all of time abiding,
Serenade, for Anda.
(bis)

(Lyrics by Ligia Grindeanu, adapted to the melody of Toto Cutugno's "Serenata")

The Cricket and the Ant

The Cricket and the Ant, in harmony they sing,
Spreading beauty in the soul,
Beloved by everyone.
They are lovely, they are tireless,
And I too am their fan!
From all things they make a feast—
They are Anda and Ștefan.

(Dedication: Ana Munteanu Drăghici)

🎵 Dedication for Anda 🎵

After so much frost and winter,
When at last the sun appears,
Lest it leave us lost in mist,
She sketches out her bright new scenes.

She presents, recites, and sings,
Morning finds her full of song—

And together, as a band,
With Retro we all sail along.

All day long along the pathway,
On her bike or on a stroll,
With her tangents, with her algorithms,
In her red coat, splendid whole.

So we all together wish her
Health and joy, and many years,
Countless meetings still to come,
Retro's laughter through the years!
Countless meetings still to come,
Always Anda through the years!

(Verses by Corina Vlad)

🎵 *Happy Birthday, Cătălin!* 🎵

Cătălin, oh Cătălin,
With your violin you shine.
With Retro you sing and play,
May you live for many a day.

In your family — joy and cheer,
Health and love throughout the year.
From the youngest to the tall,
Your gift of music charms us all.

Our hearts begin to resonate,
With your strings that vibrate,
Every tone you find with ease —
Cătălin, may you live in peace!

When we miss a semitone,
You frown gently, not alone,
Then you bring back harmony,
Mingling sound with poetry.

Happy birthday, health and light,
Play your violin tonight.
Everything turns bright and true,
When the crowd applauds for you.

Chorus 1
Applause, applause — let it resound!
Cătălin, you are profound.
A virtuoso, shining bright,
May you live in joy and light.
With Retro concerts ever near,
Let the whole wide world now hear.

Chorus 2
Many years, oh many more,
Healthy, happy as before.
May your life be song and rhyme,
Music flowing all the time.
On the violin's sweet strings,
Endless celebration rings!

♫ *A Scented Romance for Carmen* ♫

I see the garden, full of bloom,
Colors dancing, sweet perfume,
And there's Carmen, lost in dreaming...
By her side stands Sorin near,
Gazing skyward, eyes sincere,
Holding gently one fair flower.

Together now we sing tonight,
With all our hearts, with all delight,
Happy birthday, joyful cheer!
May you stay just as you are,
Like a gift, a shining star,
Carmencita, blossom rare.

You wear a smile that's bright and warm,
Every thought a gentle charm,
Today we celebrate you.
Two dear daughters, love so near,
Family bonds you hold so dear,
Lucky Sorin stands beside you.

Together now we sing tonight,
With all our hearts, with all delight,
Happy birthday, joyful cheer!
May you stay just as you are,
Like a gift, a shining star,
Carmencita, blossom rare.

Time is a friend that walks with you,
With your family strong and true,
And the best friends all around.
You are the light that softly shines
On our Retro ties that bind,
Happy birthday, dearest Carmen!

Together now we sing tonight,
With all our hearts, with all delight,
Happy birthday, joyful cheer!
May you stay just as you are,
Like a gift, a shining star,
Carmencita, blossom rare.

THE TREASURE CHEST OF MEMORIES

Here we open our Treasure Chest of Memories — the Retro notebook where moments were scribbled down with joy, laughter, and friendship. Now, these notes have been lovingly gathered into this book, so we can relive them together, again and again.

📖 *June 24–25, 2017* **Starved Rock – Camping Trip**

"A night of twenty years,
Watch the play, dear mother, and ask no more.
It's very simple – tonight is mine."

This was the very first outing of the Retro Muse Society, thanks to Corina's initiative. We gathered — young and old, everyone who could make it (sadly, not all who wanted to) — and somehow, we turned the dream of singing all night by the fire into reality.

And so, now (around 7:30 a.m.), only Charley - our cute little dog - and I are awake, and I can quietly write whatever comes to mind. Only the little birds are singing for me, and the Sun is gently stroking me with its warm rays. Everyone else is still asleep. There is so much beauty all around, you can almost *hear* the grass growing.

After we all gathered around 3:30 p.m., we went on a hike to Illinois Canyon — spectacular, full of challenges (three little streams to cross), stories to tell, and pictures to snap. What a wonderful group we are: Corina with Sergiu (and the cauldron 😊), Sorin with Carmen & Gina (and the bacon), Ștefan with Anda

211

(me), and Sonia, our daughter (with Charley and the sour cherry liqueur).

After our "mountain trails," we set up camp at a crossroads and got busy right away: adventures, fire, a table loaded with chicken, mushrooms, bacon, sausages, and a colorful mix of vegetables on the grill. And then the highlight: singing by the fire, sharing ideas, laughter, and just a little bit of exhaustion.

I don't even know when it ended (did it really end?) because I went into the tent early to calm Charley down. We'll find out today. We plan to continue with a hike at Matthiessen State Park, where we hope Ligia, Iulian, Adelina, Alex, and Lola will join us. The adventure of the Retro Muse Society goes on...

📖 *June 25, 2017* **Corina's Voice**

Whispers of wind, sparkles of sunlight, dreamy glances, shivers that flood your soul when you hear those wonderful songs. Moments that pass through time and space — yet stay alive in the depths of the heart. Dreamy moments, longing moments, moments of love.

And I melt for folk — for everything — oh, I can't stop, I want more! More folk, more of you, you beautiful people. With the Retro Muse Society, life is in full bloom. Everything runs smoothly, and you're reborn from the fire. Games, music, laughter, move you from your place. On the trails, through the canyons, in flowered valleys, You lose yourself in song and giggle with the dawn. Come on, boys and girls, let's truly live life. Romanians we are, and Romanians we'll always be.

We remain
Eternal
Young
Romanians!
Youhuuu!

As for hiking — words can hardly express the bliss of the landscapes: canyons, waterfalls, warm water inviting you to taste its whispers. New ideas for future projects take shape among the wild bats that catch your eye — and you lose yourself in the horizons of imagination.

It was beautiful, it is beautiful, it will be beautiful — the beautiful story of the Retro Muse Society. To be continued...

📖 *November 8, 2017* **Anişoara's Voice**

A Gathering with Music and Poetry at Corina and Sergiu's Home

An intimate "supper" of ideas and feelings, expressed through poetry and music, harmonized within the **Retro Muse Society**!

After the successful performance of the now-beloved Retro Circle, held in the library hall at the Romanian Heritage Center on the fourth of November, the artists of words and sounds gathered together for counsel.

They met for this special "last supper" of words and music, hosted with both spiritual and traditional hospitality. Like a beehive, the buzz of opinions filled every corner of the welcoming home.

Plans are now in motion for a Christmas concert, sprinkled with poetry dedicated to the great feast of the Birth of Our Lord Jesus Christ — music pieces, poems, creativity, lively discussions, and, why not, a glass of wine.

"Poetry is the music of the soul — especially of the great and sensitive soul."

A dreamlike journey for the Retro Muse Society, of which I feel a part — a spectrum of light within the spiritual sphere of the Romanian soul, never and nowhere a stranger, for it is eternal.

VOICE OF THE AUDIENCE – *from the impression's notebook*

Here are some of the beautiful words our audience has shared with us — heartfelt memories we cherish and keep in our Treasure Chest of Memories.

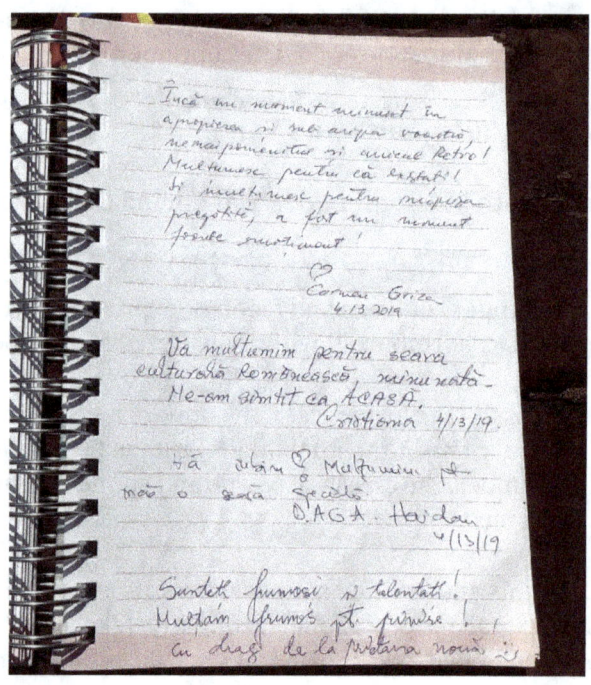

Another special moment spent close to you and under your wing, the one and only Retro Muse Society!
Thank you for existing!
And thank you for the beautiful surprise —
it was such a moving experience.
Carmen Griza, April 13, 2019

Thank you for the wonderful Romanian cultural evening.
We truly felt at home.
Cristiana, April 13, 2019

We love you!
Thank you for yet another special evening.
D.A.G.A Haidău – April 13, 2019

You are beautiful and talented!
Thank you so much for the warm welcome!
With love, from your new friend 💛

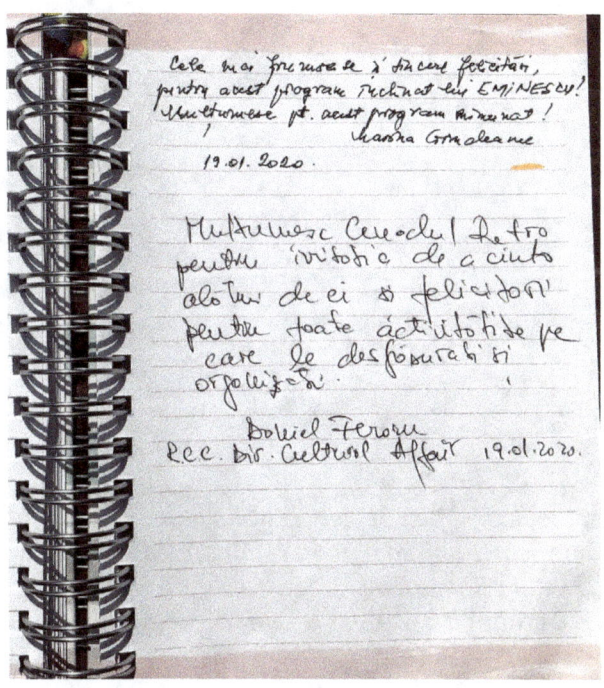

My warmest and most sincere congratulations
for this program dedicated to EMINESCU!
Thank you for such a wonderful event!
Marina Grindeanu – January 19, 2020

Thank you, Retro Muse Society, for the invitation
to sing alongside you — and congratulations
for all the activities you organize and bring to life.
Daniel Feraru – Director of Cultural Affairs, R.C.C. – January 19, 2020

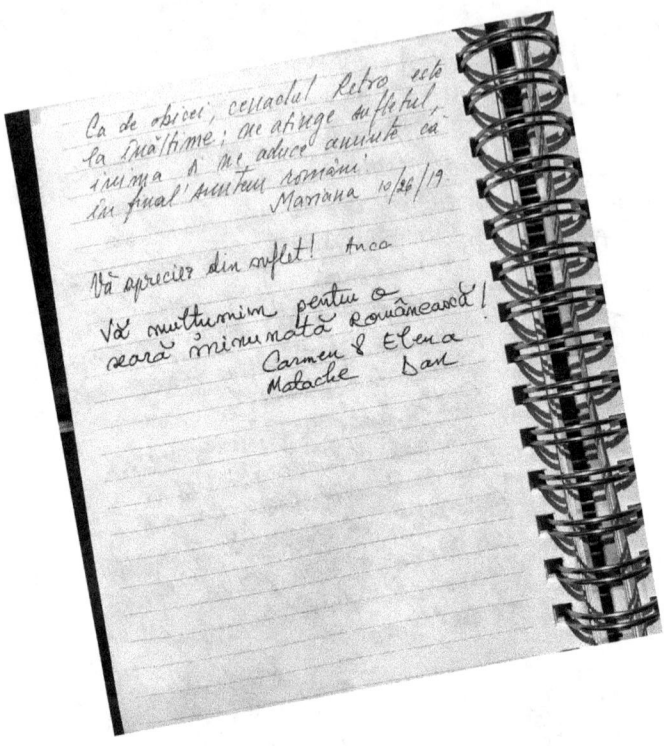

As always, the Retro Muse Society is at its best —
touching our hearts and souls, and reminding us that,
in the end, we are Romanians.
Mariana – October 26, 2019

I appreciate you with all my heart!
Anca

Thank you for a wonderful Romanian evening!
Carmen Matache & Elena Dan

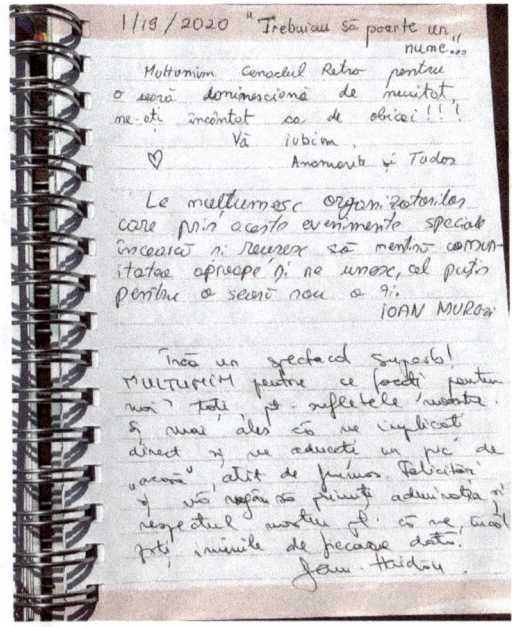

January 19, 2020 – "They Had to Have a Name…"

Thank you, Retro Muse Society, for an unforgettable Eminescu evening —you enchanted us as always!!! We love you.
Anamaria & Tudor

My thanks to the organizers, who through these special events try — and succeed — to keep the community close, bringing us together for at least an evening or a day.
Ioan M.

Another wonderful performance! THANK YOU for all that you do for us, for our souls — and especially for involving us directly and bringing us a little piece of "home" in such a beautiful way. Congratulations, and please accept our admiration and respect for warming our hearts every single time.
The Haidău Family

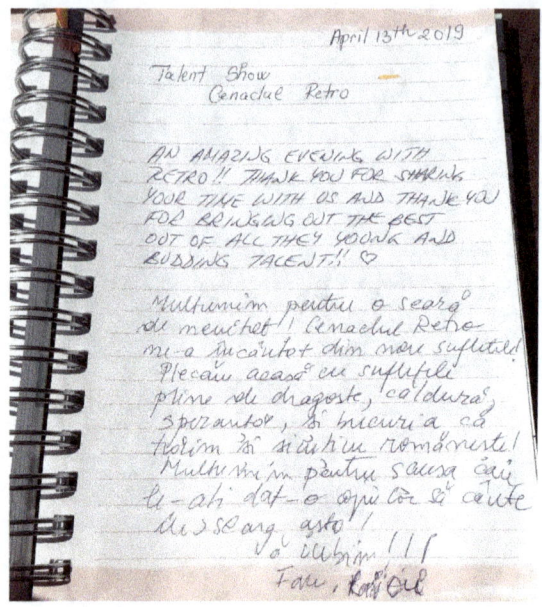

April 13, 2019 – Talent Show

AN AMAZING EVENING WITH RETRO!!
THANK YOU FOR SHARING YOUR TIME WITH US
AND FOR BRINGING OUT THE BEST
IN ALL THE YOUNG AND BUDDING TALENT!!

Thank you for an unforgettable evening!
The Retro Muse Society once again filled our hearts with joy!
We go home with hearts full of love, warmth, hope,
and the happiness of living and feeling Romanian!
Thank you for giving the children the chance to sing tonight!
We love you!!!
The Raicu Family

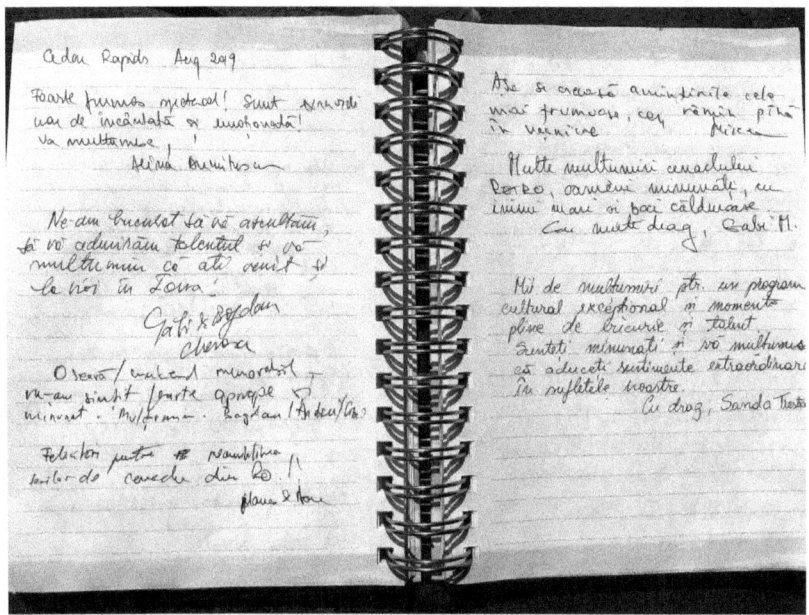

Cedar Rapids – August 2019

Such a beautiful show! I was absolutely delighted and moved!
Thank you!
Alina Dumitrescu

We were so glad to listen to you, to admire your talent,
and we thank you for coming to us here in Iowa.
Gabi & Bogdan Cherăscu

A memorable evening and weekend.
We felt so close and had a wonderful time.
Thank you – Bogdan, Andrei, C.

Congratulations for bringing back the memory
of those cenaclu evenings from back home!!
Nana & Dan

This is how the most beautiful memories are made —
the kind that last forever.
Mircea

Many congratulations to the Retro Muse Society —
wonderful people, with big hearts and warm voices.
With much love, Gabi M.

A thousand thanks for an exceptional cultural program
and moments full of joy and talent.
You are amazing, and I thank you for bringing
such extraordinary feelings into our hearts.
With love, Sanda Trestian

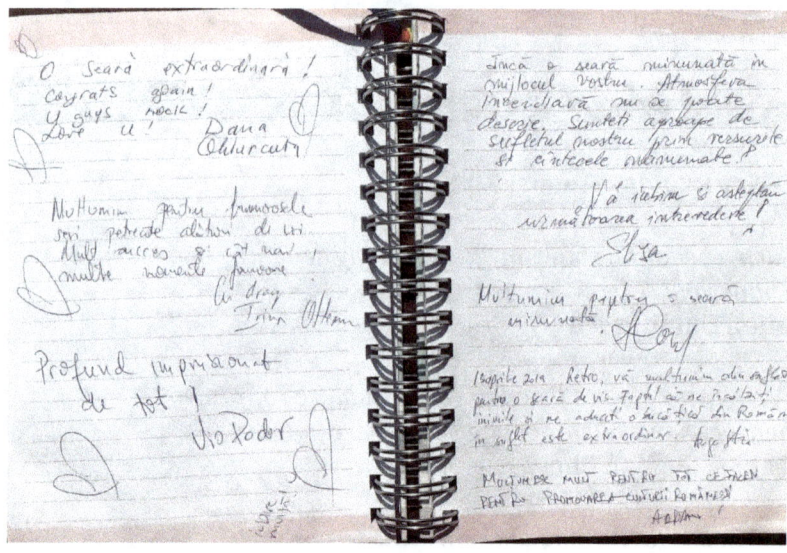

An extraordinary evening!
Congratulations once again —
you truly rock! We love you!
Dana Ghiurcuţa

Thank you for the beautiful evenings spent with you.
Wishing you great success and many more
moments filled with joy!
With love, Irina Olteanu

I was deeply moved by everything!
Vio Podar

Another wonderful evening in your midst.
The atmosphere was electric — impossible to put into words!
Through your beautiful songs and lyrics,
you stay close to our hearts.
We love you and look forward to the next gathering!
Elisa

Thank you for a truly wonderful evening!

April 13, 2019

Retro, we thank you from the bottom of our hearts
for a dreamlike evening.
The way you warm our hearts and bring us
a little piece of Romania is truly extraordinary.

Thank you so much for all that you do
to promote Romanian culture.
Adrian

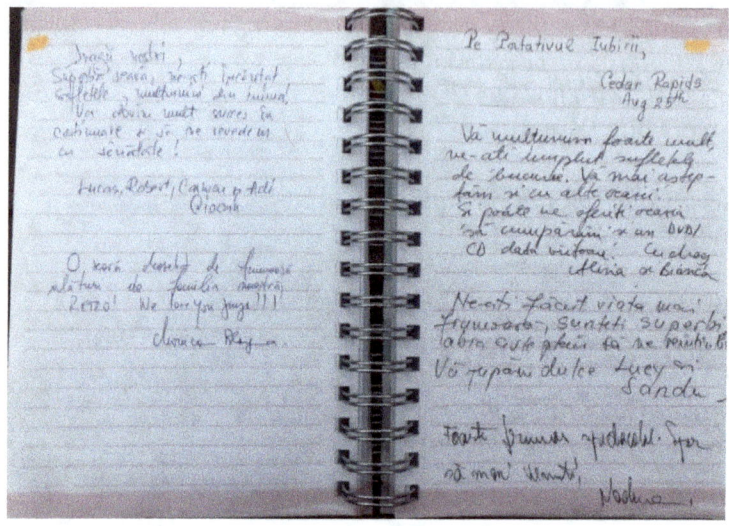

Our dear friends,
What a superb evening — you delighted our hearts,
thank you from the bottom of our souls!
We wish you continued success
and hope to see each other again in good health!
Lucas, Robert, Carmen & Adi Ciocan

A particularly beautiful evening
spent with our RETRO family!
We love you guys!!!
Monica Blaga

On the Staff of Love – Cedar Rapids, August 25

Thank you so very much —
you filled our hearts with joy.
We look forward to welcoming you again,
and maybe next time you can offer us the chance
to buy a DVD or CD!
With love, Alina & Bianca

You made our lives more beautiful — you are wonderful!
We can't wait to meet again. Sweet kisses!
Lucy & Sandu

A very beautiful performance.
I hope you will come again!
Nadina

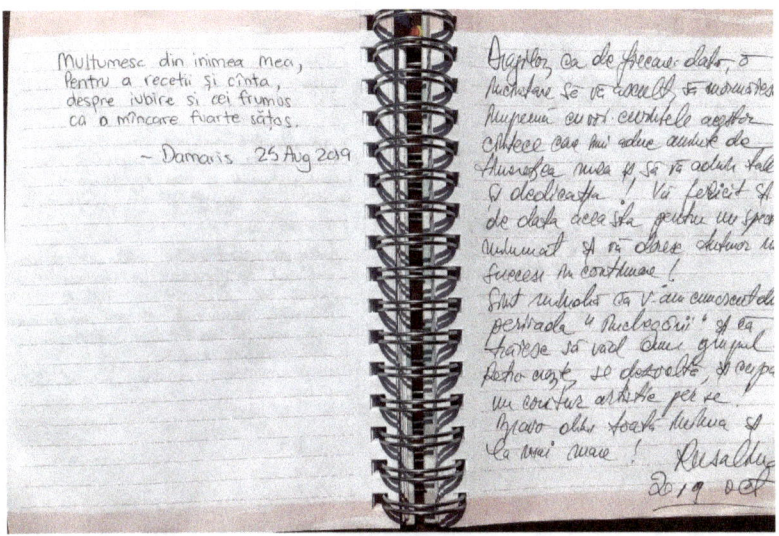

"Thank you from the bottom of my heart
for the singing and reciting
about love and all that is beautiful —
like a meal that fills the soul."
Damaris – August 25, 2019

*(**Note:** Damaris was born in the U.S. to Romanian parents,*
and she does not speak Romanian. Her effort to express her feelings
after the Cedar Rapids concertwas truly impressive.)

*My dear friends, as always, it is a delight to listen to you,
to hum along with the words of these songs
that bring back memories of my youth,
and to admire your talent and dedication!

I congratulate you once again for a wonderful performance
and wish you all much success going forward!

I am proud to have known you from the early days,
when the group was just taking shape,
and to see how Retro has grown, developed,
and gained its own unique artistic identity.
Bravo from the bottom of my heart — and here's to even more!*
Rusalina – October 2019

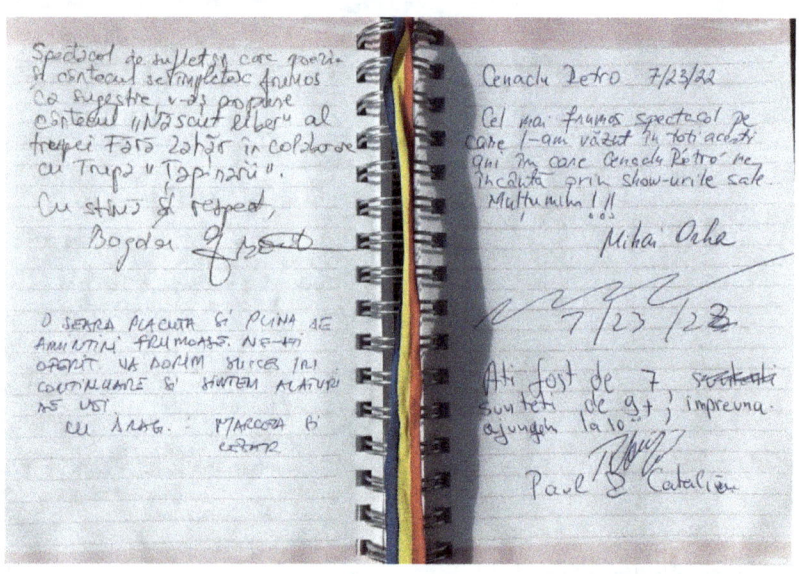

Poets Chatting About the Loves of the Muses
Chicago – July 2022

*A soulful performance where poetry and song
are beautifully intertwined.
As a suggestion, I would propose the song
"Născut liber" ("Born Free") by the band Fără Zahăr,
in collaboration with the band Țapinarii.*
With respect, Bogdan Groza

*You offered us a pleasant evening
filled with beautiful memories.*

*We wish you continued success and want you to know
we are cheering you on!*
With love, Marcela & Cezar

Retro – July 23, 2022
*The most beautiful performance I've seen
in all these years of enjoying Retro's shows.
Thank you!!!*
Mihai Orha

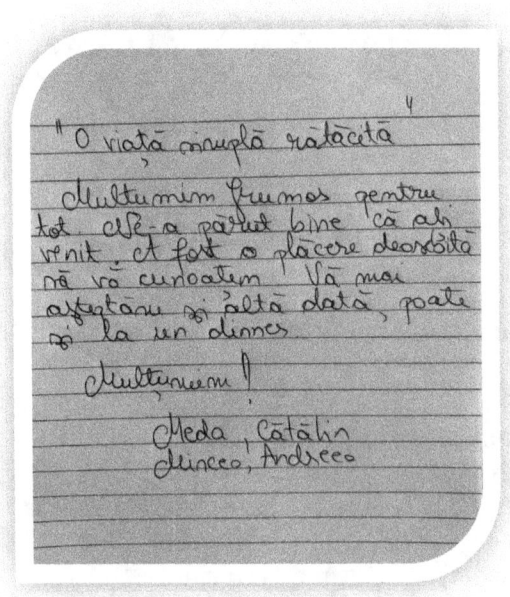

Picnic at the Farm – September 4, 2022 – Wisconsin
"A Simple Life, Found Again"

*Thank you so much for everything.
We were so glad you came — it was a real pleasure to meet you!
We hope to welcome you again sometime, maybe even for a dinner.*

**With thanks,
Meda & Cătălin, Mircea & Andreea**

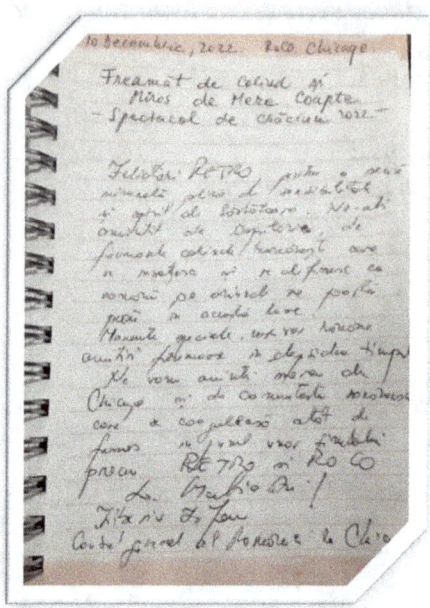

Rustle of Carols and the Scent of Baked Apples – December 10, 2022

Congratulations, Retro, for a wonderful evening,
full of sensitivity and the spirit of the holidays.
You reminded us of childhood, of the beautiful Romanian carols
that accompany us and define us as Romanians,
wherever life may take us in this world.

Special moments that will remain
beautiful memories in the hourglass of time.

We will always remember Chicago
and the Romanian community that gathers so beautifully
around symbols such as RETRO and ROCO.

Happy Holidays!
Tiberiu Trifan – Consul General of Romania in Chicago

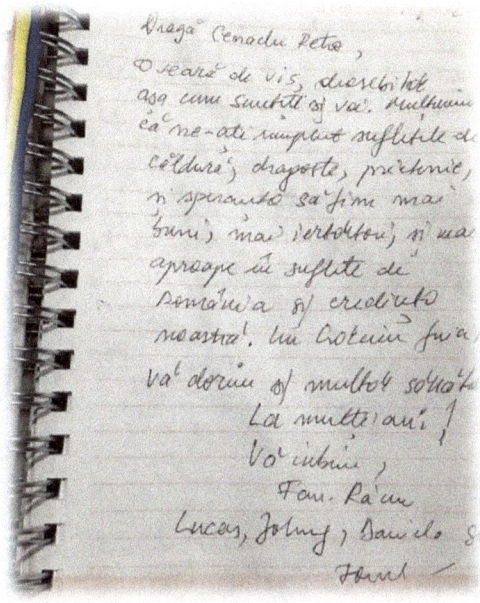

Dear Retro,

A dreamlike evening — as special as you are.
Thank you for filling our hearts with warmth, love, friendship,
and the hope to become better, more forgiving,
and closer in spirit to Romania and to our faith.

We wish you a Merry Christmas and good health.
Happy New Year! We love you!

The Raicu Family
Lucas, Johny, Daniela & Ionel

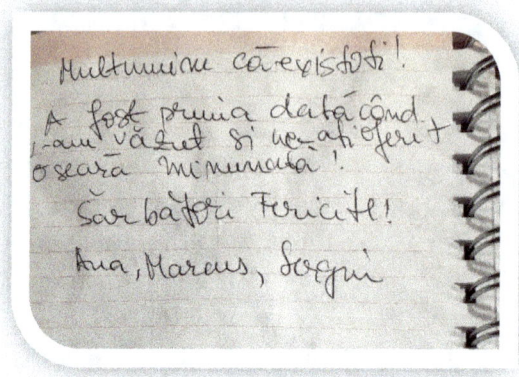

Thank you for existing!
This was the first time we saw you,
and you gave us a truly wonderful evening!

Happy Holidays!

Ana, Marius & Sergiu

Artwork lovingly created by Anișoara

Whimsical Ceramic Art by Iva

A Beautiful Painting by Geta

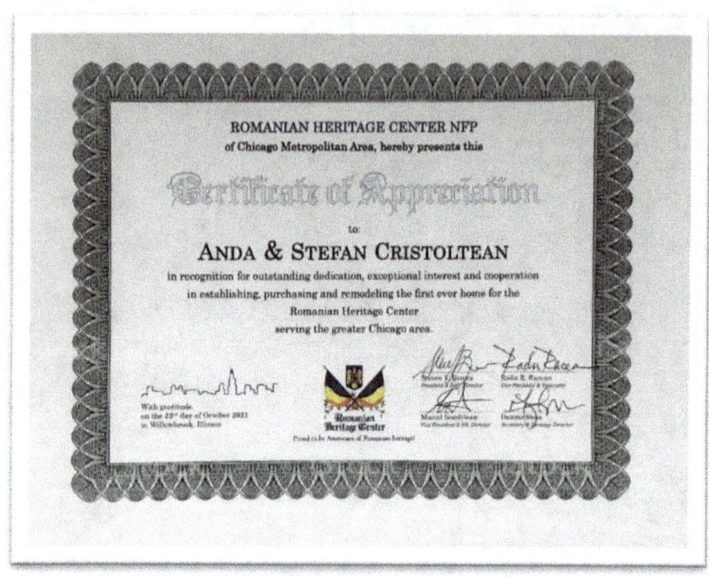

🎸 🎶 The Story Behind Our Logo

Created by Dana Negruş

Before you read this story, take a moment.
Look carefully at our logo.
What do you see? What do you *feel* it expresses?

After one of our shows, **S** came up to me and said:

"Well, well — you folks are so progressive!
I have to say, I really noticed your logo.
Very daring!"

I was surprised.
Yes — I think our logo is beautiful and perfectly in tune with
our mission.

Then he grinned:

"You know, that girl lying on the sand... on the beach..."

I blinked.
I looked at the logo, then back at **S**.
Where was this girl, this sand, this beach?!

And then I just burst out laughing:

"It's a guitar, a vinyl record, the guitar strings...
and the word RETRO so nicely framed inside it!
But of course, everyone is free to imagine whatever they
want..."

I'm still smiling as I write this.
And I wonder — what do *you* see in our logo?

ROMANTICS, SLIGHTLY GROWN UP

Here you'll meet the members of the Retro Muse Society — each in their own words. Short autobiographical sketches, little glimpses of lives and passions.

Many of these first appeared on our website (cenaclulretro.org), like love notes to our younger selves. Some have gone on to publish more, pursue new adventures, or accomplish remarkable things, but here they are, still curious, creative, and deeply engaged.

This chapter is a tapestry of voices and experiences, full of references to Romanian poets, musicians, and prestigious awards that have shaped these lives. While some names may be unfamiliar, each one carries a story, a spark, or a rhythm that resonates beyond borders.

Open these pages and meet the voices that make Retro, well... Retro.

Ana Munteanu-Drăghici
Ana Munteanu-Drăghici is a poet and writer from Sighișoara, a soul deeply rooted in Romania's artistic spirit. She is a member of the Writers' League of Romania, president of the *"N.D. Cocea – Anotimpuri"* Literary Circle, and vice-president of the *"Creneluri Sighișorene"* Literary Association. Ana has published two volumes of poetry — *Testamentul Iubirii (The Testament of Love)* and *Nirvana* — works that have

earned her numerous literary awards and a place among Romania's respected voices.

A founding member of the Retro Muse Society, Ana occasionally writes under the pen name *Ana de Sighişoara.* She is a lyrical artist of rare sensitivity and erudition, her gift for recitation often compared to that of Romania's great stage actors. For the members of RETRO, she is a true treasure.

Even when her travels keep her in Romania and far from RETRO gatherings in person, Ana remains deeply connected — her heart, words, and presence always felt, even from afar.

Sonia Maria Anda Cristolţean
Anda's artistic journey began in the 2nd grade, when she first discovered the classical guitar. Before long, she was performing at city events with a group of mandolins and guitars (State Philharmonic, Satu-Mare). Growing up under the spell of *Cenaclul Flacăra*'s music left a deep and lasting mark on her, shaping the way she felt and shared the world. Anda carried her guitar everywhere — and it was that very guitar that led her to meet Ştefan, the man who would become her life partner.

Together, they embarked not only on the adventure of marriage, but on a shared artistic path. As dancers in the ensemble of the Cluj-Napoca School of Popular Arts, they traveled to many cities across Romania and the world, proudly sharing the richness of Romanian tradition and culture at countless festivals and events.

In 1996, they settled in Chicago and for several years led the Miorița dance group at the. Holy Nativity Church, continuing to nurture Romanian cultural life abroad.

In 2016, Anda and Ştefan gave new life to the movement, founding what is now known as *Cenaclul RETRO.* Through this circle, Anda hopes to revive the spirit of *Cenaclul Flacăra* and inspire all those who love beauty — leaving future generations a living fragment of Romanian culture, memory, and song.

The following is **Călin Marincaş**, speaking in his own voice:

Who am I — the one that I am? I was born between the Carpathians, carrying with me a love for song and poetry. My high school and university years were filled with the music of Iris, Compact, Semnal M, Holograf, and the unforgettable performances of Cenaclul Flacăra.

My love for poetry and music springs from the shivers they awaken — deep within me and in the living vibration of the world around me. Through them, I find both roots and flight, silence and voice.

Corina Vlad

Corina is originally from Satu Mare and has always carried within her a love for nature, music, and poetry. She discovered her passion for folk music at Chicago's Old Town School of Folk Music and continued her journey as a member of the *Vox Maris* and *Retro* circles. As she herself says: *"When I'm with Retro, time stands still — these are suspended moments of being."*

When she is not with *Retro,* Corina expresses her calling through the art of therapeutic massage — a way of channeling the energy of positive thought into healing touch. She describes herself as having the soul of a child, delighting in life's smallest wonders, a joy that she often captures in her poetry.

Ligia Ana Grindeanu

Ligia Ana Grindeanu is both a pediatrician and a poet — a heart equally devoted to healing and to words. She is the author of the poetry volume *"Beyond Silence"* (Casa de Editură Mureş, 2003), a collection that reflects her deep inner world.

Ligia has been writing and reciting poetry since childhood and is a member of the *"N.D. Cocea – Anotimpuri"* Literary Circle in her hometown of Sighişoara. Even after moving across the ocean, she continued to nurture her love of Romanian literature, becoming a founding member of the *Dor* literary circle in Iowa City, a member

235

of *Cenaclul Retro* in Chicago, and Director for Poetry and Literary Creation at *Seara Culturală Românească.* She participates actively in and organizes cultural events in Romanian communities and churches.

Her poems have been published in *Cuvântul Liber, Glasul Cetății, Ambasador, Târnava, Vatra Veche, LitArt, Creneluri Sighișorene,* and she is featured in the anthologies *Anotimpuri sub turnul cu ceas, Veșnicia Secundei, Efigii Lirice, Colecția Grai Românesc,* and *Vise Târzii.* She is currently preparing a new poetry volume entitled *"Seasons of Longing."*

Through her presence, Ligia brings a quiet strength and a gentle voice to *Cenaclul RETRO,* reminding everyone that poetry is not only written — it is lived.

Decebal Sorin Griza

Sorin is originally from Reșița, a place surrounded by the mountain trails of Romania — a landscape that shaped his love for music and freedom. He first picked up the guitar in high school, where, like many teenagers of the time, he would sing songs by The Beatles, Phoenix, and *Cenaclul Flacără* in school hallways and on trips with friends.

During his university years, Sorin played in the student rock band *Argus* as well as in the folk music ensemble of the Timișoara Medical School. After moving to the United States, his artistic journey paused for many years — until June 2017, when he joined *Cenaclul RETRO* as a bassist.

Since then, Sorin has been a steady presence, weaving together music, family, career, and dedication to the Romanian community — proving that passion, once awakened, never truly fades.

Ştefan Cristolţean

Ştefan's musical journey began in the 7th grade, when he received an electronic keyboard made in the USSR — his first window into the world of sound. In high school, he picked up the guitar, and during his military service, he found the time to refine his style and deepen his connection to music.

But Ştefan's passions have always gone beyond music. During his university years, he was a folk dancer with *Mărţişorul* in Cluj-Napoca, and after graduation with *Someşul-Napoca* in the same city. With both ensembles, he traveled across Europe and to the United States, proudly showcasing Romanian folklore at international festivals.

In 1996, together with his wife Anda, he settled in Chicago, where for several years they led the Mioriţa dance group at the Holy Nativity, carrying forward the traditions of home.

In 2004, Ştefan stepped briefly into the world of television, playing Richie in the series *"My Life is a Sitcom II."*
In 2010, he founded and directed the children's music group *Cireşarii,* planting seeds of Romanian song in a new generation.

A year later, he launched the musical-literary circle *Vox-Maris,* which later became a Folk-Rock band. Ştefan performed with this band until 2015, and recorded the album *"Travelers Through Dreams."*

In 2016, Ştefan revived the circle under its new name — *Cenaclul RETRO.* Through it, he seeks to rekindle the spirit of *Cenaclul Flacăra* and offer future generations a living legacy of Romanian music, poetry, and culture.

🎵 Cătălin Lari

Cătălin Lari discovered music at the age of six, when he first began studying the accordion in his hometown of Năsăud. At ten, encouraged by his teacher, he left for the Music High School in Cluj-Napoca, where he began violin studies — later discovering the viola, which became his instrument of choice. Even during his student years at the Gheorghe Dima Academy of Music, he was already performing with renowned institutions such as the Dinu Lipatti Philharmonic, the Ștefan Ruha Chamber Orchestra, the Transylvania Philharmonic, and the Black Sea Philharmonic.

In 2003, Cătălin crossed the ocean to continue his musical journey, receiving a scholarship to pursue further studies in the United States. He earned a Master's degree in Music from Pittsburg State University and a Certificate of Music Performance from DePaul University by 2007.

Over the years, he has collaborated with numerous symphonic and chamber ensembles, including the Pittsburg State Symphony, Springfield Symphony Orchestra, Fort Smith Symphony, DePaul Symphony, and Chicago Civic Symphony Orchestra.

In recent years, Cătălin has dedicated himself to teaching violin and viola at various studios and private schools in Chicago — including Ten Happy Little Fingers, which he runs together with his wife, Călina, as well as Music Connection, Music Expressions, and, more recently, Northside Music Academy.

He first met the members of *Cenaclul RETRO* at their performances in 2019, but truly became one of them after the memorable January 2020 show dedicated to Mihai Eminescu. Since then, Cătălin has poured his heart into every project and concert, promoting Romanian artistic creation abroad.

For him, *Cenaclul RETRO* is "a true infusion of Romanian music and poetry, a place where one rediscovers the most beautiful and rare emotions, inspired by the longing for the land of our roots."

ꙮ Constantin Cătălin Nicolae

Constantin Cătălin Nicolae is a professional actor, a graduate of the Faculty of Letters and Arts at "Lucian Blaga" University of Sibiu, where he studied Acting under the guidance of Professor Florin Zamfirescu.

He has performed both in Romania and in the United States, in theatre as well as in film productions. Among his stage and screen credits are:
"Mad Forest" (Raymond Hadges Theatre, Richmond, Virginia),
"Audiția" (National Theatre "Radu Stanca," Sibiu),
"O Scrisoare pierdută" (Sibiu, Romania),
"Yellow Rain" (film, directed by Jose de Avila, Chicago),
"The Muslim Brotherhood" (film, Tower Production, Chicago),
"Brazil's Roswell" (film, Tower Production, Chicago),
and *"My Best Friend"* (film, directed by Cătălin Bugean), which won the award for Best Comedy at the Los Angeles Film Awards (February 2018).

Together with his wife, Laura Șișu, he founded Ro Act Theatre in Chicago — a Romanian theatre company dedicated to staging productions in Romanian for the local community as well as for theatre lovers in general.

Cătălin was among the earliest collaborators of *Cenaclul RETRO*, taking part in the 2017 and 2018 performances, and remains a valued artistic partner of the group.

ꙮ Laura Șișu

Born in Brăila, Laura Șișu is a professional actress, a graduate of the Theatre Acting program at "Lucian Blaga" University of Sibiu, class of Professor George Ivașcu (2004).

Her stage career spans both Romania and the United States, with memorable performances in productions such as:
"Audiția" (directed by George Ivașcu, Sibiu, Romania),
"Iubirile lui Anatol" (directed by Cristian Juncu, Sibiu, Romania),
"Pilafuri și parfum de măgar" (directed by Silviu Purcărete, Sibiu

and St. Petersburg, Russia),
"Gândacii" (directed by Tompa Gabor, Sibiu, Romania),
"Bashavel" (New Castle, England, 2003),
"Seara de ajun în familie" (Chicago, USA),
"Oase pentru Otto" (Ro Act Theatre, Chicago),
"Aici nu se simte" (Ro Act Theatre, Chicago),
and *"Dragoste cu năbădăi"* (after Chekhov's *"The Bear"* and *"The Proposal,"* Ro Act Theatre, Chicago).

Together with her husband, actor Constantin Cătălin Nicolae, Laura is co-founder of Ro Act Theatre in Chicago, a company dedicated to staging Romanian-language productions for the local community and for lovers of theatre and culture everywhere.

Beyond the stage, Laura is also a gifted pop and folk musician — both as a vocalist and guitarist — having graduated from the Hariclea Darclée Arts High School in Brăila, with a specialization in music pedagogy.

A beloved collaborator of *Cenaclul RETRO,* Laura brings the group a unique charm and a signature style all her own. She took part in the 2017 and 2018 performances, adding her voice and presence to the cenaclu's spirit of artistic celebration.

🌙 Alina Celia Cumpan

Alina Celia Cumpan is a poet of exceptional talent — one who, as Nicu Alifantis wrote in the introduction to her poetry volume *"Har risipit,"* "takes refuge in verse at night" and "creates poetry about feelings, thoughts, emotions, and dreams."

In a 2015 interview given at the launch of her book, when asked where she finds her inspiration and talent, she replied with disarming sincerity that "the talent does not come from me — I only write what the angels dictate." Alina attributes her gift for writing and the talent with which she has been blessed to God.

Originally from Caraș-Severin, Alina is a graduate of the Faculty of Political Science in Timișoara, the Romanian Diplomatic Institute in Bucharest, and holds a Master's degree in Public Administration Management.

In addition to *"Har risipit,"* Alina has published two other volumes of poetry: *"Între două lumi și mine"* (2007) and *"Selfie Altruist"* (2017). She is also the president of the Autentic de Limba și Cultură Română Society in Chicago and a proud member of *Cenaclul RETRO.*

Alina's presence at the cenaclu's 2017 and 2018 performances brought a touch of grace and depth, her poetry offering the audience a glimpse into a world where emotion meets divine inspiration.

Marius Stan

Marius Stan describes himself as a writer in love with mathematics — a mind where science and art meet. A graduate of the Faculty of Physics at the University of Bucharest, he went on to earn a Ph.D. in Chemistry from the Romanian Academy. Marius has published eight books, over eighty scientific articles, and has delivered more than 150 presentations at international scientific conferences.

Between 2008 and 2011, he became widely known for his role as Bogdan in the Emmy Award–winning television series *"Breaking Bad."*

In Romanian literature, Marius is the author of the short story collection *"Câteva zile"* (2013) and the poetry volume *"Un foc viu"* (2015), both published by Helis Press — works in which the precision of the scientist meets the sensibility of the poet.

✍ Traian Alex Bălan

Originally from Bucharest, Traian Alex Bălan spent many of his childhood summers in Transylvania — a place that left a lasting mark on his heart. He first discovered the guitar at the age of twelve at the *Mihai Eminescu* Cultural Center in Bucharest and began writing poetry during high school, later taking part in the *Cântarea României* Festival and the Student Creation Festival.

After moving to the United States, Traian took a long pause from artistic pursuits. His return to music and poetry came as a homecoming of the soul — inspired by meeting the members of *Cenaclul RETRO,* where he reconnected with his first loves: the guitar, the word, and the stage.

✍ Monica Topârcean-Blaga

Monica's love for music began in early childhood. At the age of six, she joined the children's choir *"Mlădiţe,"* with whom she made numerous recordings for Radio Romania and Romanian Television — including appearances alongside actor Iurie Darie on the popular children's program *"Matineu Duminical."* With the same group, she performed with Mihai Constantinescu and Zoe Dumitrescu at music festivals throughout Bucharest.

Throughout her school years, Monica sang in local choirs, often performing as a soloist. She later attended the Popular School of Arts in Bucharest, specializing in light music, where she studied under vocal coach Zina Dumitrescu, jazz composer Marius Popp, and composer Alexandru Simu. During this period, she participated in several music festivals across the country — in Bucharest, Botoşani, Galaţi, and Constanţa — and in 1985, she won the Youth Prize at the Bucharest Light Music Festival with Ion Cristinoiu's song *"Oare de ce?"*

During her university years, Monica became the lead vocalist of the artistic ensemble of the Ministry of Internal Affairs in Bucharest, performing at shows organized for the military and in the *Cântarea României* festival series. It was here that she met her future husband, Lucian Blaga — a fellow member of the artistic club — beginning not only a life partnership but also a creative one, as Lucian's compositions inspired Monica to write lyrics for his music.

After graduating in Romania, Monica went on to earn an MBA in England, pursuing a professional career in London and later in Chicago. Though she stepped away from the public stage for many years, she never stopped writing lyrics to Lucian's music.

In 2017, through Lucian, Monica met the members of *Cenaclul RETRO,* whose passion reignited her own and inspired her to sing once again — with the hope of many future collaborations.

Lucian Blaga

Lucian's musical calling was discovered at the age of five, when his aunt — the celebrated singer Mia Braia — overheard him humming a melody and noticed how he stood transfixed by the piano at a family musical soirée. Mia suggested to Lucian's mother that he be tested for musical aptitude at the George Enescu Music High School in Bucharest — a test he passed with flying colors. Thus began his lifelong journey in music.

Lucian went on to study piano at the *George Enescu* Music High School and later at the *Ciprian Porumbescu* Conservatory, where he graduated Magna cum Laude with two master's degrees: one in Music Pedagogy and another in Jazz and Light Music Composition, under the guidance of composer Anton Şuteu.

His love for pop and jazz inspired him to begin composing at the age of fourteen — a passion that reached a peak in 1993 when he won First Prize and the Trophy at the Mamaia Light Music Festival (Creation Section) with the song *"Din tot ce-a fost,"* performed by Luminiţa Anghel. That same year, Lucian participated in Romania's first-ever Eurovision National Selection with the song *"Dintr-un vis,"* performed by Monica Anghel. In 1995, he became a member of the Union of Romanian Composers and Musicologists and again won recognition at the Mamaia Festival, this time with Third Prize for the song *"Cât aş vrea,"* performed by Adrian Daminescu.

In Romania, Lucian also performed as a keyboardist with several rock groups. Between 1989 and 1991, he was a member of Vali Sterian şi Compania de Sunet, recording the album *"Nimic Fără Oameni."* He later performed with the bands Barock and Sens, sharing the stage with legendary Romanian rock groups such as Holograf, Iris, Compact, and Roşu şi Negru. At the same time, he collaborated with well-known singers including Elena Cârstea, Sanda Ladoşi, Adrian Daminescu, Monica Anghel, and Carmen Trandafir.

Together with his wife, lyricist Monica Topârcean-Blaga, Lucian moved to Chicago in 1996, where he earned a Master's degree in Music Theory from Roosevelt University. Despite living in the United States, he continued collaborating with Romanian Television and Radio Romania International, composing songs for Romanian artists and creating jingles for various radio programs.

Today, Lucian continues to compose and to teach piano, music theory, and composition. He is especially joyful to have recently joined *Cenaclul RETRO* — a group that inspires him musically and artistically and with whom he shares a special friendship.

THROUGH THE YEARS...

RETRO Performances – Sharing Harmony with Our Audience

Everything that follows was adapted in December 2022.

An Anniversary Performance - *January 15, 2017*
Organized on the 167th anniversary of Mihai Eminescu's birth

This event marks one of the early milestones in the history of the RETRO Literary and Music Circle — an exceptional performance organized in collaboration with the Eminescu Circle, celebrating the birth of Romania's greatest poet.

Special guests included Nicoleta Roman, Roxana Iacob, and Liviu Roman. The performance was hosted at the Romanian Orthodox Church Holy Nativity, in Chicago,
At that time, the group was still known as Vox Maris, adopting the name RETRO after the following performance in March 2017.

From the Harmony of Spring Chords, *April 1, 2017*
A modest offering to the season of love from the members of Cenaclul RETRO, joined by dear friends and valued collaborators of that time, at the Romanian Heritage Center.

Harmonies with Cenaclul Retro - *June 4, 2017*

Voice of Ligia

Our story continued on June 4, 2017, with the "Harmonies" show, hosted by St. Mary's Romanian Orthodox Church in Chicago, through the generosity of Father George Ursache and Presbytera Ramona Ursache.
The guitar chords of Laura Șișu, Traian Bălan, Corina Vlad, Ștefan Cristolțean, and Sorin Griza delighted the audience. Alina Celia Cumpan, Marius Stan, and Ligia Ana Grindeanu shared the emotion of their own poetic creations, while Anda Cristolțean, Cătălin Nicolae, and Călin Mărincaș recited selections from the classics.

Writer and journalist Ion Berghia reminded us that "our language is a treasure" and that "poetry is the good sister of music."
The show was presented by Ligia Ana Grindeanu and Anda Cristolțean, with a colorful visual palette offered by Oana Moise.

We were blessed with a warm and receptive audience who applauded wholeheartedly and sang along with us to beloved songs about love, youth, hope, nature, and longing for home.
We were honored to have with us the Consul General of Romania in Chicago, Mr. Tiberiu Trifan, and Mrs. Consul Mihaela Deaconu. We thank them for their presence and for their encouragement to continue this spiritual initiative within the Romanian community.

Euro-Balkan Folk Festival - *September 16, 2017*

On the evening of Saturday, September 16, 2017, the musical group of Cenaclul RETRO performed a memorable recital alongside renowned performers and ensembles from across America, representing the diverse nationalities of the Euro-Balkan region, on the stage of the Chicago Euro-Balkan Folk Festival.

Laura, Corina, Lucian, Ştefan, Traian, and Sorin performed beloved Romanian folk-rock songs as well as their own original compositions, to the delight of a public eager for tradition and beauty.

Autumn Harmonies - *November 4, 2017*

The evening was dedicated to poetry, music, and the colors of autumn.
The program was inspired by Nichita Stănescu's *Emoţie de toamnă* (*Autumn Emotion*):

Autumn has come, cover my heart with something,
with the shadow of a tree, or better yet, with your shadow.

I fear that I might not see you again, at times,
that sharp wings will grow on me up to the clouds,
that you will hide within a stranger's eye,
and it will close with a wormwood leaf.

And then I will draw near to stones and be silent,
take words and drown them in the sea.
I whistle to the moon to rise and turn it
into a great love.

This evening of autumn reflection blended poetry and song, creating a space where the spirit of Nichita's verse met the warmth of RETRO's music.

Open the Door, Christian - *December 16, 2017*

Voice of Sorin

We extend our heartfelt thanks to our dear audience for the overwhelming presence with which they honored us, and for the warmth of spirit that embraced us throughout this unforgettable evening — one filled with deep emotions, impossible to put into words, where our souls seemed to merge and rise in tears of exaltation.

We humbly apologize to those who were unable to join us because the venue quickly became too small to accommodate everyone and they had to turn back. We promise to reward them tenfold at our future events, with the highest-quality Romanian music and poetry.

In Love with Spring, - *April 15, 2018*

Voice of Olezia

Congratulations, Cenaclul RETRO!
You warmed our souls with your songs, poems, satires, and with the atmosphere you created — full of love and warmth as we awaited the spring!

The love within your hearts moved us so deeply tonight. From your souls to ours — thank you!
Yes, truly, longing for spring…
Thank you all for this delight!

Thank you, Anda, the coordinator of souls, radiant in the red of love — a true doll, even if you call yourself wooden!
Thank you, Marius, spring's eternal lover — may we raise a glass of red wine thinking of home… longing for home.
Thank you, Ligia, so delicate and expressive, awaiting those *"blades of grass smelling of home."*

Thank you, Cătălin, who made us laugh until our faces ached —
what a delight to listen to you!
Thank you, Sorin — warm and modest, "God's bread," as they say
in Transylvania — dressed in the most Romanian way, in a
traditional *ie*, and singing with a pure, heartfelt voice.
Thank you, Corina — another champion of love, dressed in red!
Thank you, Ștefan, with your striking red guitar, who truly
brought us back to the retro style!
Thank you, Traian — a strong, clear voice, reminiscent of Baniciu.
Thank you, Lucian — quietly yet masterfully conducting the
whole musical flow.
Thank you, Laura — a strong, clear voice, forever in love with love
itself.
Thank you, Călin, always the soul of optimism.
Thank you, Monica — a natural, warm voice, perfect for the most
challenging songs.

Each of you was extraordinary! True-hearted Romanians!
And we thank you, from the bottom of our hearts — myself and
everyone present.
The show was a success — you brought the audience to their feet!

Cenaclul Retro Responds

We, in turn, thank Olezia for sharing these beautiful thoughts
and impressions.
We promise to continue to rise to the same high standards, for the
audience that loves us — and whom we love just as much.
We cannot exist without you.

In love with spring, we asked winter to delay the chill of her
innocent snowflakes. She graciously left her coats at the door,
eager to float on the wings of music and poetry in a magical,
fairytale-like evening.

It was a fiery night, one that will remain forever in our book of
memories.
The joy and emotion we felt are difficult to put into words,

watching how the audience blossomed with every song, every verse, and rediscovered themselves in the love story we had prepared for them.

You are an *extraordinary* audience, one that loves the infinite — together with Cenaclul RETRO.

We thank our sponsors and friends who supported us in every way and contributed to the success of this event:

- Our gracious host, Cerasela Stan (Stan Mansion)
- Sophicle
- American Family Insurance (Adriana Deaconu)
- Diversital (Mariana Torz)
- Design Granite and Marble (Cătălin Nicolae)
- Ro Act Theatre
- Romanian American Network & Tribuna US (Steven Bonica)
- The ART of a Smile Dental Studio (Dr. Diana Răcean)
- Sound system: Cătălin Nicolae & Valer Pîrvu
- Photography: Florin Romoșan
- Video recording: Iulian Grindeanu & Radu Răcean

Thank you all — and don't forget, our story continues...
Follow us here, and on Facebook at **Cenaclul RETRO.** 🖋

Autumn Story - *October 20, 2018*

Dear friends,

Autumn has come again...
We invite you to join us for a story inspired by the nostalgic
memories of our childhood and teenage autumns, as well as by
the beautiful autumns of these lands — so very much like the
ones back home.

We are waiting for you with open hearts!

A Christmas Evening - *December 16, 2018*

Dear friends,

Cenaclul RETRO warmly invites you to *"A Christmas Evening"* — with you and for you!

Let us sing carols together under the fir branches, remembering Romanian traditions and the heartfelt warmth that wrapped the winter holidays back home.

Everyone is welcome — and the little ones will receive a special keepsake, lovingly prepared by Santa Claus himself.

Talent Show - *April 13, 2019*

Dear friends,

While waiting for spring to fully bloom, we invite you to spend a cultural evening together in a warm, family-like atmosphere at the Romanian Heritage Center library.

Everyone is welcome — children, teens, and adults alike — to share an artistic moment according to your own inclination, passion, and talent.

This is not a competition — there will be no jury and no critiques, only appreciation. So, leave behind any shyness or stage fright and come enjoy an evening where performers and audience become one.

Those who wish to take part in the program are kindly asked to send us your chosen acts via Cenaclul Retro's Facebook Messenger, including the title, duration, and whether you will need a backing track or instruments for musical performances.

Admission is free. A light snack and a donation toward room rental are welcome.

We thank all participants and supporters for their wonderful performances and generosity during this Talent Show evening. The petals of hope came to life through the dedication of our young talents.

Bravo to Dănel Haidău, Rebecca Răcean, Lucas and Johnny Raicu, Robert and Lucas Ciocan!!!
Bravo to Cristina Haidău, Daniela Raicu, Carmen Alina Ciocan, Georgeta Hațegan Pupek, Diana Răcean, Dana Ghiurcuța, Nicolae Bogdan Groza, Irina Don, Adrian Donisa, Anda & Ștefan, Sorin Griza, Carmen Griza, Lucian Blaga, Monica Blaga, Traian-Alex Bălan, Corina Vlad, Călin Mărincaș, and Radu Russell Răcean!

On Love's Staff - *May 18, 2019*

Dear friends,

Cenaclul RETRO invites you to an evening of music and poetry, right in the heart of spring — "On Love's Staff."
As always, we will sing and share stories together, in a romantic evening filled with smiles and surprises.

Encore Performance in Iowa

On Love's Staff – Iowa Tour, Cedar Rapids - *August 25, 2019*

"Carry love across the ocean." – *Ligia Grindeanu*

As always, we listened — and we carried love across the Mississippi.
We built bridges, forged friendships, and met wonderful people with beautiful, big hearts, full of longing for Romanian music and poetry.
Thank you for existing and for being part of the RETRO story.

We are deeply grateful to the cultural organization in Iowa for the warmth and enthusiasm with which they welcomed and supported our performance of **"On Love's Staff"** in Cedar Rapids, Iowa.
We were overjoyed to be with you here, in the heart of the continent — far from home, yet so close to what "home" truly means for all of us.

Together, we transcend the ephemeral through the eternity of soulful values!

Shades and Tones - *October 2019*

Voice of Olezia

An unforgettable October evening!
With rain!
Yes! It rained tonight!
It rained applause! It rained autumn emotions!
It rained smiles, and it rained sighs—laughter mixed with tears of longing and pain.

Yes! This bundle of souls in love with beauty — the Retro Muse Society — once again lifted us to our feet and moved us to tears!

Thank you, Retro, for this wonderful evening!
Thank you for reminding us where we came from — we, the wandering sons and daughters!
Thank you for singing to us our history and traditions!
We will never forget that we are Romanians! And through you, our hearts will always remain tied to the soil of our homeland.
Yes, we are proud to be Romanians!

And the guitars played! And the voices chirped!
And smiles bloomed, and tears fell, and emotions — autumnal, patriotic — swept through us.
And then... the applause!
In an autumn symphony of love.

Who doesn't love love?
Yes! Yes! Yes! That shiver that rushes through you, from head to toe...
Yes! Retro Muse Society! Thank you!
Everything you do is a pure, selfless gift, full of love and beauty.
Thank you!

Autumn has come! And we want more autumn nights like this one!
We need Romanian song!

Bravo, Retro!

With gratitude,
Anda & Ştefan, Ligia & Iulian, Corina, Radu, Traian, Sorin, Marius Călin

And thank you, Roxana — what an incredible voice!

Thank You, Lord, for everything — and for this night!

Late at night, over a cup of wine, we are reborn,
Honoring
The Living
Romanian
Spirit
Wherever we are...

"How could you go, how could you forget
The rain that kissed the mountain crest,
Autumn setting in the vine,
The woven threads on blouses fine." — Ligia Grindeanu

Carolers with Dreams - *December 21, 2019*

A Retro Holiday Wish – excerpt
Carolers with dreams,
Knocking on your window bright,
Come sing with us,
It's storytime tonight!

Breathe in words of love and cheer,
Of hope and joy that draw us near,
Then raise your voices, loud and clear —
These are the songs that keep us here.

When a carol taps your pane
On this magic Christmas Eve,
Step softly through the years gone by —
Dreaming carolers, we still believe.

With all our hearts, we thank you for sharing your words and
feelings with us.
Here's our gift back to you — a musical hug for everyone whose
heart beats in time with Retro:

Thank you for sparking our inspiration.
With you beside us, we find our strength
And keep the music going.

Retro wishes you a Merry Christmas!
May your hearts be warm, your dreams come true,
May love and light find their way to you —
And may your days be filled with all that's beautiful!"*

✦ **Happy New Year 2020!** ✦

They Had to Have a Name - *January 19, 2020*

Tonight...
Eminescu
with the Retro Muse Society.

Once again...
we leave fulfilled, joyful, and proud to be born Romanians!

You are wonderful, Retro Muse Society!
— *Olezia*

A Park Story with the Retro Muse Society – *October 3, 2020*

Our First Postponed Show

Out of an abundance of caution regarding the epidemic and following the rules set by the Park District, we must postpone our autumn concert to a future date — which we will announce as soon as possible.

Thank you for your understanding, and we wish you a beautiful autumn filled with music and poetry in your hearts.

We can't wait to gather again and sing with you under the open sky! 🌿 🎵

🖼 The Enchanted Grove – Private Event - *July 2021*
A magical summer gathering, filled with music, laughter, and friendship.

DUMBRAVA MINUNATĂ
Ana Munteanu Drăghici
with **Cenaclul Retro &
Ligia Grindeanu**
Chicago, Illinois

SIGNED BOOKS 'IN DUMBRAVA MINUNATĂ'
Thank you for the hospitality,
wonderful people, and the
beautiful grove in the Chicago area!
The arts joined hands under the
arched vaults under the proud sky
of the trees.
A lovely Sunday, the 17th!

The beautiful Sunday of July 17th, 2021, became a Sunday for the soul. It joined with the concert of the birds in the grove, with the literary and musical program. Torches were lit, guarding the music of the soul, of song, of poetry, and of the muses. The audience breathed together with the orchestra, the soloists, the reciters, and the creators.

The verse *"I am alone, far away"* — sung with grace — melted into a gift of friendship, as if to confirm that:
"Distances grow near, when thoughts call them closer."

And the thoughts and feelings expressed in the poems we recited brought forth the revelation of closeness — in space and in spirit.

There is a continent of the soul, unique to the Romanian heart, that no ocean can divide. And so, those chosen souls stepped toward us, became close to us, seeking to know our poetic horizon. Generations, open and receptive, to the depths of the soul gifted through verse!

Voice of Ana Munteanu Drăghici

Calina Lari
1d · 🌐

Cenaclul Retro **is back! We had such a great time Saturday night attending their concert!**

> We sang with them,
> (all people at our table
> sang their hearts out -
> sorry Retro for
> harmonizing with you),
> clapped with them, tapped
> our feet with the rhythm,
> and enjoyed beautiful
> Romanian songs and poems!

🌿 **In the Enchanted Grove, Iowa Tour** - *August 1, 2021*

The Enchanted Grove: Summer Ballads, Poetry & Music with the Retro Muse Society

We invite you to our magical gathering: *The Enchanted Grove*, a charming afternoon of music and poetry with the Retro Muse Society from Chicago.

This special event is organized together with *Cenaclul Dor* and the *Romanian Cultural Organization of Iowa City.*

✨ **Featured Book Releases:**
📖 *Seasons of Longing* – by Ligia Ana Grindeanu, Ardealul Publishing, 2020
📖 *The Heavenly Garden* – by Ana Munteanu Drăghici, Vatra Veche Publishing, 2020

📍 **Location:** Downtown Public Library – Whipple Auditorium
450 5th Ave SE, Cedar Rapids, IA 52401

Bring your family, your friends, and your good summer vibes — we'll be waiting for you in *The Enchanted Grove!* 🌳 🎶

Together Again with the Retro Muse Society! – *September 25, 2021*

Join us for an **open-air celebration of music and poetry** under the big blue sky!
📍 **Where:** Performance Pavilion, Heritage Park
201 Community Blvd, Wheeling, IL 60090

👜 **Bring:** your brightest smile, a cozy blanket or a folding chair, and maybe a snack to share.

Let's fill the park with songs, laughter, and friendship — the perfect way to feed our souls and celebrate the beauty of nature together.

🎶 **Let's make the park sing!**
🎤 **Admission:** Free – everyone's invited!

Poets Chatting with Their Beloved Muses – *May 7, 2022*

"After so much cold and fog,
The sun appears again..."

Dear friends,
Cenaclul Retro invites you to share **"Tea with the Muses."**
Let's greet spring together with music and poetry under the
warm roof of Holy Nativity Church in Chicago.

A Second Pause, Before the Song

Dear friends,
We're sorry to say that our May 7, 2022 gathering must wait —
but only for a while.

The muses are restless,
whispering verses and humming refrains,
and we promise they will join us soon.

A new date will be announced shortly.
Until then, keep your hearts tuned —
the next meeting will be all the sweeter!

Ligia

Ode to the Violin

In the silence of words
The violin is heard,
A bow across time,
The concert is postponel
For another season,
You and I only in thought
It was not easy, and yet ve chose
To make of hope

The final word,
In the chord of love
The guitar still plays
You have received theinvitations
Written by hand
With blue ink
Dipped in destiny

Ligia Ana Grindeanu
Chicago, October 11, 2020 9:00 PM

Ligia

History repeats itself.
I vote for the violin,
the guitar and poetry
— in one word, Retro   9:04 PM

Catalin Lari:
"To heck with history, I'd rather have another event in Iowa!"

Ligia:
"I think it's better postponed. The intention is to come back another day."

Catalin Lari:
"I think so too, but I still haven't come to terms with the idea…"

Poets Chatting with Their Beloved Muses – *July 23, 2022*

Moment – *"See how many people we made happy?" I can almost hear Ştefan say.*
What a dreamy evening... with music, poetry, dear friends, and poets chatting with their beloved muses...
We were delighted to see many of the cenacle's collaborators in the audience, as well as a few members of the Vox Maris band. Adi even helped us with the sound setup...

Since this seems to be the last performance from these five years that appears in this book, I'll share a little more with you...
We invite you to chat with the beloved muses...

✦ *Poets Chatting with Their Beloved Muses*
Show – July 23, 2022

Cenaclul Retro: *The Bard from Mircești*

Ștefan: Welcome to a gathering with poets, musicians, and beloved muses alongside Cenaclul RETRO. We are happy to be here with you — far from home, but close to everything that "home" means to all of us.

Cătălin: *Violin Solo –* **Ballad** (Ciprian Porumbescu)
Ligia: *At the Chat Table* (excerpt) – Ligia Ana Grindeanu

Anda: The title of this show is inspired by Ligia's verses, which you've just heard, from her book *Seasons of Longing*, published in 2020 by Ardealul Publishing House. We invite you to meet the beloved muses – a heartfelt gift of music and poetry for those here with us and for all who have supported us through the years. Welcome to our show. We hope you enjoy Romanian music and poetry.

Radu: *And If –* Mihai Eminescu
Călin: *Allow Me to Tell You –* Matei Vișniec
Ștefan: *Romanian Pastel –* Gheorghe Zamfir
Corina: *Two Hands –* Bosquito
(invitation to dance)

Anda: Thank you to the dancers — you are wonderful! Don't leave just yet, keep dancing — next up: *Love at First Sight.*

Sorin: *Love at First Sight –* Ilie Micolov
(invitation to dance, Radu leads – boys/girls dialogue voices)

Anda: Next, we have a song performed for the first time, sung by Corina, with lyrics from her debut volume *Living in Bright Flames.*

Corina: *I Will Love You –* Corina Vlad
Radu: *Ode in Ancient Meter –* Mihai Eminescu (violin background)

Ligia/Sorin: *At the Chat Table* – Ligia Grindeanu & Sorin Griza
Ștefan: *Tell Me Who You Are* – Semnal M
Anda: *Marriage Proposal* – Nicu Stancu
Sorin: *Live the Moment* – Sorin Griza

Ligia: About *Live the Moment* – music & lyrics by Sorin Griza
Ligia: *My Story with Blue Eyes* – Ana Munteanu Drăghici
(violin background: Cătălin)

Radu: Yes, girls' eyes have always inspired artists. I wonder whose eyes inspired Ștefan?

Ștefan: introduces the next song and presents the official video, projected on screen.

Ștefan: *Your Brown Eyes* – Ștefan Cristolțean
Anda: *The Commandment or the Sin* – Parody
Anda & Ștefan: *The Commandment* – Licuța Pântia / Anda & Ștefan
Ligia: About *The Moment* – music & lyrics by Corina Vlad
Corina: *The Moment* – Corina Vlad
Călin: *When You Need Love* – Mircea Cărtărescu
Corina: *Chasing the Wind*
Sorin: *The Coming Rain* – Pasărea Colibri

Anda: Sponsor Presentation
Ligia: *Treasure Chest of Memories / The Heart of Cenaclul Retro*

Break: 15 minutes – video clips by technical team

Instrumental + Presentation of Cenaclul Retro

Ligia: Quote – "Romanians are born poets." The members of Cenaclul Retro have prepared this show…

Anda: begins the introductions, Ligia continues
Anda: Cenaclul Retro celebrates five years of harmony this year…

273

We will soon prepare an anniversary show, but until then, sing with us — *Ah, what times those were...*

Sorin: *About the Horse* – humorous moment (may include audience interaction)

Ligia: We invite you into *The Enchanted Glade*, a song from our student years, adapted and kept alive by Anda and Ștefan, and gifted to you today.

Anda: *The Enchanted Glade*

Ștefan: Another story-song I composed at the beginning of our journey in America... actually, the song is called *You're All I Have,* but it became *There's Nothing in My Fridge.* Let's sing it together!

Ștefan: *There's Nothing in My Fridge* – Ștefan Cristolțean

All: *Mocirița*
Ligia: *Only Thoughts* – Ligia Ana Grindeanu
Ștefan: *Charlie Chaplin*
Radu: *Thoughts*

Ștefan: Hoping that this show has made you feel at home, I invite you to join me for *On My Street,* a song I composed on foreign streets, but with my heart and mind back on the street of my childhood in Cluj. Let's sing it together.

Ștefan: *On My Street*

Anda: Thank you for joining us on Retro Street tonight. We close with the hope that we will meet again soon. Thank you to the Holy Nativity Church y for hosting us. The church brings people closer. As you know, all funds from tonight's ticket sales are donated to the Church of the Nativity. Thank you for coming... and staying.

Ligia: Only together with you can we move forward. The heart of Cenaclul Retro beats for all of us. We invite you to write in the

Guestbook, called *The Treasure Chest of Memories.* We look forward to seeing you at our future shows — we are planning an anniversary performance this fall. Details to follow. Stay with us for a final story...

Encore: *Andrii Popa*

Program written by Ligia & Anda, adapted for this book.

PRESENTATION: July 23, 2022
• The sweet voice of the violin carries us on wings of longing... **Cătălin Lari**
• A young brother who believes in justice... **Sorin Griza**
• The living fire of the moment, the Forest Girl... **Corina Vlad**
• A dreamy princess from the Medieval Fortress of Sighişoara, the heart and poetic soul of the cenaclu... **Ligia Grindeanu**
• Ana of Sighişoara, the Lady of Poetry, is with us in spirit... **Ana Munteanu Drăghici**
• Lost in the American whirlwind, but found again in Retro... **Radu Răcean**
• Beautiful ladies, he invites you to dance on the wings of poetry... **Călin Mărincaş**
• From behind the camera, right into the spotlight... **Iulian Grindeanu**
• Everything turns into a story through colors and shades with... **Anda Cristolţean**
• Eternally in love with brown eyes, the Leader of Cenaclul Retro... **Ştefan Cristolţean**

We also thank those involved in organizing:
Steliana Mărincaş, Carmen Griza, Sergiu Vlad, Alexandru Grindeanu, Paul Cristolţean, Rebecca Răcean, Adrian Nechiti.

We carry in our hearts every moment spent with you at Taifas, together with the beloved muses 📖

The members of Cenaclul Retro prepared this performance with much dedication, respect, and admiration for the Romanian verses—written, spoken, and sung.

 is with **Cenaclul Retro** and **8 others.**
1h · 🌐

Thank you, Thank you, Thank you, Cenaclul Retro!
It was a wonderful evening!
A beautiful show, from your hearts to ours!
Music and poetry and dance and humor... at Taifas with us, the audience!
Thank you, Cenaclul Retro!

 Olezia Comsulea is with **Cenaclul Retro** and **8 others.**   •••
1h · 👥

⭐Thank you, because once again we went home more fulfilled, more relaxed, with smiles on our faces, with souls filled with peace and beauty, proud to be Romanians!
🔴Brown eyes and blue eyes, in love at first sight with you, Cenaclul Retro, we savored such wonderful moments on your stage!
🙌Thank you, Cenaclul Retro!

Anakin

Good Morning, Rebels,
We had a full evening;
in fact, the whole week
was full of rehearsals,
emotions and much hard
work from everyone.
Great progress was evident
compared to the fall
performance.

Have a beautiful Sunday.
Be Blessed!

I am sending a few photos
with the impressions
written in the memory

✦ What began as a night of poetry and music turned into a shared confession of feelings, a dialogue between verses, smiles, and reflections. Here is how that evening unfolded...

Ligia

It was truly beautiful at the poets' table,
sharing the stage with musicians.
Only those who know
can feel a tear when it's time to cry,
and only those who truly know
can smile when it's time to smile.

Corina

It was an evening that recharged my batteries,
worn down by the daily rush.
The Cenaclu means recited and sung verses,
an amalgam of emotions,
sometimes joyful, sometimes sad.

🟦 Corina
We would not value the sunrise
if we didn't know the sunset,
just as daytime is the smile of the night.
I am grateful for Retro moments,
as part of this gift called LIFE.
I will always love you all! 🧡

Ligia
It's good to let ourselves
feel joy and embrace
authentic emotions.
That's the kind of joy
we find in the Retro Circle
11:42

Sonia
Congratulations to
the poets, the
musicians, and the
muses — and above all,
to the lovers.
You were magnificent.
"We'll love you, Retro
Muse Society,
In every season,
We'll love you always
❤️
—as Corina's poetic
confession says.   4:02 PM

Monica
Dear Anda, congratul-
ations once again on
the wonderful perfor-
mance last night!
It truly filled our hearts.
As I told you before —
you are a natural,
a born artist who lights
up every stage. ✨

St. Andrew Church

Congratulations and gratitude to all for
this noble work of keeping a wonderful
Romanian tradition alive and known!
May our Lord Jesus Christ give you
strength and protect you.

■ Vio
It was superb! Extraordinary!
What a joy to have you among us!

■ Anda & Ştefan
The pleasure is ours, Vio.
Only together can we continue our mission.

■ Vio
It truly was superb.
I am so happy — and I can hardly wait
until we meet again,
to rejoice in another fabulous performance!
Thanks to everyone for the passion you poured into it.
You are true professionals — congratulations!

*Could this be the last performance before the appearance of this
book? I have just learned that we were invited to give a show near
Kenosha, Wisconsin, this coming September... A picnic on the farm...*

*And so, our story goes on...
With a touch of organization — and so much more enthusiasm.*

■ Anakin
My dears, I've just sent you an email with the list so far.
Add to it, and tomorrow we'll decide how and what. 😘

279

🟦 Corina
Thank you, Ștefan.
Thought to thought, with joy.
I was just about to write during my break...
While working, I closed my eyes and smiled.
Why?
Because I was in an explosion of existential joy,
and I thought of you! and I couldn't let it pass
without sharing it. 🔥

A Day in the Country, Farm Picnic - *September 4, 2022*

We invite you to join us for a picnic hosted by the Romanian
community in Kenosha, WI — outdoors in the fresh grass, in a
rustic setting, accompanied by guitar chords.

📅 **Sunday, September 4, 2022**
🕐 **12 PM – 6 PM**

For details and registration, please send us a message or email us
at cenaclulretro@gmail.com.

Rustle of Carols with the Scent of Baked Apples
December 10, 2022

@ ROCO Chicago, 5406 N Kedzie Ave, Chicago, IL 60625,
United States

Admission to the show is free. Seating is limited, so please RSVP
at https://www.rocochicago.org/retro_dec22

Free parking is available during the event – details at
https://www.rocochicago.org/parking

Perhaps this is the last show captured in these pages... or maybe
just the last one *so far.* Our story certainly doesn't end here — it
continues, more harmonious and more beautiful than ever.

This event was special because of the people who shared it with
us. So many members of our community — talented, generous,
and full of love for the art of words and music — brought their
gifts to the stage. Their presence and participation gave the
evening something truly unique.

The stage was open to everyone, and the spontaneous moments
from the audience brought laughter, color, and joy to the entire

hall. And the children — oh, the children! They were unforgettable, their innocence and energy filling the room with light. This night reminded us why we gather, why we sing, why we share stories. It reminded us that Retro Muse Society is not just about music or poetry — it's about building memories together.

Song for the Audience
We thank you tonight, and we sing with joy,
This song we composed, just for you — oh, what a joy!
You listen with love, you brighten our way,
Through you we relive those moments of longing that make us sway.

Chorus:
Retro wishes you a Merry Christmas,
Warm hearts and all your dreams fulfilled,
Endless love and shining thoughts to guide you,
May your days be bright and beautiful!

Through every verse, with you we're reborn,
You are wonderful, you keep our spirits warm.
We thank you so much, for the light you bring,
With you by our side, we'll always find strength to sing.

Casian
Today at 8:47 AM

I followed the society's page.
It was fabulous.
I am proud and happy to
know you are the promoters
of this artistic and cultural
act.
I appreciate you as much as
I love you.
I miss you very much and I
am extremely eager to see
you again.
I hug you with longing.

PUBLICATIONS

Here follow a few publications that honored us with heartfelt words and thoughts.
They are shortened here for space reasons, but we warmly invite you to visit the Cenaclul Retro page at www.cenaclulretro.org to read the full articles.

📰 Publication: *Creneluri Sighişorene / Cultural Journal*, Romania
📅 July – December, 2013

The following piece turns its gaze toward Ştefan's life and poetry, tracing the lyrical threads that run through his creative journey and illuminate the sensibility of his voice.

Editor ASOCIAŢIA LITERARĂ „CRENELURI SIGHIŞORENE"
Redactor-şef Gabriella Costescu • ISSN 2343 – 7693•Nr. 3 (iulie –decembrie) 2013

Welcome to the World of Poetry, Ştefan!

The art of words shares the same dreamlike realm as the art of sound, and Ştefan Cristolţean masterfully embraces both. In his poem, metaphorically titled *"The Kneeling Mountain"*, passion runs through every line, carrying a powerful patriotic message. The personification of the mountain brings dynamism to the poet's lyrical voice, inviting readers to become its "fortress" and awakening a deep sense of national consciousness.

In *"The Punctuation Marks"*, one can appreciate, even from a didactic perspective, the subtlety and social awareness embedded in the verses. Cristolțean, a poet and a parent, crafts lines that resonate with both personal insight and societal reflection. Similarly, in *"Among the Stars"*, he explores themes of departure and longing. Concrete and abstract imagery intertwine seamlessly, as in the line: *"On the ridge of the air I set out without thought"*, and the striking metaphor: *"I crossed three shades of wind"*, which captures the richness of the emotional experience.

The poems convey the yearning of the one who, in the end, recognizes that:
"There is light here too, / and the place from which I left / looks like a firefly."
This is the light of distant places that nonetheless remains close to the heart. Cristolțean's inspiration even extends into Shakespeare's language, demonstrating not only his adaptation to life in America but also a spiritual connection to universal literary tradition.

His poetry embodies a sacred devotion to beauty, truth, and faith. Composed in a classical style, with rhythm and rhyme that lend musicality, these poems are inherently singable. Many have been given voice through Cristolțean's own musical compositions and refined performances. While his art is not confined by traditional methods, it achieves profound emotional impact through simplicity and sincerity.

Rooted in the Transylvanian spirit, the poems carry the depth of Ardelean sobriety and the nostalgic romanticism of a sensitive creator. Through them, readers find reflections of themselves, and performances of music and poetry bring the verses to life for wider audiences.

It is particularly commendable that Ştefan Cristolţean's work has been published in *"Creneluri sighişorene"*, preserving his voice on the literary and cultural landscape of our Transylvanian town.

Ana Munteanu Drăghici

Confessions

The cheerful echoes of the first group of archaeologists on the hill with the tunnel still resonate through the cultural and medieval heart of Europe. Sighişoara does not forget, and it knows how to honor the bold—those who bring ever more relics into the light. The town sends forth its cultural envoys in search of all who have contributed to or uncovered a chapter of its history. During her travels to distant lands, Mrs. Ana Munteanu-Drăghici met, by no mere chance, the one who, with a scythe in hand, had cleared a patch of rough July grass that would become an archaeological site for years to come.

That scythe wielder was me, Ştefan Cristolţean, a student at the Technical University of Cluj-Napoca at the time. Even now, as I write these lines, I feel the weight of that scythe. The whistle of the blade through the grass still rings in my ears, mingled with the laughter of friends—some ironic, some envious, others astonished. I felt like Ion from *"The Curse of the Land"*, stubborn yet vibrantly alive. My hands, weary from the day's excavations, would revive each evening by the campfire, dancing across the chords of a twelve-string guitar. My childhood friend Casian would join in, and together, our music became a ritual, connecting us to the spirits of our ancestors.

Though my professional path led me into the scientific world, I fully embraced the cultural sphere as well. I graduated from the Technical University of Cluj in 1993 and earned a Master's degree from the International Technical University in Brussels. Born and raised in Cluj-Napoca, the letter "U" carries for me far more meaning than a mere symbol of the alphabet. During my student years, I danced in the "Mărțișorul" ensemble, later performing with "Someșul-Napoca." My mother taught me piano and violin during middle school, and though I was no virtuoso, my father rejoiced every time I played. I took up the guitar in my final years of high school and during military service. It is the instrument that has brought me countless joys and even won the heart of my wife, Anda. Today, we live in Chicago and have three children.

The fusion of music and dance opened unexpected doors: it helped me secure an audition for a role in a TV series aired on ABC Family in 2004. Poetry has floated among my musical notes ever since I picked up the guitar, waiting patiently for a messenger of words to release its full expression. At the first *"Vox Maris"* literary circle (Chicago, May 2011), the intertwining of music and poetry became a powerful catalyst, allowing my imagination to flow freely. There, I met Sighișoara's cultural envoys, Ana Munteanu Drăghici and her daughter, Ligia Ana Grindeanu, messengers of the art of words.

That gathering was transformative. Alongside my friend Dan Păduraru, with whom I had been performing for over a year, we met two more cultural envoys, Adrian Nechiti and Dan Rizo. For the first time, we played together as if we had been performing for a lifetime. From that experience, the four of us founded the Romanian folk-rock band in the diaspora, *"Vox Maris Band."* Later, two more members, Dan and Marcel, joined, and we enjoyed unforgettable performances across Chicago, Portland, and Houston.

My family holds a sacred place in my heart. I strive to teach my children—Andrei, Paul, and Sonia—to embrace life's joys: music, sports, and knowledge. My wife, Anda, continues to inspire and support me in my passions. I remain a devoted supporter of Cluj University and play football and hockey weekly.

Ștefan Cristolțean, Summer 2013

Note: *The excerpts are presented **in their original Romanian**, preserving the rhythm, tone, and authenticity of the publications in which they first appeared.*

Muntele îngenuncheat

Plângea un munte-ngenuncheat,
De umbra vorbelor grele,
Că noi românii l-am trădat,
Pentru o pungă de lovele.
El ne-a ales pe-acest pământ,
Să-i fim poporul lui cel sfânt,
Şi-n vremuri grele ne-a păzit,
În codrii lui ca-ntr-o cetate,
Să nu pierim din lumea asta
C-ar fi o mare nedreptate.
Nu ne-a cerut nimic în schimb,
Şi ne-a dat tot ce a putut,
Semeț în orice anotimp,
Ne-a fost străjer de la-nceput.
Şi dintre noi au luptat mulți,
Să-l țină falnic printre munți,
Deci trebuie înconjurat,
Şi toti să-i fim cetatea lui,
Căci Dumnezeu ni l-a creat
Să nu îl vindem nimănui.

Chicago 17.09.2013

Între astre

Din adâncul luminii am plecat ademenit de-ntuneric,
M-au atras licăriri din tabloul feeric,
De la-nceput am ştiut că-i departe,
Dar nu m-am descurajat,
Nu ştiam ce e zi, ce-i noapte.

Pe coama de văzduh am pornit fără gând,
Şi-am străbătut trei nuanțe de vânt,
Nu sunt culori din vreun spectru anume,
Şi nici nu sunt note muzicale aş spune,
Erau parca idei şuierind.
Nu!
Poate că totuşi mă grăbesc,
Când explic ceva neconcludent, Şi parcă
nici nu am fost prea atent.

Acum simt că ma apropii de destinație

Şi chiar dacă nu mai vreau să fac nici o
comparație
E lumina şi aici,
Iar locul de unde am plecat,
Arată ca un licurici.

Chicago 23. 08. 2013

Semnele de punctuație

Nişte semne de punctuație,
Pline de inspirație,
Au plecat într-o călătorie.
Erau ca pe o câmpie,
Plina de umbre întortocheate,
Pe alocuri îngrămădite, dar bine aşezate
Care uneori se repetau,
Şi din când în când, brusc se terminau.

Aşa că toate au ales,
Să dea un înțeles,
Scorniturilor întunecate,
Dar e grea viața în două dimensiuni,
Să n-ai cum să sari să vezi ce şi cum,
Să aşezi şi să grupezi,
Înşiruiri de forme fără rost,
Şi să dai până la urmă un sens,
Sau o idee cu folos.

Deci în lumea furnicilor de pe hârtie,
Ele au un scop clar, se ştie,
E oarecum la alegerea lor,
Să dea rostul cuvintelor.

Chicago 30. 08. 2013

◯ *These poems carry Ştefan's voice into the printed page —*
delicate yet enduring.

📧 Publication: *Creneluri Sighișorene / Cultural Journal*, Romania

📅 Autumn 2017.

CRENELURI SIGHIŞORENE

Editor ASOCIAȚIA LITERARĂ „CRENELURI SIGHIŞORENE"
Redactor-șef Gabriella Costescu ●ISSN 2343 – 7693●Anul V Nr. 11 (Iulie-decembrie) 2017

LIGIA ANA GRINDEANU

La taifas

Mi-e dor de-o ninsoare la
mine acasă,
Cu brazi aplecați peste
ramuri de vis,
Atât de aproape de clipa
năiastră
Cum cerul, la munte, de
pise.

Poeți la taifas cu iubirile
muze,
Visând la poteci petrecute
de cerbi
Și zgomotul cerului întors
din pădure,
Anotimpuri- ecouri pe
veci...

Acolo m-aș duce să uit și
să plâng,
Icoane să caut, în
genunchi, printre frunze,
Să fie amiază, să uit să
mănânc,
Cu lacrimi pe-obraz,
călăuze...

Și sete să-mi fie la izvor de
lumină,
Cuvânt de-nceput de
poem,

În clipa cea grea, care știu
c-o să vină,
Mă-nvalui și strig și sunt
eu!

Iowa City, ianuarie, 2005

Lacrimă și cânt

Mă simt lacrimă și cânt
Mă adie un cuvânt
Dar mă las în grija zării
Să-mi aducă lăutarii.

Mă simt lună, dar și soare
Și mă rog la-ntinsa mare
Să-mi dea valuri de iubit
Castele de-mpodobit.

Prea rămân cărările
Și ne pleacă zborurile
Sărutul culorilor
Din prea plinul zorilor.

Cum să pleci și cum să uiți
Ploaia cum cădea în munți,
Toamna apunând în vie
Țesătura de pe ie.

Pâinea cum se coace-n
vatră
Izvor luminând pe piatră
Jocul ierbii despletit
Legendele-n chip zidit.

Nu te-ntoarce prea târziu
Când e totul un pustiu...
Vino când lumina cade
Peste luncile din sate.

Iowa City, 14 martie, 2007

Mai rămâi, colindă...

Colindă, colindă,
Pentru a câta oară
La vreme de seară
Te cânt și te plâng

Departe de țară...

Colindă, colindă,
Cu brazi încărcați
Și luceferi frați
Amintiri arzânde
În pridvoare sfinte.

Colindă, colindă
Mai rămâi în tindă
Preț de-o mângâiere
Ninsoarea se cerne
E încă devreme...

Iowa City, 8 ianuarie, 2004

Ora exactă a plecării

Aș fi rămas cu tine
Dacă mi-ai fi iubit
Clipele
Numărate în palmă.

Oriunde îmi întorceam
privirea
Ceasurile lumii
Arătau ora exactă
A plecării.

Undeva ne grăbeam,
Poate frica de un mâine gol
Și fără chemări
Poate pustiul s-a ascuns
între noi
Construind castele de
nisip,
În care doar amintirile
Își reazimă fruntea.

Cam atât am avut să-ți
spun,
Pădurea se pregătește de
toamnă,
Gândul meu se pregătește
de uitare,
Cuvântul se pregătește de
necuvânt.

💬 *Here's a taste of the lyrical world of Ligia, presented in the original Romanian.*

📰 Publication: *Romanian Tribune / Magazine*, published in the US, Chicago

📅 November 2017

💬 Excerpt: The journal noted the unique blend of song and verse that defines Cenaclul Retro, calling it a celebration of art in harmony. *"A brief note highlighting the seamless interplay of music and poetry at our Retro events."*

The article was later republished in *Creneluri Sighişorene*, a cultural journal in Romania.

Armonii de Toamnă
O seară de neuitat cu Cenaclul „Retro"

„A venit, a venit toamna, acopera-mi inima
cu ceva,
Cu umbra vreunui copac, sau mai bine,
sau mai bine cu umbra ta..."
(Nichita Stănescu)

Stimati cititori,

Am avut plăcerea de a participa sâmbătă 4 Noiembrie 2017, la spectacolul organizat de Cenaclul „Retro" in biblioteca sediului Romanian Heritage Media Center din Niles, sub găzduirea d-lui Steven Bonica, redactor şef al ziarului „Tribuna Românească" din Chicago.

In appearing in print, Corina's voice is both preserved and set free
— a reminder that poetry, once spoken, longs to live also in ink,
where it may be found again by unknown hands and new hearts.

CORINA VLAD

S-a născut în Satu Mare. De mic copil s-a bucurat la maxim de lucrurile mărunte din lumea înconjurătoare,a îndrăgit muzica, poezia și natura.

Suflet timid, dornic de afirmare, Corina și-a regăsit EUL odată cu stabilirea sa în SUA în anul 2004. Din 2016, este membră activă a Cenaclului „Retro" din Chicago, implinindu-și visul de a cânta la chitară. În același timp, compune și poezii.

Așa sunt eu

Nu mi-e rușine să admit
Sunt o romantică avidă
Căci dacă simt, știu că exist,
Știu că trăiesc, sunt vie!
Nu trec nepăsătoare
Prin istovitul ceas prielnic.
Respir, iubesc și tot admir
Lucrul duios, vremelnic!
Trăind frumos, pulsez prin timp
Orice ieșire a firii
Nu vreau să pierd acel copil
Ce saltă-n inima tăcerii!

Așa sunt eu, un suflet viu!

Veselia sufletului

Veselia sufletului
Se măsoară în trăiri
De licăriri în gol închis
Și nostalgii în timp deschis!

Zâmbind, plutești peste uitări
Pierdute în amurgul serii
Și te cobori, zvâcnind flori
Scrutând valsorile tăcerii!

Ah, ce duios la tine-n suflet
Înmuguresc frunzișuri goale,
Copacii împânzesc înaltul
Seninului ce curge-n zare!

Un fir de iarbă te-mpresoară
Și-ți mângâie obrajii arși
De-a soarelui săgeți de aur
Ce scânteiază iarăși, azi!

Veselia sufletului
Se măsoară în trăiri
Cu sclipiri de vis simțit!

Mâini în dar

Mâini în dar am dobândit
Aripi de cer desprinse-n trup
Chemări mărețe spre împliniri
Slujind un vis în fiecare zi!

Fără de ele aș fi neant
Scăldat de valul desecat
Aș fi fost stol căzut din zbor
În drumul meu spre depărtări!

Mâini ce lucrează,
Mâini ce dansează,
Mâini ce se joacă,
Mâini ce visează,
Mâini care cântă
Pe-al strunelor dor
Mâini care scriu
Gânduri nespuse în zori.
Mâinile mele, trăirile mele...

📰 Publication: *Dor de Basarabia* Magazine, Chişinău

📅 August 2017

💬 The article's warm words captured the essence of Retro: poetry and music intertwined, shared with joy and authenticity.

Note: *Dor de Basarabia*, published in Chişinău, bears a name that itself is a song of yearning. "Dor" — that untranslatable ache of the heart — joined with *Basarabia*, a land of memory and belonging, together conjure a longing for roots and horizons. Issued from Moldova's capital, the magazine carries with it both remembrance and presence, a bridge between past and present, heritage and hope.

Seri culturale la Chicago

În faţa spectatorilor evoluează membri ai Cenaclului „Retro". La microfon - consulul general Tiberiu Trifan. Sala de festivităţi a Bisericii „Sfi

📰 Publication: *Romanian Tribune / Magazine*, published in the US, Chicago

📅 December 2017

💬 *Excerpt: Coverage of our Christmas concert, highlighting the children's participation and warm community spirit.*

6   Nr. 297 ● Anul 16 Nr. 22 ● 16-31 decembrie 2017   TRIBUNA Românească

Deschide ușa creștine – Spectacol de colinde cu Cenaclul Retro

„Îngerii cu flori în mână,
Împletesc mândră cunună
Pre cunună-i scris frumos:
Astăzi s-a născut Hristos..."

Deschide ușa creștine,

Traian a cântat apoi cântecul propriu „Vine iarnă, nu te mai preface" pe versuri de Lucian Vâlea, o poezie a iubirii neînțelese și a lipsei de romantism în timpul iernii.

„Primiți cu colinda" se aude o voce dincolo de ușa laterală a sălii. „Primiți" am

„Sculați gazde din pătuc", o altă colindă tradițională din Ardeal a fost interpretată de Ștefan cu acompaniamentul întregului grup. Anda a recitat apoi poezia „Vreau" de Adrian Păunescu, o poezie trecută a iubirii pierdute.

a cuplului Monica și Lucian Blaga este o creație superbă cu versuri minunate care ne îndeamnă la rugăciune în noaptea de Crăciun și a fost interpretată de vocea angelică a Monicăi.

Doamna Ana de Sighișoara a recitat

A Journey through Music and Poetry

🖼 Publication: *Creneluri Sighișorene / Cultural Journal*, Romania
📅 Spring 2021
💬 *This article, written in Romanian, gathers the verses of Ligia, Ana and Corina — a lyrical thread spun into print, where their poetry steps beyond the stage and takes root on the page.*

CRENELURI SIGHIȘORENE

Editor ASOCIAȚIA LITERARĂ „CRENELURI SIGHIȘORENE"
Redactor-șef Gabriella Costescu ●ISSN 2343 – 7693●Anul VIII Nr. 18 (ianuarie - iunie) 2021

DE PESTE OCEAN

LIGIA ANA GRINDEANU

Membru nou al Asociației Literare „Creneluri Sighișorene"

Cu toate că avem o colaborare... cam dintotdeauna cu Ligia Ana Grindeanu, oficial s-a înscris în Asociația Literară „Creneluri Sighișorene", doar din luna ianuarie 2021.

S-a născut la 24 octombrie 1971, la Sighișoara, fiica poetei și scriitoarei sighișorene Ana Munteanu Drăghici. A urmat Școala Gimnazială „Nicolae Iorga" și Liceul Teoretic „Joseph Haltrich" din Sighișoara.

Este absolventă a Universității de Medicină și Farmacie „Iuliu Hațieganu" din Cluj-Napoca, activă în viața culturală atât în orașul natal cât și peste ocean. Locuiește de ani buni în Chicago – SUA, unde este medic specialist pediatru.

Este membră a Cenaclului „N.D. Cocea-Anotimpuri" din Sighișoara, membru-fondator și președinte a Cenaclului „Dor" din Iowa City și membru-fondator a Cenaclului „Retro" și „Seara Culturală Românească" din Chicago. Ligia este implicată în organizarea de întâlniri literare și spectacole în comunitatea românească din Chicago SUA.

A publicat de asemenea și în editoriale mureșene precum și Poeme în antologiile:
- „Anotimpuri sub turnul cu ceas –Veșnicia Secundei";

- Efigii Lirice.
- Vise Târzii.
- România, țara mea de dor;
- Scriitori români uniți în cuget și simțiri la Centenarul Marii Uniri;
- Antologia Poeților Români Contemporani din Întreaga Lume;
- Poeți și Prozatori Români în Regal Eminescian
- Românul s-a născut Poet, Antologia „Universum" – Canada.

Cărți publicate:
- „Dincolo de liniște" – Casa de editură Mureș, 2003
- „Anotimpuri de dor" – editura „Ardealul"

Aproape de cer

Jumătate cer, jumătate piatră,
Harpă a naturii
Învăluită în nori
Ce aproape e cerul de noi...
Pădure de veghe și aripa dor
Șoaptele apusului
Căzut într-un somn,
În care lumina își caută fior.
Drum spre Atlantic,
drum spre Pacific
Gândurile curg
spre aceleași cărări.
Urcușuri abrupte - treptele vis
Piatră de piatră și destin de destin.
Insule albe-tăcute așteaptă
Primăvara promisă-n adânc
La întâlnirea cu zarea,
Într-o scurtă paradă
Delicată și mândră e floarea.

Noua apariție editorială, punte de legătură între Sighișoara și Chicago. „Anotimpuri de dor" poate fi găsit de către iubitorii de versuri care cred în puterea de vindecare a Cuvântului la Librăria „Hyperion" din Sighișoara.

Ceea ce ni se întâmplă

Ceea ce ni se întâmplă
Nu ajunge
Ziua cu ore
Miezul clipei- scrum
În necroite zale, la răscruce
Iubirile au parcă gust de fum.
Eu te visam

În cartea nedeschisă
Adus de-albastre regăsiri șirag
Și-am înțeles târziu
Că nu sunt tristă
Șoptitul dor
Ți l-am adus în prag.
E dansul tău
Ți-e lumea la picioare
De-ai încerca
Să-ți cânți iubirea iar
Eu ți-aș ieși cu râurile-n cale
Lumina să o treci peste ocean.

Gândurile

Gândurile-țipete de ploi
Într-un glas răstălmăcit de muze
Eu pe un continent de piatră gol
Tu visând la-ntinsele peluze.

Când să mi te-apropiu, ești suspin,
Un profil dintr-o poveste veche
Și încerc să-mi amintesc
de-un timp
Când citeam în astrele pereche.

Ochiul tău încremenind în sete
Ți-a purtat zadarnicul păcat
La o margine de câmp
atât de verde
Și atât de aproape de inserat.

Lasă merii cei desprinși din teaca
Vântului adulmecând livezi
Lasă-i jos, aproape de tăcere
Și să-i strângi în brațe,
să nu-i pierzi.

Erai mai frumos pe caii repezi
La izvoare pregătind un zbor
N-a mai fost decât lumina pietrei
Gândurile-țipete de ploi.

CORINA VLAD

S-a născut în România, dar este stabilită în SUA din anul 2004.

A publicat în revista „Creneluri Sighișorene" din România, în revista „Poezii pentru sufletul meu" din Canada cât și pe diverse platforme on-line în limba română și engleză.

Este membră activă a Cenaclului „Retro" din Chicago în cadrul căruia interpretează piese folk ale cântăreților consacrați, dar este și cantautoare „pe-al corzilor meridian, glasul dulce peste ocean", cum frumos o numește Ana Munteanu Drăghici. Poeziile Corinei sunt expresia stărilor și a trăirilor sufletești adunate în sertarele inimii, de cele mai multe ori gasindu-și popas în mijlocul naturii, ca parte integrantă din existența ei.

Întâmplare?

Pe a timpului cărare
Este oare întâmplare
Să te simți și mic și mare
Savurând a ta chemare?

În a vremii nepăsare
Este doar o descărcare
Să mai cazi în apăsare
Privind totul cum dispare?

În a razelor visare
Să fie pură sfidare
Când te pierzi în relaxare
Lăsând totul în uitare?

Nu-i nimic o întâmplare,
Să nu-ți fie cu mirare,
Tot ce tu trăiești în zare
Este-o binecuvântare!

Și de-ar fi

De-i veni la mine pe-nserat
Ți-oi cânta de dor nu de oftat,

De-i veni la mine în pridvor,
Ți-oi vorbi de-al nostru drag amor.

Și de-ar fi să-mi spui că mă iubești
Te-aș purta pe plaiuri din povești,
Și de-ar fi să mă săruți cu foc
Ți-aș cădea în brațe ca-ntr-un joc.

Și de-o fi să stai să nu mai pleci
Te-aș cinsti să nu poți să rănești
Și de-o fi să dăinuim pe veci
Am rămâne-un basm din vechiul vers ....

Furori

Furori printre frunze-mbrăcate-n culori
Mângâiate de vântul ce-ți cântă-n viori,
Pe-un colț de plai, într-o gură de rai
Ascult al tăcutului grai!

Foșnesc ale cerului albe visări,
Comori nestemate, în suflet cântări
Întinsă pe zestrea de petec străbun
Mai stau, căci tânjesc să rămân!

Clipe-amorțesc în acord cu suflarea
Ce-o-nghet pe moment, ador încântarea,
Pământul e rece dar focul din trup
Arde al aurei scut!

Mai stau, savurez divinul din tot,
Îl simt ca un trăznet prin trupul pivot,
Se face târziu dar nu, nu vreau să plec
Pe-al naturii refren mai petrec....!

Apariții editoriale:

„UNIVERSUM"

Există un univers al sufletului ce tinde spre astralul ceresc prin arta cuvântului! Antoligia de Literatură Contemporană, cuprinzând autori români de pretutindeni, ne-a situat în „Universum", această carte în care ne-a fost dat să ne întâlnim cu cei dintr-un nimb cu noi, prin înrudire spirituală. Suntem mamă și fiică, respectiv Ana Munteanu Drăghici și Ligia-Ana Grindeanu, născute în aceeași zi și aceeași lună, a două zeci și patra zi a lunii Octombrie. Astfel ne spunem reciproc „La mulți ani!" Fiind născute „sub zodia versului", tindem spiritualicește și spre eternitate prin harul artei cuvântului. Venim din orașul cu glas medieval, numit „Mărgăritar al Transilvaniei", Sighișoara, din România, patria noastră și a Nadiei Comăneci, care a adus aură acestei „Grădini a Maicii Domnului".

Plutire de dor...
(Ana Munteanu Drăghici)

Pe luciul de ape o frunză plutește
Ivită din pomul vieții stârnit
De vântul aprig al cărărilor vieții
Spre drumul uitărilor, nestăvilit...

Culorile se-ntorc
în oglinzile firii.
Verdele crește în undele reci
Ca să redea tinerețea privirii!
Apele fac din privire poteci...

Galben din amiezile vieții
Aurește sub razele soarelui viu.
Mă-mbrățișează aduceri aminte,
Clipa privește
spre ceasul pustiu...

Un ruginiu se topește-n tăcere
Pe nicovala arzând neiertări...
Frunza se-adună în răsuflare
Purtată de apele altor zări.

Suntem un strop de dor în plutire,
Cântecul frunzei purtând anotimp,
Între suspinul ivit din iubire
Și umbrele mărilor trimise de-
Olimp...

Întru iubire

Privirea ta să-mi fie stea
Spre dăinuire
Fără sfârșit să ne vorbim
Cu tăinuire.

Să-ncrucișăm pașnic în doi
Spadele noastre,
Ce ucigând orgoliul din noi
În lumea-albastră,
Va-ngemăna clipe de vis
Iubirea noastră ...

Gloria perfecțiunii Nadiei Comăneci, ca gimnastă, la marile competiții de la Montreal, Canada, a făcut pe tot globul pământesc cunoscută țara noastră! A avea numele înscrise într-o magnifică antologie, publicată la Montreal-Canada-2020, înseamnă a ne reîntoarce în timp spre a reveni în actualitate cu aplauze pentru Nadia Comăneci, dar și pentru realizatorii cărții „Universum", respectiv redactor coordonator Mihaela Miha Miha C. D, senior editor coordonator Johnny Ciatlos-Deak și întregii echipei editoriae „Globart"!

Cu adevărat, potrivit afirmației lui P.T. Barnum, citat în deschiderea cărții „Literatura este una dintre cele mai interesante și semnificative expresii ale umanității". Dacă sufletul cititorului va fi deschis de o singură literă luminată din scritura noastră, înseamnă că ne vom întâlni prin lumina puterii cuvântului în constelația cerească a firii!

**Ana Munteanu Drăghici &
Ligia Ana Grindeanu
Iunie 2021, Chicago**

Tribuna Românească on Its 18th Anniversary
Chronicle of the Celebration Evening

The second set of video messages presented to the audience came from the team of the Retro Literary Circle: Anda and Ștefan Cristolțean (the founders), Corina Vlad, Ligia Grindeanu, Ana Drăghici Munteanu, and Călin Mărincaș. Last but not least, the audience also enjoyed a message from the chronicler and folk musician Radu Răcean.

With sincere appreciation and gratitude,
Tribuna Românească
Steven & Simona Bonica – Editors-in-Chief, Chicago
Timotei Dinică – Editor-in-Chief, Bucharest

📑 Publication: *Creneluri Sighişorene / Cultural Journal*, Romania
📅 *June, 2020*
💬 *Excerpt: Reflections on Cenaclul Retro's role in connecting Romanian culture abroad with tradition and creativity.*

Dialoguri literare și muzicale

cu Cenaclul „Retro"

Cenaclul „Retro" din Chicago nu şi-a dezis crezul, desfăşurându-şi continuu activitatea, sub genericul:

📑 Publication: *Creneluri Sighişorene / Cultural Journal*, Romania
📅 *December, 2021*
💬 *Excerpt:* In its warm words, the article captured the spirit of Retro: the intertwining of poetry and music, shared with joy and authenticity.

Din Nou Împreună cu Cenaclul „Retro"

Mulțumim, Cenaclul Retro! Mulțumim pentru încă un spectacol minunat! Mulțumim că existați și ne încălziți sufletele cu focul iubirii de artist! O după-masă de vară târzie în care vântul toamnei a încercat sa ne pătrundă și sufletele! Noroc... cu haiducii Cenaclului „Retro" care ne-au amintit să trăim clipa!

A HANDFUL OF THOUGHTS

OR – Through the Eyes of Others…

A playful idea designed to delight everyone who has contributed to the success of the Retro Muse Society over these past five years. Below, you will find the message sent back in January 2022, along with the "handful of thoughts" that followed.

Dear Retro,

I invite you to take a moment behind the curtain. I am working on a project (for if I didn't complicate things, I wouldn't be myself…) and I need everyone's participation, as much as possible.

Please fill out the following form with your impressions, thoughts, verses, or beautiful words, describing everyone (or just some) from Retro. Nothing elaborate—a single word is enough. Try to leave out your own name; the others will describe you.

I will keep all responses anonymous, but I plan to use them to create a *"Handful of Thoughts"* in celebration of the five-year anniversary since we first became the Retro Muse Society.

Thank you,
Anda

GO RETRO!

Alina Celia Cumpan
A hopeless romantic
An immigrant on the planet, unconventional in verse, stylish; she carries culture like a map with love.
Alina is contagious through passion and courage.
A fighter.
A sensitive poet, devoted to Romanian traditions.
Tradition and poetry, love and longing for Romania! Charming on stage, both sweet and bohemian.
Involved.
Poetic sensitivity with a longing for the mioritic lands.

Ana Munteanu Drăghici
Soulful poetry.
A person without whom value would have no meaning.
Mrs. Ana from Chicago brings sensitivity to the forefront.
Blue dreams, with love on her lips, a masterful blending of words and muses.
Ana from Sighişoara, the lady of poetry, encourages and inspires our artistic endeavors.
Ana from Sighişoara, carrying the treasures of the muses.
Charismatic.
The lady of poetry, an inspiration and mentor to all of us.

Anda Cristolțean
An eternal pilgrim on the wings of time...
Anda brings us closer through style and elegance.
Delighted on the path, she organizes scenarios, recites, and sings along vacation trails, always playful!
Devotion, talent, warm and noble soul, promoting beauty and harmony.
"Lady in Red," the charming little ant.
Devoted.
Our common denominator, the one who unites and encourages us to continue the Retro adventure.

Călin Mărincaș

Time traveler.
Playful and mischievous, with his heart on fire.
Călin is an assertive presenter!
Transforms good cheer into pages of stories.
Enthusiasm and friendship.
The poet's grandson, a messenger of verse.
Easygoing.
Cheerful, optimistic, and an exceptional dancer. Pages from a story...

Cătălin Lari

In music, his soul speaks.
A warm joker who tames any rebellious bow.
Talent and sensitivity on the violin staff, a gifted musician.
Cătălin Lari, relevant, from the shore of thought to the infinite expanse.
Through music, rediscovered! From violin strings flow the seconds of dreaming...
Musician and instrumentalist, violinist and ceterist, loving father and husband, but above all, a wonderful human being.

Iulian Grindeanu

A discreet mediator, bearer of the arts.
A warm and talented mind.
Warm as a summer breeze.
Iulian absorbs and radiates solar energy.
He walks "behind the lens," giving eternity to memories.
Observer and observed; the photos and recordings from Retro events testify.
Classy.
An ardent supporter of the Circle, the one who gives us priceless video memories.

Corina Vlad
Carries a living fire in her soul.
A big heart, a wandering mind, and a tear on a flower.
Corina has a crystal-clear voice.
A voice as pure as spring waters, a soul filled with childhood and innocence.
On the meridian of strings, her sweet voice crosses the ocean.
Cheerful.
A fire that continuously burns in the hearth of music and poetry.
Missing childhood? Call Corina.

Cătălin Nicolae
Refined humor.
Bubbly like a glass of fine champagne.
With or without a beard, Cătălin conquers the stage and the audience.
Skilled actor, serious in gaze, ready to help whenever needed.
A charming actor.
A loving actor and bringer of humor.
Eloquent.
Accomplished actor, master of improvisation.

Ligia Grindeanu
Messenger of the muses through the tear of poems.
Poetic soul.
A voice that carries the blue serenity of poetry and the delightful scent of green fir.
Ligia is our guide through the land of white stone.
A wild angel, gentle and serene, weaving sublimely through seasons of longing.
Serene.
A poet of exceptional sensitivity but with the strength of character to tame even the "boar with silver tusks."

Ștefan Cristolțean

The talented cricket, admired by all of us.

Exceptional talent.

The bond and soul of Retro. A great guy from Cluj, whom I wish I had met sooner.

Ștefan has immense musical talent, from Cluj!

Provides solutions, concludes discussions with solos, carries his beloved guitar, singing winged dreams.

He gives and devotes: a talented singer-songwriter and leader of the Retro Circle.

Relaxed.

Founder, organizer, rocker, manager, and above all, a Transylvanian with a heart of gold.

Monica Blaga

Nightingale on the branch of the soul.

Sweet springtime voice.

With her wonderful voice, Monica sings and enchants us.

Her voice is a piano string, at home and on the frontier.

A marvelous voice.

Organized.

An extraordinary voice, with exceptional talent.

Lucian Blaga

The perfectionist teacher, at the keys of artistic nature.

Lucian tells stories with his fingers.

The piano is his sacred altar, every day of the year.

Talented composer and pianist.

Meticulous.

Composer and piano master, expert in his field.

Sorin Griza

Famous human doctor, artist with fan appeal.

Embodiment of gentleness.

A big heart always open.

Sorin is a Phoenix bird from Banat.

Modest and gentle, with a big heart; never brings upset, plays patiently from the bass.
Sings and delights us: music, performance, outreach.
Enthusiastic.
Loyal friend, perfectionist, exceptional guitarist, the "mayor" of Retro.

Laura Şişu
The art of sound captures the actress who embraces us with a melodious voice.
Emotion in song.
Sensitive, yet strong.
Laura is a golden quince at our window.
A 20-year-old girl who brings emotion even to a shadow.
A wonderful voice, loves the stage, and shines on it.
Honest.
Accomplished performer, through her songs she brings us into a "twenty-year-old world."

Sergiu Vlad
Discreet supporter of the Circle, gallant, even builds the stage.
Always close to the heart of Retro.
Sergiu is silent with meaning.
He acts quietly.
A golden soul.
An exceptional friend, with body and soul alongside Retro.

Radu Răcean
Patriot through his singing, always carrying the tricolor.
Gratitude to you, Radu!
A great soul, beating for those around him.
Radu is passionate like a literary circle.
With the flag forward and faith in the sacred, he wants to sing anything.
Sings and interprets with great passion; his enthusiasm keeps us

motivated to continue Retro's mission.
Dreamer.

Traian Alex Bălan
A Roman emperor's name; listening to him, you are a music lover.
Simplicity.
Traian's timbre is poetic and poetic (Poesis).
Charming, he looks at you, smiles beautifully, speaks in verses, and entices you.
A folk music enthusiast, with beautiful performances and compositions.
Composer and performer with a unique, melancholic touch.

Marius Stan
Distinguished creator, captivating reciter.
Perfectionist.
Spiritual and prepared.
Recites under his lashes, scolds, and lifts you.
Verses and performance from the perspective of a scientist.
Approachable.

Message – OR – When You Least Expect It
On the Anniversary... Retro, Happy Birthday!!!

Every story begins with: "Once upon a time"... just as the story of the Retro Muse Society in Chicago began... five years ago.
Once upon a time... like never before (for if it weren't, it wouldn't be told)... there was a group of wonderful, soulful, and passionate people—romantic and dreamy troubadours—trying to bring a piece of Romanian culture across the ocean through music and poetry.

Professionals, and beyond, bearers of joy and good cheer; these people deserve encouragement and support, because we need culture, so that we never forget who we truly are in our hearts: Romanians... wherever we may be!

Alina Celia Cumpan
A young poet who writes in both Romanian and English, exploring emotional states with daring metaphors. She has a special passion for words, building and unbuilding them, playing with our longings:
"Through sun... and through rain,
Longings grow within us..."

The story continues through the words and creations of two poets, mother and daughter: **Ana Munteanu Drăghici** and **Ligia Grindeanu**.
Ana Munteanu Drăghici, known as the Lady of Romanian Poetry, teaches us how life should be understood and lived, through her vitality and zest for life, attuned to all that is beautiful: music, poetry, and authentic Romanian feelings.
Her daughter, Ligia Grindeanu, inheriting her mother's talent, adds a special refinement and sensitivity, both through her creations and her ethereal, gentle presence... like a Snow Queen, with clear blue eyes like mountain lakes. Carrying Romanian longing across the ocean, Ligia bridges two worlds through emotions that often leave a lump in the throat and a nostalgic smile:
"How to leave... and how to forget,
The rain falling on the mountains,
Autumn setting in the vineyard...
The weaving on the blouse..."

A masculine presence, authentic, through recitations of poems inherited from family as well as other Romanian poets, with a Transylvanian voice: **Călin Mărincaș** carries friendship and good cheer.

Marius Stan
Actor, writer, reciter, passionate about mathematics and science...
a combination of firmness and flexibility, with a rich cultural and
intellectual background, emphasizing quality, structure, and
discipline. Observant and visionary, he organizes and reorganizes
until everything takes the desired shape.

Corina Vlad
Bearer of the living fire, through feelings carried on wings of love,
hope, and joy... A childlike, pure, and trusting soul, music and
poetry lover, always discovering new dimensions. She brings
energy and positivity to every performance.

Monica and Lucian Blaga
Music professionals—a composer and a singer with a warm,
unique voice—whose collaboration with Retro added
professionalism, understood and appreciated in context.

Anda Cristolțean
"The Little Ant," always working, building and rebuilding,
developing ideas and projects, concerned with artistic, aesthetic,
and cultural organization at all levels.

Ștefan Cristolțean
"The Cricket" with his guitar... passionate about everything he
does, confident in himself and in others, giving encouragement
and courage. A broad artistic and human understanding of the
socio-cultural context, flexible, able to adapt quickly, offering
solutions to move projects forward.

The story continues with **Sorin Griza**, a "young brother who
believes in justice," often smiling with sadness when hopes
seemed misleading... passionate about music and audiovisual
projects, a bearer of friendship and loyalty, giving the best of his
time and knowledge to those around him, patient, trusting,
helpful.

Cătălin Nicolae
Bringer of smiles and laughter to the audience, a charismatic actor who spreads joy in every performance, sharing stories from his life adventures.

Cătălin Lari
Joined Retro bringing the sweet voice of the violin and professionalism, contributing to a fruitful collaboration.

Traian Bălan
The troubadour with a scarf, the "Mircea Baniciu" of the Circle, always accompanied by provincial sadness, nostalgic obsessions, longings, and memories that cling to him.

Radu Răcean
Rediscovered joy, song, and poetry with Retro, believing he was lost in the American whirlwind, but in fact, he rediscovered the longings of his homeland and people, which had always been in his heart.

Iulian Grindeanu
Active participant, attentive viewer from behind the camera lens.

Sergiu Vlad
The man you can rely on to lend a hand wherever needed.

Congratulations, Retro, congratulations to all, and may you continue to carry the story forward... through the joy and beautiful energy you have always brought to your performances. Happy anniversary and many more performances!

Laura and Constantin C Nicolae
Artistic Director

Epilogue

This journey has been far from easy, yet along the way I have encountered incredible people whose support has meant the world to me. I want to take a moment to express my heartfelt gratitude.

Thank you to Laetiţia Alex-St. Patrick, who read the uncensored edition of this book and offered the most insightful advice on both content and publication.

Thank you to Patty McAnally, who, despite not speaking Romanian, patiently and enthusiastically guided me through the labyrinth of editing. I learned so much from her, and I am delighted that she can now read about the Retro Muse Society in English.
Thank you to Michael Latza, a fellow author, for sharing invaluable insights on pagination, cover design, and publishing in general.

Thank you to Corina Vlad for all her guidance on publishing the book in Romanian, and for the joy and enthusiasm she brought to the process.

To the members, collaborators, and supporters of the Retro Muse Society—thank you for your passion and energy. To everyone who attended our performances, participated, got involved, or simply watched from across the ocean, supporting us with the simple joy of being part of our journey—even virtually—you all helped create this book.

I also wish to thank those who requested not to be mentioned anywhere in this book. It gives me great satisfaction to honor their wishes.

With deep gratitude,
                    Sonia Maria Anda

Peek into our story, laugh with who we were
We've caught some years, and back to you they stir
Our gentle hours, our wild, untamed ways
Memories dancing through sunlight and haze...

                    - Adapted from the lyrics of Adrian Păunescu

Dear Retro,

Thank you for being.
Thank you for surrounding us with beautiful, kind, and talented
souls...
for teaching us to grow, to love more deeply, and to be better.

Art never dies—and through it, we too touch immortality.

With love, from all of us—both the rebels and the romantics—in
Retro

The Mission of the Retro Muse Society:

Our deepest wish is to bring beauty into your lives and light into
your hearts.
We invite you to hum cherished songs together,
to recall the verses stored in our home libraries,
to craft new lyrics and melodies,
and to feel the Romanian spirit within.

We are reborn by honoring the richness of Romanian
experiences—wherever in the world we may be...

www.ingramcontent.com/pod-product-compliance
Lightning Source LLC
Chambersburg PA
CBHW060409130626
46555CB00005B/2010